THE PRE-FORECLOSURE PROPERTY INVESTOR'S KIT

How to Make Money Buying Distressed Real Estate... *Before the Public Auction*

THOMAS J. LUCIER

WILEY

John Wiley & Sons, Inc.

Published by John Wiley & Sons, Inc., Hoboken, New Jersey.
Published simultaneously in Canada.

For general information on our other products and services please contact our Customer Care Department within the United States at (800) 762-2974, outside the United States at (317) 572-3993 or fax (317) 572-4002.

Wiley also publishes its books in a variety of electronic formats. Some content that appears in print may not be available in electronic books. For more information about Wiley products, visit our web site at www.wiley.com.

Library of Congress Cataloging-in-Publication Data:

Lucier, Thomas J.
  The pre-foreclosure property investor's kit : how to make money buying distressed real estate . . . before the public auction / Thomas Lucier.
      p. cm.
  ISBN 0-471-69279-4
  1. Real estate investment—United States.   2. Foreclosure—United States.
I. Title.
  HD255.L829 2005
  332.63'24—dc22
2004021911

Printed in the United States of America.

10   9   8   7   6

To my wife and business partner,
Barbara V. Lucier,
who has steadfastly stood shoulder-to-shoulder
with me through the good, the bad, and the ugly!

CONTENTS

v

PART II
MY 14-STEP PROCESS FOR INVESTING IN
PRE-FORECLOSURE PROPERTIES

CONTENTS

due diligence before you ever make a written offer to purchase a pre-foreclosure property. • How to use the Internet to perform due diligence on pre-foreclosure properties. • Eight things that you must check for when performing due diligence on pre-foreclosures. • Where to find the names of all the property owners in your county. • How to conduct an online property records search. • The six states that don't require the public disclosure of real estate sales information. • What to do when your county's property records aren't available online. • How parcels of land are identified for tax purposes. • How to use grantor and grantee indexes. • Twelve ways to locate the owners of abandoned properties in foreclosure. • The two types of real property liens. • Fifteen liens to check for when researching pre-foreclosure property titles. • Thirty-four common abbreviations used in property title documents. • How title companies index documents in their property records databases. • Why it is best to have title searches done at the county public records library. • The two most common types of property title searches. • How to hire an experienced title abstractor to perform your title searches on pre-foreclosure properties. • Online sources of free public property records.

Twelve major defects that are often overlooked during property inspections. • How to inspect suspicious properties for environmental contamination. • How to find a competent property inspector. • Why it is best to use inspection checklists to conduct your property inspections. • Phase One Environmental Audit Checklist. • Thirteen Property Inspection Checklists.

The definition of market value. • Eight factors that you must consider when estimating a pre-foreclosure property's current market value. • The difference between assessed value and appraised value. • Why you must pursue only properties that have a relatively low debt to value ratio. • Common methods used by appraisers to estimate property values. • How to use the comparison sales method to estimate a pre-foreclosure property's current market value. • Online sources of property appraisal information. • Why you must always deduct the needed repair costs from the seller's estimated equity. • Four steps to estimating a pre-foreclosure property's current market value. • How to get free building replacement cost estimates. • Online sources for construction replacement cost calculators. • Online sources of comparable property sales data. • Current Market Value Worksheet.

What you must always do before making final payments to
repairmen and contractors. • Daily Repair Cost Worksheet.

How to calculate the resale value of a property. • How to
package properties to highlight their best features. • The
three best ways to market properties online. • How to use
the Internet to market your properties globally. • How to
create a property for sale web page to advertise your
properties online. • How to use URL forwarding for
property for sale domain names. • How to create a list of
potential buyers by having visitors to your web site
complete a buyer e-mail notification form. • What you
must include in your property for sale e-mail
fact sheet. • How to effectively use classified newspaper
ads, property for sale signs, word-of-mouth advertising, and
outgoing telephone messages to market your properties. •
Four qualifying questions that you must always ask
potential buyers. • How to sell your property through real
estate brokers without signing a listing agreement. • How
to make money assigning your purchase agreements
to third-party buyers. • What you must know about the
vacancy exclusion clause in insurance policies when selling
vacant properties. • How income from the sale of real
estate is taxed by the Internal Revenue Service. • Online
sources of tax information. • Outgoing Telephone Sales
Message Script. • Participating Broker Agreement. •
Assignment of Real Estate Purchase Agreement.

Over 100 real estate-related web site URLs that every
serious pre-foreclosure investor needs to have bookmarked
on his or her personal computer.

PART I

GETTING STARTED AS A PROFITABLE PRE-FORECLOSURE INVESTOR

How You Can Make $60,000 a Year Investing in Pre-Foreclosure Properties Part-Time

First off, I want to take this opportunity to thank you for investing your hard-earned money in a copy of *The Pre-Foreclosure Property Investor's Kit*. I also want to congratulate you on making a very wise investment decision! As you will soon find out, this book lives up to its title. It is packed with step-by-step instructions, ready-to-use worksheets, checklists, letters and agreements, and practical, no-nonsense advice on how to buy properties directly from owners with mortgage or deed of trust loans that are in default and facing foreclosure.

The Definition of Pre-Foreclosure

First things first: Before I begin to tell you how you can make $60,000 a year investing in pre-foreclosure properties part-time, I need to give you a brief description of what the term *pre-foreclosure means*. Pre-foreclosure refers to the period of time during the foreclosure process between when a lender files a foreclosure lawsuit or a notice of default in the official public records and the date the property is scheduled to be sold at a public foreclosure auction or trustee's sale. The entire foreclosure process is covered in great detail in Chapter 4.

Why the Pre-Foreclosure Stage Is the Time to Buy during the Foreclosure Process

The real trick to consistently making money in real estate is to find a steady source of readily identifiable property owners who have a compelling reason to sell their property. This type of property owner is known in the business as a *motivated seller*. And that is exactly why I like investing in pre-foreclosure properties. Pre-foreclosures provide a steady source of readily identifiable motivated sellers in the form of property owners with mortgage or deed of trust loans that lenders have publicly declared to be in default and facing foreclosure. As you will soon learn, the future looks bright for pre-foreclosure property investors in the know. The coming months and years could provide a record number of opportunities to buy properties, at a discount, directly from motivated sellers who have a very compelling reason to sell their property. In Chapter 2, you will get the lowdown on exactly why you should never bid on properties at public foreclosure auction or trustee sales or buy lender-owned repossessed properties.

The First Step to Making $60,000 a Year Investing in Pre-Foreclosures Part-Time

I do not know about you, but to me, $60,000 a year is nothing to scoff at, especially from a part-time job. And if you are willing to apply the information and advice that is contained in this book, and work hard, and don't quit the first time you run into an obstacle, you can reasonably expect to earn $60,000 a year investing in pre-foreclosures part-time. The $60,000 annual income figure that I am using in this chapter to illustrate the profit potential that pre-foreclosure properties can provide to hard-working investors is not based on wishful thinking or pie-in-the-sky logic. Rather, it is based on local foreclosure market conditions and how much time, money, and energy the average investor has to dedicate to investing in pre-foreclosures. For example, in lower cost housing markets, an investor might have to do six $10,000 deals in order to earn $60,000 annually. To accomplish this, an investor would have to buy and resell one pre-foreclosure property every two months. In more expensive housing markets, it could very well take an investor just four $15,000 deals to earn $60,000 annually. This would require completing one deal every three months. And, in high-end markets, an investor could do two $30,000 deals or even earn $60,000 from a single property. Please keep in mind that individual results will vary and that many people may not reach $60,000 in profits during their first year in business. But, what if you earn only a "measly $20,000" during your first year? I am willing to bet that most of the people reading this book could put an extra $20,000 in annual income to good use.

Why Now Is One of the Best Times Ever to Invest in Pre-Foreclosure Properties

Today's soft economy, lax lending policies, predatory lending practices, and historically low interest rates are causing overextended homeowners to default on their mortgage and deed of trust loans in very large numbers. As I write this, the Mortgage Bankers Association of America has just reported in their quarterly National Delinquency Survey that a near record number of single-family homes were in foreclosure during the last quarter of 2003. Also, other organizations that monitor residential loan trends are not making any rosy predictions about any possible future decline in the number of mortgage foreclosures. In fact, the number of home loans foreclosed on each year has steadily increased over the past 20 years. According to the U.S. Census Bureau's statistical abstract, the number of homes in foreclosure in 1980 was 114,000, while the number of homes in foreclosure in the year 2001—the latest year in which information is available—was 555,000. This is an increase of over 250 percent. The main reason that I do not see any letup in the number of foreclosures in the foreseeable future is because of the unbridled spending habits of most Americans, which are fueled by easily accessible credit in the form of credit cards. Far too many homeowners today are in debt up to their eyeballs and living on borrowed money, well beyond their financial means. They are living in houses they really cannot afford. And until Mr. and Mrs. America learn how to live a lifestyle that is based solely on their actual income, and not on the credit limits of their fantastic plastic credit cards, the number of foreclosures nationwide can only go one way: straight up!

Six Factors Contributing to the Skyrocketing Number of Foreclosures Nationwide

The following is a list of the six main factors that most financial experts claim are contributing to the skyrocketing number of mortgage and deed of trust loan foreclosures nationwide:

1. *A downturn in local economic conditions:* Many local economies that are not well diversified and are overly dependent on one or two types of low-tech industry are experiencing a downturn due to foreign competition and the

ever-growing practice of outsourcing jobs offshore to countries like Mexico and India. This has resulted in massive layoffs that have caused many borrowers to lose their homes through foreclosure.

2. *Overextended first-time homebuyers:* An aggressive push for homeownership on the part of state and federal government agencies and lenders has helped a record number of first-time homebuyers buy homes of their own. However, most first-time homeowners do not have the cash reserves necessary to pay for emergency home repairs and the other unexpected costs that are a part of homeownership. And, once they get behind on their bills and miss a loan payment, they are usually never able to make up the missed payment and they end up in foreclosure.

3. *Predatory lending practices:* So-called predatory lenders prey on borrowers with low credit scores, excessive debt, and past bankruptcies and foreclosures that keep them from being able to obtain conventional loans at market terms and rates. They make what are called subprime loans that typically have repayment terms that include extremely high late payment fees and interest rates that cause many borrowers to eventually have their loans foreclosed.

4. *Government-backed loan programs:* Government-backed home loan programs such as Federal Housing Administration (FHA) insured loans and Department of Veterans Affairs (DVA) guaranteed loans have less stringent qualification standards than conventional loans that are not backed by any government agency. Lax loan underwriting standards result in lenders making loans to borrowers with marginal credit, less than stellar job histories, and higher than normal debt ratios. This is proving to be a recipe for financial disaster for many borrowers who end up in foreclosure.

5. *Loans with high loan-to-value ratios:* Conventional and government-backed loan programs offer loans at 95 to 100 percent of the value of the property securing the loan. The practice of making loans to borrowers who pay little or nothing as a down payment has led to many borrowers just walking away from their home the first time they experience any type of financial difficulty.

6. *Historically low interest rates:* The lowest interest rates in 40 years have allowed borrowers to buy larger, more expensive homes than ever before. However, most residential loans are based on two incomes. The problem with large loans that are based on two incomes is that when one of the borrowers loses his or her source of income, the borrowers usually cannot continue to make their loan payment on just one borrower's income and wind up having their dream home foreclosed.

The National Delinquency Survey

As I briefly mentioned, the Mortgage Bankers Association (MBA) compiles and publishes the quarterly National Delinquency Survey (NDS) that shows the seasonally adjusted delinquency rate for mortgage and deed of trust loans on one-to-four-unit residential properties. According to the MBA, the NDS currently covers more than 32 million loans that represent about half of all outstanding first-lien residential loans in the United States. The loans surveyed are reported by approximately 130 lenders, including mortgage bankers, commercial banks, thrifts, and life insurance companies. To review the National Delinquency Survey, log on to the MBA Web site: www.mortgagebankers.org and click on News Room and scroll down until you find the NDS.

Nothing Illegal or Unethical about Buying Property from Owners in Foreclosure

In spite of what many uninformed people may believe, there is nothing inherently illegal or unethical about buying properties directly from owners with mortgage or deed of trust loans that are in default and facing foreclosure. The fact of the matter is that the vast majority of pre-foreclosure property investors nationwide are honest, ethical business people, who provide much needed debt relief to tens of thousands of financially distressed property owners annually. And during the course of reading this book, you are going to learn how to be a profitable investor without having to resort to the vulture tactics that are commonly employed by predatory foreclosure investors. Treating property owners in foreclosure in an honest, ethical manner is not only the right thing to do, but also the best way to avoid being the subject of the lead story on your favorite local television evening news broadcast exposing sleazy real estate investors who prey on homeowners in foreclosure.

It Takes Knowledge and Persistence to Be a Profitable Pre-Foreclosure Investor

Trust me; you do not need a degree from Harvard Law School in order to make money buying properties directly from owners with mortgage or deeds of trust loans that are in default and about to be sold at a public foreclosure auction sale. Please do not get me wrong: Finding, researching, inspecting, negotiating, buying, and reselling pre-foreclosure properties can be a lot of hard work. But it can also be a very lucrative line of work, provided you are knowledgeable, well organized, and have the good old-fashioned stick-to-itiveness that is necessary to be a profitable pre-foreclosure investor in today's competitive foreclosure market.

How I Got Started Buying Pre-Foreclosure Properties 20 Years Ago

When I started out as a real estate investor in 1980, there were no books available on how to buy properties directly from owners in foreclosure before the auction. In fact, everything that I read on the subject of investing in foreclosures told me to buy property on the county courthouse steps at public foreclosure auction sales. I attended a few public foreclosure auction sales, but I was not impressed by what I observed. I saw investors get caught up in the frenzy surrounding the competitive bidding process and end up overpaying for property. So, I decided to forget about investing in foreclosures. However, in 1985, Archie, one of my birddogs in South Tampa, called and told me about a single-family house on Fitzgerald Street, near MacDill Air Force Base, that was scheduled to be sold at a public foreclosure auction sale in 30 days. Archie also told me that due to the husband being injured on the job, the owners were six months behind on their house payments, and the owners had decided to vacate the house and move in with relatives before the scheduled sale date. The next day I mailed the owners a short note that read: "What do I have to do to buy your house?" I enclosed a business card and told them to call me anytime. I received a telephone call from the wife two days later. She told me that she and her husband did not understand how I could possibly buy their house while they were six months behind on their payments and owed the bank over $3,000 in loan payments, late fees, accrued interest, and legal fees. I told her that it was possible, and I made an appointment to meet with her and her husband. That evening, I negotiated a deal where the owners sold me their equity in exchange for my bringing their loan current and assuming their non-qualifying Veterans Administration (VA) mortgage loan. As far as I understood it at the time, I had done nothing more than take over a delinquent loan from a homeowner in distress. Now in hindsight, I realize I had done my first pre-foreclosure property deal without even knowing it. However, I quickly realized that the concept of taking over loan payments from financially distressed property owners had a lot more profit potential than bidding against every foreclosure investor in Tampa on the Hillsborough County Courthouse steps. And, I have been refining the process of buying properties directly from owners in foreclosure ever since I struck that first deal back in 1985!

How I Made a $14,000 Profit on My First Pre-Foreclosure Property

I turned around and resold the house on Fitzgerald Street one month later to a staff sergeant in the United States Air Force for a $14,000 profit. Here's an in-depth, step-by-step analysis of the actual transaction:

1. *The type of property:* The property was a three-bedroom, one bathroom single-family house of concrete block construction.

2. *How the property was found:* The property was found by what is known in the business as a property locator or birddog, who was paid a $300 finder's fee on the day the transaction closed.

3. *The type of existing loan:* The existing loan on the property was a fixed-rate, 30-year, non-qualifying VA-guaranteed mortgage at 12 percent interest.

4. *The cost to reinstate the existing loan:* I paid the lender $3,125 to reinstate the loan. I was able to get the lender to waive $875 in legal fees.

5. *The cost to close the transaction:* I paid a total of $850 in closing costs to include a title search, title insurance, and title transfer taxes.

6. *The purchase price of the property:* I bought the house for the amount of the existing loan balance, which was $28,250.

7. *The cost of buying the owner's equity:* The owners agreed to accept my cost of reinstating and assuming their mortgage as payment for their equity. They just wanted to get the lender off their back and avoid having a foreclosure on their credit report.

8. *The cost of buying subordinate liens:* Surprisingly, the only outstanding lien against the property was a delinquent property tax bill of less than $150 for 1984. The owners had claimed the property as their homestead, so the first $25,000 of assessed value was exempt from taxation.

9. *The cost of fixing up the property:* There was no fix-up cost as I sold the house in an as-is condition.

10. *The total cost to acquire the property:* The total cost to acquire the house was $4,125.

11. *How the purchase was financed:* I paid the lender $45 to assume the existing fixed-rate, 30-year, non-qualifying VA-guaranteed mortgage at 12 percent interest.

12. *The resale price of the property:* I resold the house in 1985 for $42,500 with owner financing.

13. *How the sale was financed:* The buyer paid $4,000 as a down payment, and I financed the purchase by using what is known as a wraparound mortgage. I lent the buyer $10,000 of my equity in the form of a purchase money second mortgage at 12 percent interest. My second mortgage was figuratively wrapped around the existing first mortgage, hence, the term *wraparound mortgage.* The property's title was transferred to the buyer, but the first mortgage stayed in my name. The new buyer's mortgage payment covered both the first and second mortgages. I paid the monthly payment on the first mortgage and kept the rest.

14. *Net profit before taxes:* The net profit before taxes was a little over $14,000 because the property was sold on a wraparound mortgage that included a $10,000 purchase money second mortgage that was amortized over 10 years, with a balloon payment due in 5 years. The interest income earned during the 5-year lifespan of the second mortgage was a little over $4,000. The buyer refinanced the loan in 1990, paid the balloon payment as agreed, and cashed me out of the deal.

Today, I value my time at $100 an hour and will not pursue a pre-foreclosure property unless I can make at least a $15,000 profit before taxes and without offering any type of seller financing. Most professional pre-foreclosure investors that I know around the country tell me that they average between $25,000 and $35,000 profit per deal.

A One-on-One Graduate Level Seminar That Is Not Available at Any College

As the old saying goes, they don't teach this stuff at Harvard Business School or anywhere else for that matter. To the best of my knowledge, there is not a single course available on how to buy pre-foreclosure properties at any fully accredited junior college, community college, college, university, or graduate-level business school within the United States. However, because you had the good sense to invest in a copy of *The Pre-Foreclosure Property Investor's Kit,* you are now going to receive the college equivalent of a one-on-one graduate level seminar on the finer points of the pre-foreclosure property investment business complete with examples of real deals. But best of all, you are going to be able to learn at your own pace and within the comfort and privacy of your home. In other words, you are going to get a useful education without having to take out a student loan to pay for it or be subjected to the usual dry, dull, useless pap that's being pushed on most college campuses today by long-winded, know-it-all professors with no practical, hands-on experience. And to top it all off, you will be able to actually put your newfound moneymaking knowledge to immediate use!

It Is Hard to Succeed When You Are Unemployed, Broke, and Have Lousy Credit

I don't know how you are wired, but my internal bullspit detector automatically goes off when I read about the exploits of some novice investor who claims to have bought his or her first pre-foreclosure property for the paltry sum of $10 and then realized a whopping $53,000 profit by magically reselling the property three days later. The fact of the matter is that in spite of what some real estate fairy tale authors may tell you, it does take a certain amount of money and credit to be a successful foreclosure investor. I don't want to come across as some sort of real estate killjoy, but for the average person with absolutely no real estate investment or business experience, it's almost next to impossible to succeed as a pre-foreclosure property investor when you are unemployed, broke, and have lousy credit. The problem is that virtually all legitimate pre-foreclosure investment strategies require a certain amount of cash—or the creditworthiness to borrow money—to implement. The best advice I can give to any aspiring pre-foreclosure property investor who is currently unemployed, flat broke, and has lousy credit is to get a steady-paying job, save your money, and rebuild your credit.

How to Invest Without a Large Income, Big Bank Account, and High Credit Score

I just gave you a reality check on why an unemployed person who happens to be flat broke and has lousy credit to boot has an extremely slim chance of making it as a pre-foreclosure investor. Now I am going to tell you how you can get started investing in pre-foreclosure properties without a six-figure income, a large bank account, and a super-high credit score. First off, the amount of money that you will need to do your first deal depends on what segment of your local real estate market you target. For example, my target market in Hillsborough County, Florida, is stable, blue-collar neighborhoods where houses sell for $90,000 to

$140,000. Please keep in mind that a house that sells for $140,000 in Tampa would cost double that amount in the Northeast and triple that price in California. And depending upon the circumstances, it usually costs me between $8,500 and $11,500 to reinstate the loan and buy the owner's equity at a steep discount. However, if I were to put the same property under contract and then turn around and assign or sell my purchase agreement for a $5,000 profit to an experienced, professional investor who has the financial wherewithal to close the deal, my out-of-pocket expenses would probably be less than $1,500. If I decided to ask a foreclosing lender to modify the terms of an existing loan so that the loan could be assumed, I would need a FICO Score of only 620 and an annual income of around $40,000 to assume the loan on reasonable terms. (The term FICO refers to the name of the company, Fair Isaac Corporation, that developed the popular credit scoring model named FICO.) So, as you can see, in my target market, you can get started as a pre-foreclosure investor with an annual income of $40,000, less than $2,000 in savings, and a FICO Score of 620. In Chapter 5, I give you complete details on realistic ways that you can finance the purchase of a pre-foreclosure property.

Learn How to Use My 14-Step Process for Investing in Pre-Foreclosures

Over the past 20 years, I have developed and refined a 14-step process for investing in pre-foreclosure properties. In Part Two of this book, you will learn chapter by chapter how to use my 14-step process and avoid the pitfalls and problems that plague most uninformed and unsuspecting novice pre-foreclosure investors just starting out. Here is my 14-step process along with a brief description of each step.

Step 1: Find Property Owners with Loans That Are in Default and Facing Foreclosure

In Chapter 7, you will learn where foreclosure notices are filed in your county and how to use them to find property owners with mortgage or deed of trust loans that are in default and facing foreclosure. You will also find out how you can access your county's public records online to obtain information on foreclosure actions on the very same day they are recorded in the official public records.

Step 2: Contact Property Owners in Foreclosure

After you have finished reading Chapter 8, you will know the methods that professional investors use to contact property owners with mortgage or deed of trust loans that are in default and facing foreclosure. There are also sample copies of six very good letters that you can send to property owners in foreclosure. Plus, you will get the scoop on how to use classified newspaper ads to find owners with delinquent loans that have not yet been made public information.

Step 3: Get the Lowdown on Loans in Default from Foreclosing Lenders

Chapter 9 contains complete step-by-step instructions on how to quickly get the lowdown on loans in default from foreclosing lenders and their attorneys and trustees. You will find out how to quickly verify loan information without having to constantly deal with snotty loan clerks who can be a royal pain in the butt.

Step 4: Perform Due Diligence on Pre-Foreclosure Properties

In Chapter 10, you will receive a mini-course on how to perform due diligence on pre-foreclosure properties. You will also learn how to use the Internet to access the numerous public records that are available online to find current information on a pre-foreclosure property and its owner.

Step 5: Thoroughly Inspect a Pre-Foreclosure Property

In Chapter 11, you will learn how to avoid being bamboozled by an unscrupulous owner trying to surreptitiously mask a pre-foreclosure property's major defects. This chapter also comes complete with 13 ready-to-use checklists for conducting your own pre-buy property inspections.

Step 6: Accurately Estimate the Current Market Value of a Pre-Foreclosure Property

By the time you have finished reading Chapter 12, you will know how to accurately estimate the current or as-is market value of a pre-foreclosure property. This is the single most important aspect of the entire buying process, so please make certain that you fully understand it before you go out on a buying binge!

Step 7: Negotiate with Property Owners in Foreclosure

Chapter 13 gives you the step-by-step guidelines on how to negotiate with property owners with mortgage or deed of trust loans that are in default and facing foreclosure. You will learn all of the little nuances that you need to know about when dealing with property owners in a state of denial.

Step 8: Get Subordinate Lienholders to Discount Their Liens by 50 Percent or More

The real hallmark of a profitable pre-foreclosure property investor is the ability to get subordinate lienholders to discount their liens by 50 percent or more. In this business, your profit margin is tied directly to how well you are able to negotiate discounts with subordinate lienholders. In Chapter 14, you will learn how to get lienholders to discount their liens by 50 percent or more.

Step 9: Negotiate with Foreclosing Lenders and Their Attorneys and Trustees

To be a successful pre-foreclosure property investor, you need to know how to negotiate directly with foreclosing lenders and their hardball attorneys and trustees. In Chapter 15, you will learn what to say during face-to-face negotiations, so that you get the best possible deal every time.

Step 10: Do a Short Payoff Sale on Pre-Foreclosure Properties with Little or No Equity

The much-ballyhooed short payoff sale acquisition technique is covered in Chapter 16. You will get step-by-step instructions and realistic advice on how to submit a short sale package that will impress lenders and get them to accept your short payoff of a mortgage or deed of trust loan.

Step 11: Prepare Your Purchase Agreements

You will get all of the nitty-gritty details on how to properly prepare your purchase agreements in Chapter 17. Please pay close attention to what is in this chapter so that you do not end up being sued by sellers claiming that you took unfair advantage of their financial situation when they were in foreclosure.

Step 12: Close on a Pre-Foreclosure Property Transaction

In Chapter 18, you will learn how to use everything that you have learned in the previous 17 chapters to close on the purchase of a pre-foreclosure property. You also get the straight scoop on how to fully protect your rights and interests so that you do not get ripped off by unscrupulous property owners when buying pre-foreclosures.

Step 13: Fix Up Pre-Foreclosure Properties for Maximum Curb Appeal and Resale Value

How to fix up pre-foreclosure properties for maximum curb appeal and resale value is the subject covered in Chapter 19. You will find out how to give a pre-foreclosure property an industrial strength cleaning and cosmetic facelift on schedule and within budget.

Step 14: Package, Market, and Resell Pre-Foreclosure Properties for Maximum Profit

The detailed information that you will find in Chapter 20 will show you exactly how to package, market, and quickly resell pre-foreclosure properties for maximum profit. You will get the lowdown on how to use the Internet to market your pre-foreclosure properties to a global audience. Plus, you will learn how to structure a tax-efficient sale so that you can keep your federal tax bill to a minimum.

Some Sage Advice for All of the Overly Skeptical People Reading This Book

First, I am very well aware that the majority of people who reside within the borders of the United States worship the trappings of wealth and are pretty much open to any cockamamie get-rich-quick scheme they perceive will give them a fast ride to Easy Street. Second, given the vast number of scams that are being perpetrated against the American public on a daily basis, I definitely believe that a cautious dose of skepticism is the first line of defense against being ripped off by scam artists. However, an overdose of skepticism can have a blinding effect and keep a person from taking advantage of the numerous legitimate business opportunities that are available every day of the week to knowledgeable and open-minded people who know a real opportunity when they see one. As far as I am concerned, one of the very worst things that any person can do is to make financial and business decisions based solely on the advice of ignorant people who have never accomplished anything worthwhile in their entire adult lives! Yet, that is exactly what happens thousands of times a day all across America. Bright, ambitious people full of pep and vinegar listen to overly skeptical cynics who repeatedly tell them that it cannot be done, and then they, too, believe that it cannot be done and end up doing nothing. So, to all of you overly skeptical people reading this book, please do yourself a huge favor, and stop listening to the world-class skeptics in your life, who are most likely immediate family members such as good old mom and dad, along with brother Bob, sister Sue, Uncle Elmo, and close, personal friends or casual acquaintances like Billy the barber, Barbie the barmaid, and Harriet the hairdresser. I am not telling you to disown your overly skeptical family, friends, and acquaintances; I am just asking you to please stop taking unsolicited financial advice from them!

No Foreclosure Investment Strategy Will Work Unless You Do

This book was written for serious, rational, reasonable, intelligent, goal-driven, reality-based, and action-oriented adults who are willing to take calculated risks in order to profit from the many moneymaking opportunities that pre-foreclosure properties provide. As you will soon find out, *The Pre-Foreclosure Property Investor's Kit* is not your typical cash-in-a-flash real estate book. In other words, if you are looking for some magic formula that will tell you how to make a million bucks from pre-foreclosures by next Thursday, you are reading the wrong book. The pre-foreclosure investment strategies that I have outlined in this book will work only if you do! So if you really want to be a profitable pre-foreclosure investor, you must first be willing to put in the time and effort necessary to fully understand the information that is contained in this book! Then, you must be willing to get up off your keister, go beyond where most people fear to tread, and put what you have learned to practical use. One of the real truisms in life is this: Action is what separates the wannabes from the doers. You can have the equivalent of a PhD in pre-foreclosure property investments and be able to recite the contents of this book verbatim from rote memory, but it would all be meaningless if you did not possess the financial courage to go out and actually buy properties from owners in foreclosure.

How to Contact the Author Directly

Please feel free to contact me if there is something that you still do not understand after reading this book twice. Unlike 99 percent of all real estate authors in America, there are no gatekeepers between my readers and me. I answer my own e-mail and telephone, and I am fully wired to communicate from anywhere within the United States. You can e-mail me directly at tjlucier@thomaslucier.com. Or, call me direct at my office in Tampa, Florida, at (813) 237-6267. No other real estate author in America offers his or her readers this free service!

CHAPTER 2

Why Most Foreclosure Investment Strategies Being Taught Today Are Too Risky, Too Expensive, and Not Worth Doing

I probably could have just as well named this chapter "Myths, Lies, and Fairy Tales: What Most Foreclosure Experts Fail to Tell People." I say this because to hear most of the foreclosure pundits tell it, you would think that making money from foreclosures is a piece of cake. Well, it is not quite the slam-dunk that they make it out to be. The truth of the matter is that most—more than 51 percent—of all the foreclosure investment strategies being taught today are too risky, too expensive, and just not worth doing. Case in point: In almost every foreclosure book in print today, all of the authors rave about the oodles of money that investors can make from foreclosure sales and lender-owned properties. And to top it off, they make the process of buying these two types of properties seem like a leisurely Sunday stroll in the park! However, in reality, finding a foreclosure bargain like the ones they describe can be harder than finding the proverbial needle-in-a-haystack. To me, the risk versus reward ratio for these two types of foreclosure properties is way out of whack. In other words, the risk potential far outweighs the profit potential! In my professional opinion, these are high-risk, high-cost strategies that are very seldom profitable. That is why in this chapter, I am going to give you the straight dope about foreclosure sales and lender-owned properties and point out the numerous potential risks, problems, and pitfalls so that you do not waste your valuable time and energy pursuing them!

Properties in Foreclosure Can Be Bought Before, During, and After the Sale

There are three stages before, during, and after the foreclosure sale when investors can buy property. However, please keep in mind that the potential profit margin of a property in foreclosure decreases as the scheduled foreclosure auction sale date gets closer. Properties can be bought during the following three stages of the foreclosure process:

1. *The pre-foreclosure stage:* The pre-foreclosure stage is the first step in the foreclosure process during which investors can buy properties directly from owners in foreclosure before the auction.
2. *The public foreclosure auction stage:* The public foreclosure auction stage is when the public is given the opportunity to bid on properties that have been foreclosed on at a public foreclosure auction and trustee sales.
3. *The post-foreclosure stage:* The post-foreclosure stage occurs after the property has been foreclosed on and taken back by the foreclosing lender. These types of lender-owned properties are commonly referred to in the foreclosure business as *other real estate owned* (OREO).

Why the Pre-Foreclosure Stage Is the Time to Buy During the Foreclosure Process

The old saying, "Timing is everything in life," applies to buying foreclosures, too! I hate to be a party-pooper, but the only way that you are ever going to make a substantial profit from foreclosures is to buy them at the right time during the foreclosure process. And buying foreclosure properties from lenders at public foreclosure auction and trustee sales is definitely not the right time. Neither is buying lender-owned properties that were never bid on at auction. The right time to buy foreclosures is during the pre-foreclosure stage. This way you:

1. Can buy properties directly from owners without having to go through third parties such as government representatives and real estate brokers.
2. Have an opportunity to buy a property owner's equity at a discount of 50 percent or more.
3. Can thoroughly inspect the property and accurately estimate repair costs before making an offer to purchase.
4. Avoid the costly competitive bidding process that is part of the public foreclosure auction and trustee sales process.

No One Ever Got Rich Buying Foreclosures at Full Market Value

To me, what really separates professional foreclosure investors from the amateurs is that the pros never, ever pay retail prices when buying foreclosures. And that is exactly why I am not a fan of the two main foreclosure strategies that are being taught today. Neither strategy offers investors a legitimate opportunity to buy properties at real wholesale prices. In other words, there is just not enough profit in most foreclosure transactions to make them financially worthwhile. For example, under a typical foreclosure or lender-owned sale scenario, an investor would be lucky to be able to buy any property below market value. I do not know about you, but I have never met anyone who has ever gotten rich in real estate from buying any type of property at full market value. There is an old adage in real estate: "You make your profit when you buy and get paid when you sell." And investing in foreclosures is certainly no different! It really comes down to this: Investors who know how to buy properties directly from owners in foreclosure at wholesale prices prosper, while investors who get sucked into paying the full retail price for properties at foreclosure sales go broke. And in most cases, what appears on paper as a profit may actually be a breakeven deal or even a loss. That's because most foreclosure investors never bother to factor in the amount of time they spend chasing foreclosures as a business expense. If they did, they would come to the quick realization that they were working for subminimum wage. I don't know about you, but to me, the prospect of working for subminimum wage has zero appeal!

Most Foreclosure Investment Strategies Are Based on Hype and Misinformation

Right from the get-go, I want to separate fact from fiction when it comes to investing in foreclosures. As I see it, most of the foreclosure investment strategies being taught today are based more on hype and misinformation than on profit potential. In marketing circles, this is known as selling the sizzle and not the steak itself. To me, what is equally as bad for aspiring foreclosure investors as the misleading marketing techniques that the get-rich-quick-in-foreclosures crowd employs is that their overhyped investment strategies provide investors with very few legitimate opportunities to actually make money from foreclosures. To parody a golden oldie titled, "Looking for Love in All the Wrong Places," most would-be foreclosure mavens who blindly follow this type of advice end up "looking for foreclosure bargains in all the wrong places."

Twelve Things Most People Are Never Told about Public Foreclosure Auction Sales

To hear the foreclosure experts tell it, you would think that public foreclosure auction and trustees' sales were the greatest thing going since Robert Allen made the public aware of the concept of buying real estate for nothing down in the early 1980s. As far as I am concerned, the foreclosure investment strategy of buying properties at foreclosure sales is just as flawed as Allen's nothing down strategy. Here is a listing of 12 things that most of the experts never mention or quickly gloss over when telling everyone how swell it is to buy properties on the county courthouse steps at public foreclosure auction and trustee sales:

1. *There is no opportunity to conduct a pre-buy property inspection.* The old adage "What you see is what you get" does not apply to properties bought at foreclosure sales. The truth is that when you bid on properties at foreclosure sales, you are buying property sight unseen because it is almost always next to impossible to get the owner or tenant occupying the property to let anyone inside to inspect the interior. The fact is that most houses that end up being foreclosed on are thoroughly trashed, and everything of value has been stripped by the hostile inhabitants. Given the high cost of property repairs, buying foreclosures sight unseen could prove to be a blueprint for financial ruin.

2. *All sales are final and without recourse.* All foreclosure sales are final, where-is, as-is transactions without any disclosures or warranties by the foreclosing lender. This means that you could very well end up buying a property that is contaminated by lead-based paint, asbestos, indoor mold, or a host of other environmentally hazardous waste materials and have absolutely no recourse against the seller. Most state property owner disclosure statutes generally do not apply to properties that are bought at foreclosure sale.

3. *Verifiable proof of funds is required in order to bid.* Virtually all public foreclosure auction and trustees' sales require bidders to show verifiable proof of funds. For example, in Florida, all bidders at public foreclosure auction sales are required to have cash or a cashier's check for 5 percent of the winning bid amount. Winning bidders have until 12:00 P.M. on the following day to pay the balance of their bid along with title transfer fees. The proof of funds requirement is designed to keep non-qualified bidders from clogging up the auction by bidding on properties they do not have the funds to purchase.

4. *There is no opportunity to use leverage.* Buying properties at foreclosure sales is strictly a cash and carry proposition. However, most beginning foreclosure investors are woefully undercapitalized and do not have the deep pockets that are needed to bid on properties. And if you are not flush with cash or do not have the equivalent of a real estate sugar daddy waiting on the sidelines, you will most likely have a very hard time coming up with the cash needed to make a large lump sum payment. In other words, you will not be allowed to give the foreclosing lender a 10 percent down payment and use what is known as leverage to have the lender finance the remaining 90 percent of the sale price.

5. *There is the possibility that the property's title cannot be insured.* Most title insurers consider properties bought at foreclosure sales to be an extraordinary and unusual risk. The term *extraordinary and unusual risk* means that the foreclosure sale must be reviewed by an underwriter before the insurer will issue a title insurance commitment. Title insurers are generally leery of foreclosure sales because of their fear that the statutory provisions regarding the conduct of the foreclosure sale may not have been properly followed. And when a title insurer's review of a foreclosure sale uncovers procedural errors that deem the sale to be flawed, they will refuse to insure the property's title.

6. *Collusion between bidders is possible.* Another potential problem associated with buying properties through a competitive bidding process is the very real possibility that a group of bidders may use collusion or bid rigging to secretly restrict or chill the competition from other bidders. What generally happens is that a group of experienced bidders will get together before the scheduled foreclosure sale date and decide the maximum amount they are going to bid on certain properties.

7. *The sale price is determined by a competitive bidding process.* Unlike the sale price of a pre-foreclosure property that is negotiated between the two principals in the transaction better known as the buyer and seller, the sale price of a property sold at a foreclosure auction sale is determined by a competitive bidding process. The bidding process can be unduly influenced by the frenzy that usually surrounds foreclosure sales and often results in the so-called winning bidder overpaying for the property.

8. *The property may not be in an insurable condition.* In case you did not know it, property and casualty insurers are very picky about the type of properties they will insure. This means that it may be impossible to obtain insurance on a run-down looking property with a trashed interior that was bought sight unseen at a foreclosure sale. In fact, insurers have gotten to the point where they now run background checks on properties to see how many

claims have been filed against a particular property. And if there have been too many claims within a two- to five-year period, they will refuse to insure the property. It is akin to the property being designated a lemon for insurance purposes.

9. *The property may be in the possession of hostile occupants.* In many cases, the winning bidder is forced to file a costly and time-consuming eviction or unlawful detainer lawsuit in order to have the previous owner, tenants, or unknown persons legally removed from the property. This can stop investors dead in their tracks and prevent them from getting the property in a marketable condition and ready for resale.

10. *It is possible that the property can be redeemed after the sale.* In 11 states, property owners who have been foreclosed on retain the right to redeem their property after the foreclosure sale has taken place. Owner redemption periods range from 10 days in New Jersey to 12 months in Alabama. Most of the states that grant property owners the right to redeem their property after a foreclosure sale also allow subordinate or junior lienholders the right to redeem property when the owner fails to do so. Finally, the Internal Revenue Service has the right to redeem any property that has a federal tax lien attached to its title within 120 days after the foreclosure auction sale date.

11. *The foreclosure sale procedure could have been flawed.* Many foreclosure lawsuits and notices of default are riddled with technical errors such as misspelled names, erroneous legal descriptions, inaccurate street addresses, and mathematical errors made in calculating loan arrearages, legal fees, and late payment charges. Furthermore, procedural errors made during the foreclosure process such as the faulty service of process on defendants and failure to adhere to statutory foreclosure sale procedures can all result in a foreclosure auction or trustee's sale being overturned on appeal. In the process of appealing the foreclosure sale, the previous owner would most likely obtain a court order forbidding the new owner from disposing of the property until the case has been heard in court. This could take months, and in the meantime, the property sits in legal limbo with the meter running.

12. *None of the terms of the sale are negotiable.* Foreclosure sale procedures are governed by state statutes, which cannot be deviated from. This means that investors have absolutely no chance to negotiate the terms of a foreclosure sale with the deputy clerks of the court, deputy sheriffs, court-appointed referees, and trustees who conduct public foreclosure auction and trustee sales.

Why Most Lender-Owned Properties Are Not What They Are Cracked Up to Be

Sure, there are a slew of lender-owned properties available for sale in most real estate markets, but only once in a blue moon is there a lender-owned property that is actually worth buying. In fact, most lender-owned properties are nothing like what they are cracked up to be in most foreclosure books and weekend seminars. For starters, lender-owned properties, especially Department of Housing and Urban Development (HUD) and DVA homes, are sold by a rigid set of rules that are strictly enforced. Second, 99 percent of all lender-owned properties are sold through real estate brokers at full market value. So, there are very few opportunities to buy a lender-owned property that has immediate resale profit potential. Here are four very good reasons why I highly recommend that you do not buy lender-owned properties:

1. *Buyers must have verifiable proof of funds in order to make written offers.* When a written offer to purchase a lender-owned property is submitted through a real estate broker, the purchase agreement must be accompanied by verifiable proof that the prospective buyer has the funds on hand to make the required down payment and pay closing costs. In addition, potential buyers must show proof that they have been pre-approved for a loan to finance the purchase. The proof of funds requirement is designed to keep non-qualified buyers from making written offers on properties they do not have the funds to purchase.

2. *Properties are sold through real estate brokers at fair market prices.* Today, almost all lender-owned properties are sold through real estate brokers at fair market prices. And as I told you at the beginning of this chapter, no one has ever gotten rich buying foreclosures from real estate brokers at full market value!

3. *There is no opportunity to inspect the property's electrical, plumbing, and mechanical systems.* All lender-owned properties are vacant and usually have the electrical power, natural gas, and water turned off. This means that investors are unable to have a property's electrical, plumbing, and mechanical systems such as heating and cooling units thoroughly inspected. To me, this is totally unacceptable, especially when it can cost thousands of dollars to have a property rewired or the plumbing and mechanical systems replaced.

4. *All sales are final and without recourse.* All lender-owned sales are final, where-is, as-is transactions without any warranties by the seller. This means that you could very well end up buying a property that is contaminated by

lead-based paint, asbestos, indoor mold, or a host of other environmentally hazardous waste materials, and you will have absolutely no recourse against the seller. Most state property disclosure statutes generally do not apply to lender-owned properties that are sold to the public.

Lender-Owned Properties Are Sold to the Public through Real Estate Brokers

Foreclosing lenders obtain property when no one bids over the lender's asking price, which usually includes the loan balance, arrearages, accrued interest, late payment charges, and legal fees. So, when you buy a lender-owned property, you are really buying a property that no one else wanted to buy during the foreclosure process. In effect, you are buying property that is left over from the preforeclosure and foreclosure sale stages. As you will read in the following paragraphs, all HUD, DVA, Fannie Mae, and Freddie Mac repossessed properties are sold where-is, as-is through real estate brokers at fair market prices:

1. *HUD-owned properties:* The management and marketing contractors who manage and sell HUD-owned houses are First Preston Management Inc. and Southeast Alliance, LLP. HUD-owned houses are sold through local HUD-approved real estate brokers. Buyers must provide proof of funds or be pre-approved for a loan before they can bid on a HUD-owned house. HUD-owned houses are sold for fair market value on a where-is, as-is basis without any warranty. To view a listing of HUD-owned houses in your state, log on to the HUD Homes web site: www.hud.gov/offices/hsg/sfh/reo/homes.cfm.

2. *DVA-owned properties:* Department of Veterans Affairs or DVA-owned properties are managed and sold by Ocwen Financial Corporation through local real estate brokers nationwide at fair market value. DVA-owned properties are sold in a where-is, as-is condition without any representations or warranties as to their condition. Buyers must provide proof of funds for a down payment and be pre-approved for a loan before they can make an offer on a DVA-owned property. Log on to the Ocwen Financial Corporation web site to see a listing of DVA-owned properties in your state: www.ocwen.com.

3. *Fannie Mae-owned properties:* Fannie Mae-owned homes are sold for full market value through local real estate brokers. All Fannie Mae-owned homes are listed in the local Multiple Listing System. Fannie Mae-owned properties are sold in an as-is condition without any representations or warranties as to their condition. Buyers must provide proof of funds for a down payment and be pre-approved for a loan before they can make an

offer on a Fannie Mae-owned property. To view a listing of Fannie Mae-owned houses in your state, log on to the Fannie Mae Homes web site: www.mortgagecontent.net/reoSearchApplication/fanniemae/reoSearch.jsp.

4. *Freddie Mac-owned properties:* Freddie Mac-owned homes are sold for full market value through local real estate brokers. Freddie Mac-owned properties are sold in a where-is, as-is condition without any representations or warranties as to their condition. Buyers must provide proof of funds for a down payment and be pre-approved for a loan before they can make an offer on a Freddie Mac-owned property. To view a listing of Freddie Mac-owned houses in your state, log on to the Freddie Mac Homes web site: www.homesteps.com/hm01_1featuresearch.htm.

CHAPTER 3

What Every Pre-Foreclosure Investor Needs to Know about Their State's Foreclosure Statute

In 1989, I wrote one of the first books published on how to buy properties directly from owners in foreclosure before they are sold at a public foreclosure auction sale on the county courthouse steps. And over the intervening years, I have received hundreds of letters and e-mails from people who have gotten into trouble because they were absolutely clueless about their state's foreclosure process, yet they approached owners in foreclosure and made written offers to buy their property. In most of the letters and e-mails that I have received, the investor was begging me for advice on either how to proceed with the transaction or how to get out of the agreement altogether without being sued by the property owner. Needless to say, this is not how aspiring pre-foreclosure property investors should go about educating themselves on how the foreclosure of a mortgage or deed of trust loan works in their state. As you will soon learn, you must obtain information about your state's foreclosure statute directly from legitimate sources. By legitimate sources, I mean your state's civil statutes, and not from some Internet message board. A word to the wise: Most of the information about investing in pre-foreclosures that is bandied about on Internet message boards is bogus hogwash written by anonymous posters whose collective knowledge on the subject would not fill a thimble.

Buying Properties from Owners in Foreclosure Requires Specialized Knowledge

The secret to being a profitable pre-foreclosure property investor is specialized knowledge. In no other type of distressed property investment is specialized knowledge so highly rewarded and ignorance so harshly punished than when buying properties directly from owners in foreclosure. In this business, you cannot afford to blindly rely on the expertise and advice of so-called real estate professionals such as real estate agents and title and escrow agents who may or may not know what they are doing. When you buy properties directly from owners with mortgage or deed of trust loans that are in default and facing foreclosure, you become involved in a sort of real estate free-for-all in which terms are negotiated one-on-one between property owners in foreclosure, who usually begrudgingly sell as a last resort, and overanxious buyers, who oftentimes do not really know what they are doing. One of the major problems in buying pre-foreclosure properties is that buyers lack the normal intermediaries they depend on in a conventional, easy-to-close real estate transaction. In a conventional real estate transaction between a willing seller and a willing buyer, real estate agents, title and escrow agents, and attorneys are readily available to hold hands and slowly walk both parties through the transaction. However, this is not the case when you buy a pre-foreclosure property that can have a myriad unique problems that must be quickly solved before the property's loan is foreclosed on and sold at public auction. And when you buy properties directly from owners in foreclosure, time is always of the essence because when most owners in foreclosure finally decide to throw in the towel and sell their property, it is almost always at the 11th hour in the foreclosure process, usually within a day or two before the public foreclosure auction or trustee's sale is scheduled to take place. As a side note, I once had to drive a property owner in foreclosure to the Tampa headquarters of the now defunct Barnett Bank, just a mere four hours before the property was scheduled to be sold at a public foreclosure auction sale at the Hillsborough County Courthouse, in order to get the sale postponed so that I could buy the property. Finally, as far as I am concerned, before you ever go out on a pre-foreclosure property-buying binge, it is imperative that you first know:

1. The type of foreclosure action that is used in your state to foreclose on mortgage and deed of trust loans.
2. How the judicial or non-judicial foreclosure process works in your state.
3. The length of time that it takes to complete a foreclosure action in your state.
4. If your state's foreclosure statute gives homeowners in foreclosure the right to rescind or cancel a purchase agreement.

The Definition of Foreclosure

Foreclosure is generally defined as: *A legal process through which property, pledged as security for a debt, a mortgage, or deed of trust loan, is foreclosed on by the lender, because the borrower defaulted by failing to meet the repayment terms contained in the loan agreement and promissory note.*

Where to Find Your State's Foreclosure Statute Online

The quickest way to find your state's foreclosure statute online is to type the name of your state followed by the words "foreclosure statute" into a search engine such as www.google.com. All state statutes are available online at the following web site: http://www.prairienet.org/~scruffy/f.htm.

The Two Types of Foreclosure Actions Used to Foreclose on Real Estate Loans

The two types of foreclosure actions used to foreclose on real estate mortgage and deed of trust loans are:

1. Judicial foreclosure.
2. Non-judicial foreclosure.

How the Judicial Foreclosure Process Works

In states where judicial foreclosure is used to foreclose on mortgage and deed of trust loans, the foreclosing lender files a lawsuit to foreclose, naming as defendant the defaulting borrower—mortgagor or trustor—and all lienholders of record having an interest in the property subsequent to the lender recording the mortgage or deed of trust. The defaulting borrower and other interested parties—defendants—are then summoned, that is, officially notified by the court of the lawsuit pending against the defaulting borrower. In addition, a notice of *lis pendens*—suit pending—is filed with the county or public recorder or prothonotary's office to notify the general public that a lawsuit is pending against the property owner. Once notified, the borrower or any other defendants named in the lawsuit normally have 20 days to formally reply to the lawsuit and present their case. If no reply is made or the judge rules against the defendant's reply, the judge then orders the mortgage or deed of trust loan to be foreclosed on and the property sold at a public foreclosure auction sale to satisfy the foreclosing lender's claim. Here is a sequential outline of what happens under judicial foreclosure when a borrower defaults on a residential mortgage or deed of trust loan:

1. The lender files a lawsuit to foreclose the mortgage or deed of trust loan with a court of competent jurisdiction.
2. The borrower responds to the foreclosure lawsuit complaint, and a court hearing date is set.
3. The foreclosure lawsuit is heard in court, and the judge either dismisses the case or orders the loan to be foreclosed on.
4. The judge rules against the defendant borrower and orders the loan to be foreclosed on and that a public foreclosure auction sale date be scheduled for the property.
5. The public foreclosure auction sale is advertised.
6. The property is sold to the highest bidder at a public foreclosure auction sale or is taken back by the lender if there is no acceptable bid from the public.
7. The judge may award the lender a deficiency judgment against the borrower if the bid the lender accepted was for less than the loan balance owed.
8. The borrower may exercise any statutory redemption rights after the sale.
9. A sheriff's deed or certificate of title is given to the highest bidder after any statutory redemption period expires.

How the Non-Judicial Foreclosure Process Works

In states where non-judicial foreclosure is used to foreclose on mortgage and deed of trust loans, the foreclosing mortgage lender or deed of trust beneficiary invokes the power of sale covenant contained in the mortgage or deed of trust, which gives the lender or the trustee holding the deed of trust the right to foreclose the loan in default by filing a notice of default with the county or public recorder's office or the prothonotary's office. Here's a sequential outline of what happens under non-judicial foreclosure when a borrower defaults on a residential mortgage or deed of trust loan:

1. The trustee files a notice of default with the county or public recorder's office or the prothonotary's office.
2. The public trustee's sale date is set.

3. The public trustee's sale is advertised.

4. The property is sold to the highest bidder at a public trustee's auction sale or is taken back by the lender if there is no acceptable bid from the public.

5. The borrower may exercise any statutory redemption rights after the sale.

6. A trustee's deed is given to the highest bidder after any statutory redemption rights have expired.

Why You Must Know If Your State Has a Home Equity Sales Contract Statute

Some states, most notably California, have home equity sales contract statutes that were enacted to prevent buyers from taking unfair advantage of homeowners in foreclosure by using high pressure sales tactics to get homeowners to sign a purchase agreement. Most home equity sales contract statutes specify that buyers making offers on owner-occupied one- to four-unit residential properties, whose loans are in default, must include a right of rescission or notice of cancellation clause in their purchase agreements. This clause gives homeowners a period of time, usually five business days, excluding weekends and holidays, after the contract was signed during which they can rescind or cancel the purchase agreement.

The Two Statutes That Regulate California Pre-Foreclosure Property Investors

The California State Legislature has enacted the following two statutes to try to protect homeowners in foreclosure from "fraud, deception, and unfair dealing" by home equity purchasers and foreclosure consultants:

1. *California home equity sales contracts:* California home equity sales contracts are covered under Sections 1695–1695.17 of the California Civil Code.

2. *California mortgage foreclosure consultants:* California mortgage foreclosure consultants are covered under Sections 2945–2945.11 of the California Civil Code.

The California Civil Code is Available Online

The California Civil Code is available online at the following web site: www.leginfo .ca.gov/calaw.html.

Where to Find Reliable Information on the Foreclosure Process in Your State

The most reliable and up-to-date source of state-by-state foreclosure information that I have found is the *Foreclosure Desk Guide*, published by the United States Foreclosure Network (USFN). The USFN is a non-profit association of law firms and trustee companies that provide loan loss mitigation and foreclosure services to the mortgage industry. The members of the USFN use the *Foreclosure Desk Guide* as their foreclosure reference guide. This cornucopia of foreclosure information covers everything from breach letters to foreclosure notices to subordinate liens and is available at the USFN web site: www.usfn.org.

The following is a state-by-state listing of commonly used security instruments, foreclosure actions, and the foreclosure statute number for each state:

State	Security Instrument	Foreclosure Action	Statute Number
Alabama	Mortgage	Non-judicial	§35-10-1
Alaska	Deed of trust	Non-judicial	§34.20.090
Arizona	Deed of trust	Non-judicial	§33.807
Arkansas	Mortgage	Judicial	§51-1106
California	Deed of trust	Non-judicial	§2924
Colorado	Deed of trust	Non-judicial	§38-37-113
Connecticut	Mortgage	Strict Foreclosure	§49-24
Delaware	Mortgage	Judicial	§2101
D.C.	Deed of trust	Non-judicial	§45-701
Florida	Mortgage	Judicial	§702.01
Georgia	Security deed	Non-judicial	§44-14-162
Hawaii	Mortgage	Non-judicial	§667-1
Idaho	Deed of trust	Non-judicial	§6-101
Illinois	Mortgage	Judicial	§15-101
Indiana	Mortgage	Judicial	§32-8-11-3
Iowa	Mortgage	Judicial	§654.1
Kansas	Mortgage	Judicial	§60-2410
Kentucky	Mortgage	Judicial	§381.190
Louisiana	Mortgage	Executive process	§2631
Maine	Mortgage	Judicial	§6321
Maryland	Deed of trust	Non-judicial	§7-101
Massachusetts	Mortgage	Judicial	§19.21
Michigan	Mortgage	Non-judicial	§451.401
Minnesota	Mortgage	Non-judicial	§500.01
Mississippi	Deed of trust	Non-judicial	§89-1-55
Missouri	Deed of trust	Non-judicial	§443.320
Montana	Deed of trust	Non-judicial	§71-1-228
Nebraska	Mortgage	Judicial	§25-2139
Nevada	Deed of trust	Non-judicial	§107.020
New Hampshire	Mortgage	Non-judicial	§479.22

State	Security Instrument	Foreclosure Action	Statute Number
New Jersey	Mortgage	Judicial	§2A-50-2
New Mexico	Mortgage	Judicial	§48-7-7
New York	Mortgage	Judicial	§1301-91
North Carolina	Deed of trust	Judicial	§45
North Dakota	Mortgage	Judicial	§32-19-01
Ohio	Mortgage	Judicial	§2323.07
Oklahoma	Mortgage	Judicial	§686
Oregon	Deed of trust	Non-judicial	§86.010
Pennsylvania	Mortgage	Judicial	§1141
Rhode Island	Mortgage	Non-judicial	§34-11-22
South Carolina	Mortgage	Judicial	§15-7-10
South Dakota	Mortgage	Judicial	§21-47-1
Tennessee	Deed of trust	Non-judicial	§35-501
Texas	Deed of trust	Non-judicial	§51.002
Utah	Deed of trust	Non-judicial	§57-1-14
Vermont	Mortgage	Judicial	§4528
Virginia	Deed of trust	Non-judicial	§55-59.1
Washington	Deed of trust	Non-judicial	§61.12.010
West Virginia	Deed of trust	Non-judicial	§38-1-3
Wisconsin	Mortgage	Judicial	§846.01
Wyoming	Mortgage	Judicial	§1-18-101

State-by-State Foreclosure Timeline

The following is a state-by-state listing of the average length of time that it takes for a loan to be foreclosed on from the time a lender files a foreclosure lawsuit or records a notice of default, to the time a public foreclosure auction or trustee's sale takes place:

State	Number of Months	State	Number of Months
Alabama	3	Georgia	3
Alaska	4	Hawaii	7
Arkansas	3	Idaho	9
Arizona	3	Illinois	10
California	4	Indiana	9
Colorado	5	Iowa	7
Connecticut	6	Kansas	4
Delaware	7	Kentucky	7
District of Columbia	4	Louisiana	6
Florida	7	Maine	10

State	Number of Months	State	Number of Months
Maryland	5	Oklahoma	7
Massachusetts	5	Oregon	5
Michigan	3	Pennsylvania	9
Minnesota	4	Puerto Rico	12
Mississippi	4	Rhode Island	3
Missouri	3	South Carolina	6
Montana	6	South Dakota	4
Nebraska	4	Tenessee	3
Nevada	4	Texas	2
New Hampshire	3	Utah	5
New Jersey	10	Vermont	10
New Mexico	5	Virginia	4
New York	10	Washington	5
North Carolina	2	West Virginia	4
North Dakota	4	Wisconsin	10
Ohio	8	Wyoming	3

Use *The Pre-Foreclosure Property Investor's Kit* to Become Your Own Expert

Last, use *The Pre-Foreclosure Property Investor's Kit* to educate yourself so that you will become your own pre-foreclosure property expert. In this business you cannot afford to blindly rely on the advice of other people who may or may not know what they are doing when it comes to buying pre-foreclosure properties. Even if they have experience with conventional real estate transactions, they may be totally clueless about how to solve the potential problems associated with buying pre-foreclosure properties. Let's face it, if you do not understand how the foreclosure process works in your state, how will you know if the person advising you is not chock full of what makes the grass grow greener? It has been my experience in life that if you cannot confirm what you are being told to do, there is an excellent chance that you will end up being what I call a mushroom investor— an investor who is kept in the dark and fed a lot of bullspit by a so-called adviser, mentor, or coach!

CHAPTER 4

Everything You Need to Know about Existing Loans on Pre-Foreclosure Properties

I know several people who work in the residential loan loss mitigation departments of large regional and national banks. *Loan loss mitigation* is the highfalutin term that lenders use to describe the process they go through to try to help borrowers avoid foreclosure. My friends in loan loss mitigation tell me that the lenders they work for are being inundated with telephone calls and e-mail messages from ignorant wannabe foreclosure investors whom they characterize as flakes and who are unceremoniously given the old bankers' blow-off. In other words, flakes making the goofy telephone calls are told that the person they need to speak with in the loan loss mitigation department will be on vacation for the next three weeks. The dopey e-mails they receive from flakes are deleted or passed around the office for laughs! This may seem cruel to some, but the fact of the matter is that lenders just do not have the time to explain basic real estate loan fundamentals to recent honor graduates of the latest foreclosure seminar that hit town. Please keep this in mind whenever you think about ignoring the advice that I am dispensing here and get the urge to call a loan loss mitigation specialist and ask him or her to play your version of the 20 questions game.

How to Avoid Being Characterized as a Flake and Blown Off by Lenders

Unless you want to be characterized as a flake and experience a severe case of banker blow-off whenever you contact a foreclosing lender's loan loss mitigation department, you must first acquire an in-depth knowledge of the types of existing loans that are on pre-foreclosure properties. First, the term *existing loan* refers to the mortgage or deed of trust loan, or loans that are recorded against a property's title to secure repayment of the loan. Most single-family residential properties in the United States have more than one mortgage or deed of trust loan. The fact is, in real estate markets with super-high appreciation rates, it is not unusual to find homeowners who have three or four loans against their homes. The most mortgage loans that I have ever seen recorded against a pre-foreclosure property in my market was three. You will find that most pre-foreclosure properties with more than two loans are usually not worth pursuing due to insufficient equity. In other words, owners have used multiple loans to suck or strip all of the equity out of their property before foreclosure actions were initiated. As I told you in Chapter 3, specialized knowledge is the key to being successful in this business, and part of the specialized knowledge that you need to acquire as a pre-foreclosure investor is a full understanding of the duties, responsibilities, and relationships of all the parties involved in a mortgage or deed of trust loan. To accomplish this, you must know all of the nitty-gritty details about mortgage and deed of trust loans, loan covenants, assumption rules, and taking title subject to existing loans. This means that you must know as much about the nuts and bolts of real estate loans and the lending process as the lenders, attorneys, and trustees you will be dealing with. In a nutshell, you must know:

1. The names given to borrowers and lenders in mortgage and deed of trust loan documents.
2. The three loan covenants that pertain to loans in default.
3. The assumption rules for conventional and government insured and guaranteed loans.
4. Why taking title to a pre-foreclosure property subject to an existing loan can be risky business.
5. About state and federal equity skimming statutes.

In 1995, I passed the licensing requirements and obtained a Florida mortgage broker license that is still active. I did this with no intention of ever working as a mortgage broker. Rather, I spent the time, effort, and money to get my Florida mortgage broker license in order to get a better understanding of exactly how the residential and commercial lending process works. I have also found it very beneficial to mention the fact that I am a licensed mortgage broker when negotiating pre-foreclosure deals with lenders and their attorneys. It gives me sort of an inside edge that most unlicensed investors don't have. And trust me, in this business you need to take full advantage of any competitive edge that you can get over other professional pre-foreclosure investors in your market.

The Two Types of Security Instruments Used to Secure Real Estate Loans

The two most common types of security instruments that are used to secure both residential and commercial real estate loans are:

1. Mortgages.
2. Deeds of trust.

Mortgage Loans

The two parties to a mortgage are:

1. The mortgagor (borrower).
2. The mortgagee (lender).

When a real estate loan is secured by a mortgage, the mortgagor signs a promissory note and mortgage that the mortgagee keeps until the mortgagor pays the loan off.

Deed of Trust Loans

The three parties to a deed of trust are:

1. The trustor (borrower).
2. The beneficiary (lender).
3. The trustee (neutral third party holding the deed of trust).

When a real estate loan is secured by a deed of trust, the beneficiary makes a loan to the trustor, and the trustor gives the beneficiary a promissory note and a deed of trust, which conveys title to the trustee, is recorded in the public records, and is held in trust by the trustee until the loan is paid in full by the trustor.

The Two Types of Lenders That Make Real Estate Loans

Residential and commercial mortgage or deed of trust loans are made by the following two types of lenders:

1. *Institutional lenders:* Institutional lenders are banks, credit unions, mortgage companies, mortgage bankers, commercial banks, pension funds, and

insurance companies that are licensed to make mortgage or deed of trust loans on residential and commercial real estate.

2. *Private lenders:* Private lenders are private individuals and privately held business entities that are licensed to make residential and commercial loans.

The Three Types of Residential Real Estate Loans

The three types of residential real estate loans are:

1. *Conventional loan:* A conventional mortgage or deed of trust loan is a loan that is not guaranteed or insured by the U.S. government.
2. *FHA loan:* An FHA mortgage or deed of trust loan is a loan insured by the Federal Housing Administration.
3. *DVA loan:* A DVA mortgage or deed of trust loan is a loan guaranteed by the Department of Veterans Affairs.

The Difference between a First, Second, and Third Loan

The numerical designations that are given to real estate loans are used to distinguish their priority, or the sequence in which they were recorded against a property's title. For example, a first mortgage or deed of trust loan that was recorded on May 11, 2004, is superior to a second mortgage or deed of trust loan that was recorded on May 18, 2004. And that same second mortgage or deed of trust loan that was recorded on May 18, 2004, is superior to a third loan that was recorded on June 1, 2004.

The Difference between a Loan Broker and a Lender

The difference between a loan or mortgage broker and a lender is as follows:

1. *Loan broker:* A loan or mortgage broker is licensed to take loan applications from borrowers and arrange loans between borrowers and lenders for a fee. Loan brokers are not licensed to make mortgage or deed of trust loans directly to borrowers.

2. *Lenders:* Lenders are licensed to make mortgage or deed of trust loans directly to borrowers.

Residential Mortgage and Deed of Trust Loan Documents Are Available Online

You can review copies of the conventional residential mortgage or deed of trust loan documents that are used in your state at the following two web sites:

1. Fannie Mae loan documents: www.efanniemae.com/singlefamily/forms _guidelines/mortgage-documents/sec_instr.jhtm1?role=ou
2. Freddie Mac loan documents: www.freddiemac.com/uniform

Loan Terminology Dictionary Is Available Online

The following web site, Home Loan Dictionary, has a loan terminology dictionary: www.bcpl.net/~ibcnet/terms.html.

Three Covenants That Pertain to Mortgage and Deed of Trust Loans in Default

The three loan covenants contained in Fannie Mae and Freddie Mac conventional mortgage and deed of trust loan documents that pertain to loans in default are:

1. *Transfer of the property or a beneficial interest in borrower:* This covenant is the dreaded due-on-sale clause that allows lenders to call a loan if the title to the property securing the loan is transferred without the lender's prior approval.
2. *Borrower's right to reinstate after acceleration:* This covenant gives the borrower whose loan is in default the right to cure the default and reinstate the loan by paying all loan payments, late fees, and legal costs incurred by the lender while the loan was in default.
3. *Acceleration remedies:* This covenant gives lenders the right, upon default, to accelerate loan payments and demand that the unpaid principal loan balance be paid in full within 30 days from receipt of notice.

Transfer of the Property or a Beneficial Interest in Borrower

This covenant is the dreaded due-on-sale clause that allows lenders to call a loan if the title to the property securing the loan is transferred without the lender's prior approval:

> *As used in this Section 18, "Interest in the Property" means any legal or beneficial interest in the Property, including, but not limited to, those beneficial interests transferred in a bond for deed, contract for deed, installment sales contract, or escrow agreement, the intent of which is the transfer of title by Borrower at a future date to a purchaser.*
>
> *If all or any part of the Property or any Interest in the Property is sold or transferred (or if Borrower is not a natural person and a beneficial interest and a beneficial interest in Borrower is sold or transferred) without Lender's prior written consent, Lender may require immediate payment in full of all sums secured by this Security Instrument. However, this option shall not be exercised by Lender if such exercise is prohibited by Applicable Law.*
>
> *If Lender exercises this option, Lender shall give Borrower notice of acceleration. The notice shall provide a period of not less than 30 days from the date the notice is given in accordance with Section 15 within which Borrower must pay all sums secured by this Security Instrument. If Borrower fails to pay these sums prior to the expiration of this period, Lender may invoke any remedies permitted by this Security Instrument without further notice or demand on Borrower.*

What You Need to Know about Reinstating Loans That Are in a Default Status

First things first: Most lenders consider a loan to be in default when loan payments are 91 days or more past due. Once a loan is in default, the borrower has a certain amount of time to cure the default by paying the loan payments in arrears, accrued interest, late payment charges, and legal fees incurred by the lender while the loan was in default. All loans contain a *borrower's right to reinstate after acceleration clause* like the loan covenant in the following section. Curing a loan default is known in the lending business as *reinstating the loan.* A lender's reinstatement or cure date is the last day that a mortgage or deed of trust loan can be brought current without having to pay it off in full. It has been my experience that government-backed loans can be reinstated within hours of the scheduled sale date, while conventional lenders are more likely to take a hardball approach and not allow a loan to be reinstated within two or three days of the sale. I cover how to negotiate with foreclosing lenders and their attorneys and trustees in Chapter 15.

Borrower's Right to Reinstate after Acceleration

This is the loan covenant that I mentioned earlier that gives a borrower with a loan that is in default the right to cure the default and reinstate the loan by paying all loan payments that are in arrears, accrued interest, late payment charges, and legal costs incurred by the lender while the loan was in default:

> *If Borrower meets certain conditions, Borrower shall have the right to have enforcement of this Security Instrument discontinued at any time prior to the earliest of: (a) five days before sale of the Property pursuant to any power of sale contained in this Security Instrument; (b) such other period as Applicable Law might specify for the termination of Borrower's right to reinstate; or (c) entry of a judgment enforcing this Security Instrument. Those conditions are that Borrower: (a) pays Lender all sums which then would be due under this Security Instrument and the Note as if no acceleration had occurred; (b) cures any default of any other covenants or agreements; (c) pays all expenses incurred in enforcing this Security Instrument, including, but not limited to, reasonable attorneys' fees, property inspection and valuation fees, and other fees incurred for the purpose of protecting Lender's interest in the Property and rights under this Security Instrument; and (d) takes such action as Lender may reasonably require to assure that Lender's interest in the Property and rights under this Security Instrument, and Borrower's obligation to pay the sums secured by this Security Instrument, shall continue unchanged. Lender may require that Borrower pay such reinstatement sums and expenses in one or more of the following forms, as selected by Lender: (a) cash; (b) money order; (c) certified check, bank check, treasurer's check, or cashier's check, provided any such check is drawn upon an institution whose deposits are insured by a federal agency, instrumentality, or entity; or (d) Electronic Funds Transfer. Upon reinstatement by Borrower, this Security Instrument and obligations secured hereby shall remain fully effective as if no acceleration had occurred. However, this right to reinstate shall not apply in the case of acceleration under Section 18.*

Lender's Acceleration Remedies

Following is the acceleration covenant that gives lenders the right, upon default, to accelerate loan payments and demand that the unpaid principal loan balance be paid in full within 30 days from receipt of notice:

Lender shall give notice to Borrower prior to acceleration following Borrower's breach of any covenant or agreement in this Security Instrument (but not prior to acceleration under Section 18 unless Applicable Law provides otherwise). The notice shall specify: (a) the default; (b) the action required to cure the default; (c) a date, not less than 30 days from the date the notice is given to Borrower, by which the default must be cured; and (d) that failure to cure the default on or before the date specified in the notice may result in acceleration of the sums secured by this Security Instrument, foreclosure by judicial proceeding, and sale of the Property. The notice shall further inform Borrower of the right to reinstate after acceleration and the right to assert in the foreclosure proceeding the non-existence of a default or any other defense of Borrower to acceleration and foreclosure. If the default is not cured on or before the date specified in the notice, Lender at its option may require immediate payment in full of all sums secured by this Security Instrument without further demand and may foreclose this Security Instrument by judicial proceeding. Lender shall be entitled to collect all expenses incurred in pursuing the remedies provided in this Section 22, including, but not limited to, reasonable attorneys' fees and costs of title evidence.

The Due-on-Sale Clause as Defined in the Federal Code of Regulations

Title twelve, Volume Five of the Code of Federal Regulations as of January 1, 2004, defines the due-on-sale clause as follows:

Due-on-sale clause means a contract provision which authorizes the lender, at its option, to declare immediately due and payable sums secured by the lender's security instrument upon a sale or transfer of all or any part of the real property securing the loan without the lender's prior written consent. For purposes of this definition, a sale or transfer means the conveyance of real property of any right, title, or interest therein, whether legal or equitable, whether voluntary or involuntary, by outright sale, deed, installment sale contract, land contract, contract for deed, leasehold interest with a term greater than three years, lease-option contract, or any other method of conveyance of real property interests.

Loan Assumption Rule for Federal Housing Administration-Insured Loans

FHA federally insured loans closed prior to December 14, 1989, can be assumed without qualification simply by paying an assumption fee or taken subject to without paying any assumption fee. FHA-insured loans closed after December 15, 1989, can be assumed only by qualified owner-occupants and contain a due-on-sale clause that bans investors from ever being able to assume them.

Loan Assumption Rule for Department of Veterans Affairs Guaranteed Loans

Loans guaranteed by the DVA that were closed prior to March 1, 1988, contain no due-on-sale clause and may be assumed by anyone without qualification by paying an assumption fee or taken subject to without paying an assumption fee. DVA-guaranteed loans originated on or after March 1, 1988, contain a due-on-sale clause requiring prior approval by the DVA or its authorized agent before any DVA-guaranteed loan can be assumed. All DVA mortgage or deed of trust loans have the following statement printed on the top of the first page of the loan document: **"THIS LOAN IS NOT ASSUMABLE WITHOUT THE APPROVAL OF THE DE-PARTMENT OF VETERANS AFFAIRS OR ITS AUTHORIZED AGENT."** In Chapter 5, I show you how to use installment sale contracts to legally get around the DVA loan due-on-sale clause.

No Stated Loan Assumption Rules for Private and Seller-Financed Loans

Private real estate loans made by private individuals and purchase money first or second mortgage and deed of trust loans made by sellers may or may not contain due-on-sale clauses. A word of caution: Many private lenders may claim that their loan contains a due-on-sale clause when in fact it does not. Therefore, it is crucial that you personally read the entire mortgage or deed of trust along with the promissory note when reviewing any loan documents for due-on-sale clauses. This is especially true with private and purchase money loan documents, many of which are poorly written and do not contain a due-on-sale clause. This means that if the mortgage or deed of trust or promissory note does not contain a due-on-sale clause, the lender cannot call the loan or stop a buyer from taking the property's title subject to the existing loan.

I once bought a property subject to an existing purchase money first mort-gage that was held by the previous owner. Both the loan document and promis-sory note were very poorly written and did not contain any type of due-on-sale clause. However, that did not stop the private lender holding the loan and note from attempting to call the loan and threatening foreclosure if I did not pay the loan in full within 30 days. I sent the nitwit a very starchy letter and told him to please have the attorney he referred to in his letter file a foreclosure lawsuit against me. I continued to make loan payments, and he continued to cash them, and the subject was never brought up again while I owned the property.

Personally Review all Loan Documents for Due-on-Sale Clauses

How do you know if a loan document or promissory note contains a legally enforceable due-on-sale clause? The best way is for you to personally review all loan documents—mortgages, deeds of trust, and promissory notes—for due-on-sale clauses. Ask sellers to show you copies of both their mortgage or deed of trust and promissory note. Your goal in doing this is to determine whether the loan in default has a legally enforceable due-on-sale clause before you contact the lender.

Taking Title Subject to Violates the Due-on-Sale Clause in Most Loans

You need to know that taking title to a property subject to an existing residential mortgage or deed of trust loan is in direct violation of the due-on-sale clause that is contained in virtually all residential loan documents used by institutional lenders. This means that when a lender discovers that a sale has taken place in violation of the loan's due-on-sale clause, lenders have the following three options:

1. Call the loan and exercise their right to accelerate payments and demand that the entire unpaid principal loan balance be paid in full within 30 days.
2. Foreclose on the loan if the new owner fails to pay it off after the lender calls the loan due.
3. Do nothing and let the new owner take over the loan payments.

Taking Title to Property Subject to Existing Loans Can Be Risky Business

Contrary to popular belief, almost all transactions that are made subject to existing loans are usually quickly discovered by lenders. The discovery almost always occurs when the lender receives a hazard insurance policy that has the new owner's name as the insured, instead of the name of the borrower of record. As far as I'm concerned, buying pre-foreclosure properties subject to existing loans without the prior approval of the lender can be risky business. In my professional opinion, there is a better than 50 percent chance that the lender will call the loan after the sale takes place and demand that the entire unpaid principal loan balance be paid in full within 30 days. I say this because the loan is already under close scrutiny by the lender because of its default status. In other words, the loan is on the lender's brightly flashing radar screen. For this reason, I recommend that if you do take title subject to an existing mortgage or deed of trust loan that is in default, you do not invest a lot of money to cure the default and reinstate a loan. This way, if the lender does call the loan and you are not able to pay it off, you will be able to keep your losses to a minimum.

It Is Not a Criminal Act to Violate a Loan's Due-on-Sale Clause

In spite of the constant bullspit being espoused by a certain Harvard Business School graduate posing as a real estate savant, violating a loan's due-on-sale clause is not against the law nor is it a criminal act punishable by imprisonment or a monetary fine! It is a breach of a covenant contained in conventional and government-backed residential loan agreements that gives lenders the option to call a loan due. For example, if a borrower violates a loan's due-on-sale covenant and it is discovered by the lender, the lender has the right to call the loan due and payable in full within 30 days. And if the borrower does not pay the loan off within 30 days, the lender has the right to declare the loan in default and file a foreclosure lawsuit or a notice of default. Please trust me when I tell you that no member of any law enforcement agency that is allowed to operate within the borders of the United States is going to haul you off to jail just because you violated a loan's due-on-sale clause. It is not going to happen!

The Difference between Assuming an Existing Loan and Buying Subject To

When buyers assume an existing mortgage or deed of trust loan, they sign an assumption agreement with the lender that makes them legally responsible for repayment of the loan. When buyers take title to a property subject to the existing mortgage or deed of trust loan, all they are really doing is taking over the loan payments without being personally liable for repayment of the promissory note.

The responsibility for repayment of the loan always lies with the last owner assuming the loan, prior to its being taken subject to. In Chapter 5, I show you how to buy property subject to existing loans.

The Definition of Equity Skimming

Equity skimming as it pertains to taking title subject to an existing mortgage or deed of trust loan that is in default is defined as:

> *A pattern of conduct in which a buyer defrauds a property owner of his or her equity interest or other value in real property under the guise of a purchase of the owner's property, but which is in fact a device to convert the owner's equity interest or other value in real property to a buyer, who fails to make payments, diverts the equity or other value to the buyer's benefit, and leaves the property owner with a resulting financial loss or debt.*

What You Need to Know about Equity Skimming

First, equity skimming is illegal in all 50 states of the United States of America. Second, equity skimming is a federal crime punishable by a fine of not more than $250,000 or imprisonment of not more than five years, or both. Equity skimming occurs when a property owner uses any part of the rents, assets, proceeds, income, or other funds derived from the property covered by a mortgage or deed of trust loan as personal funds. In a typical pre-foreclosure property equity skimming scam, a scam artist takes title subject to an existing mortgage or deed of trust loan that is in default for little or nothing down. The scam artist then either resells the property on a wraparound mortgage or all-inclusive trust deed and collects loan payments or rents it out and collects rental payments for months on end without ever making a single loan payment to the lender. This goes on until the lender finally forecloses on the loan and evicts the unsuspecting owner or tenant. In the meantime, the poor sap whose name is on the loan now has a foreclosure listed in his or her consumer credit file and is more than likely on the hook for a deficiency judgment from the lender. Don't do it!

The Federal Equity Skimming Statute

Under Chapter 12, United States Code, Section 1709-2, equity skimming is defined as:

Whoever, with intent to defraud, willfully engages in a pattern or practice of—

(1)   purchasing one-to four-family dwellings (including condominiums and cooperatives) which are subject to a loan in default at time of purchase or in default within one year subsequent to the purchase and the loan is secured by a mortgage or deed of trust insured or held by the Secretary of Housing and Urban Development or guaranteed by the Department of Veterans Affairs, or the loan is made by the Department of Veterans Affairs,

(2)   failing to make payments under the mortgage or deed of trust as the payments become due, regardless of whether the purchaser is obligated on the loan, and

(3)   applying or authorizing the application of rents from such dwellings for his own use, shall be fined not more than $250,000 or imprisoned not more than 5 years, or both. This section shall apply to a purchaser of such a dwelling, or a beneficial owner under any business organization or trust purchasing such dwelling, or to an officer, director, or agent of any such purchaser. Nothing in this section shall apply to the purchaser of only one such dwelling.

CHAPTER 5

How to Finance the Purchase of a Pre-Foreclosure Property

In spite of what you may have heard from those slick-talking real estate audiotape salespeople who are constantly spouting off in television infomercials about how anyone with a pulse can make a cool million buying real estate for nothing down, your chances of pulling off a nothing-down deal on a pre-foreclosure are slim and none. As I told you in Chapter 1, it does not take a six-figure income, a humongous bank account, and a super-high credit score to get started as a pre-foreclosure investor. But this is not a business where the average person can just buy a $99 starter kit, like some multilevel marketing schemes promote, and be on their merry way to riches. The truth of the matter is that to purchase a pre-foreclosure property, you will need to be able to come up with enough money to reinstate the loan that is in default in order to stop the lender from foreclosing on it. Depending on the repayment terms of the mortgage or deed of trust loan that is in foreclosure and the total amount that the lender wants to cure the loan default, it could cost you between $5,000 and $10,000 to reinstate the loan and put it back in the lender's good graces. I do not know about you, but to me, this is not exactly chump change. This is why, in this chapter, I am going to give you the lowdown on various ways to finance the purchase of a pre-foreclosure property, as both an investor and an owner-occupant, that make financial sense.

The Three Types of Residential Real Estate Loans

The three types of residential real estate loans are as follows:

1. *Conventional mortgage loan:* A conventional mortgage or deed of trust loan is a loan that is not guaranteed or insured by the U.S. government.

2. *FHA mortgage loan:* An FHA mortgage or deed of trust loan is a loan insured by the Federal Housing Administration (FHA).

3. *DVA mortgage loan:* A DVA mortgage or deed of trust loan is a loan that is guaranteed by the Department of Veterans Affairs.

Where to Find Information on Loan Programs Nationwide

Nowadays, lenders have loan programs that are geared toward people with little money and less than stellar credit. You can find loan information on all of the various types of residential loan programs that are available nationwide from the following web sites:

Fannie Mae: www.fanniemae.com/homebuyers/homepath/index.jhtml?p=Homepath

Freddie Mac: www.freddiemac.com/sell/factsheets/frm.htm

FHA: www.hud.gov/buying/insured.cfm

DVA: www.homeloans.va.gov/veteran.htm

Freddie Mac and Fannie Mae Limit Investors to 10 Loans at One Time

The Federal National Mortgage Association (better known as Fannie Mae), and the Federal Home Loan Mortgage Corporation (Freddie Mac), are congressionally chartered corporations or government-sponsored enterprises that buy existing mortgage and deed of trust loans from lenders who originate loans in the primary mortgage market. The loans are then pooled and resold as mortgage-backed securities to investors on the open market. Fannie Mae and Freddie Mac resell loans in what is known as the secondary mortgage market. In order to be sold on the secondary market, a mortgage or deed of trust loan must conform to these two organizations' loan underwriting standards. Fannie Mae and Freddie Mac each limit the number of outstanding loans that a borrower can have as an individual or joint owner at one time to 10. The 10-loan limit applies to one- to four-unit residential properties. This means that a borrower could have his or her personal residence and nine investment properties financed with either Freddie Mac or Fannie Mae conventional mortgage or deed of trust loans.

Most Lenders Do Not Have the Authority to Foreclose on FHA and DVA Loans

Most pre-foreclosure investors are under the false belief that a lender servicing an FHA or DVA loan can initiate foreclosure proceedings as soon as the lender declares the loan to be in a default status. The fact of the matter is that, in most cases, before any loan can be foreclosed on, it must first be reviewed by the FHA or DVA regional loan office that has jurisdiction over the state where the property is located. The only exception to this policy is certain direct endorsement lenders who have been authorized to foreclose on loans they have made, once they are in a default status. And depending on the workload at the regional office, the loan review process could take up to several months. In the meantime, the irresponsible property owner who has not bothered to make a loan payment in several months is provided with free housing at the expense of the good old American taxpayer. This happens all of the time because the federal bureaucracy, at all levels, is nothing more than a gigantic paper mill that moves at a snail's pace. I remember getting a telephone call in response to one of my classified ads, which was aimed at homeowners who were delinquent on their mortgage payments, from an owner who claimed that he had not made a loan payment on his FHA mortgage in over nine months. To top it off, HUD had not even gotten around to sending this guy a notice of intent to foreclose. I told him to call me back after he had received official notice from HUD that the party was over and he had a letter from the lender stating what he owed them.

How Investors Can Legally Assume FHA Loans as Owner-Occupants

Let me state here and now that I loathe ethically challenged real estate investors who resort to loan fraud in their quest for real estate riches. And today, thanks to a few crooked investors, the majority of honest investors, like me, can no longer assume FHA and DVA loans. In fact, since 1989, HUD has had a ban on private investors assuming FHA loans. Today, the only way that a pre-foreclosure investor can legally assume an FHA mortgage or deed of trust loan that is in default and facing foreclosure is as an owner-occupant, who is purchasing the property to be used as his or her principal residence. The best part about assuming existing FHA loans as an owner-occupant investor is that there are no published restrictions on how many times an individual can buy and resell properties with an FHA loan. And unlike the original borrower of an FHA loan, there is no published residency requirement that requires the owner to stay in the property for a set period of time before it can be used as a rental property. The only financial test that an owner-occupant buyer must pass in order to assume an FHA loan is a creditworthiness review, which is not supposed to take HUD or a direct endorsement lender more than 45 days to complete. However, I know an investor in Dallas, Texas, who bought a pre-foreclosure that had an FHA-insured mortgage as an owner-occupant investor, and it took HUD over two months to do a creditworthiness review on him so that he could assume the loan. Another big advantage of buying pre-foreclosure properties with an easily assumable loan is that they appeal to homebuyers who may not be able to qualify for a new conventional loan. This way, an investor can quickly resell the property by having a creditworthy buyer assume the existing loan and avoid the time-consuming rigmarole of going through the loan qualification process. According to the assumption requirements published in *HUD Handbook 4330.1 REV-5 Administration of Insured Home Mortgages,* in cases where an owner-occupant is assuming an FHA loan from another owner-occupant, the creditworthiness review requirement stays in effect for the life of the loan. Finally, unless an all-expense-paid stay at Club Fed appeals to you, do not commit loan fraud by stating to HUD and the lender that you are buying a pre-foreclosure property to be used as your primary residence when, in fact, you are buying it as a non-owner-occupied investment property.

The Problem with Assuming DVA Loans as a Non-Veteran Owner-Occupant

Non-veteran owner-occupants can legally assume a DVA loan; however, the DVA will not release a veteran property owner from being liable for repayment of the loan when it is assumed by a non-veteran. And sometimes this can be a real sticking point with owners in foreclosure who are concerned, and rightfully so, about the loan coming back to haunt them at a later date when the new or subsequent owners fail to make their loan payments and wind up in foreclosure themselves. The only way that I know to overcome this common objection is to agree in writing that you will let only another veteran formally assume the loan. This way, the new veteran owner would be on the hook with the DVA for all future loan payments and not the original borrower, whose name is on the loan documents.

A Legal Way for Investors to Get Around the Due-on-Sale Clause in DVA Loans

First, when you purchase a pre-foreclosure property on an installment sale or land contract, such as a contract for deed (CFD) or an agreement for deed (AFD), you retain an equitable interest in the property and have all of the rights of equitable ownership, including the right to deduct loan interest payments and property depreciation on your federal tax returns. However, under a CFD or AFD, the title to the property is not transferred to the new owner at the time of purchase. Instead, the property's title is transferred after the buyer has met all of the terms spelled out in the land contract. As a pre-foreclosure investor, what I like most about installment sale contracts is that they do not violate the due-on-sale clause contained in DVA loans. Section 12 of DVA Circular 26-90-37, September 25, 1990, reads as follows:

> Sale Agreements Not Subject to 38 U.S.C. 1814. When a borrower sells on an installment contract, contract for deed, or similar arrangement in which title is not transferred from the seller to the buyer, this is not considered a "disposition" of residential property securing a GI loan as stated in 38 U.S.C. 1814, and therefore does not require approval by VA or the loan holder prior to the execution of such an agreement. However, any borrower considering a sale in this manner should be cautioned that under such an arrangement he or she remains liable for repayment of the loan. Even if the agreement calls for the contract purchaser to make payments directly to the GI loan holder, the holder is not required by VA to change its records, and the contract seller is responsible for forwarding payment coupons and other information to the contract purchaser. Depending on the particular circumstances of a case, a holder may agree to change the account address to read in care of the contract purchaser, although the contract seller must promptly advise the holder of any change in his or her address.

Require That Loan Payments Be Made through a Licensed Loan Servicing Company

The only way to avoid being a victim in any type of equity-skimming scam when buying pre-foreclosures under an installment sale agreement is to require that all loan payments be made directly to a licensed loan servicing company. The loan servicing company, in turn, would take the money they receive from you as loan payments and use it to make loan payments directly to the lender. This way, you have verifiable proof that the loan payment is being made, and you are not funding the property owner's equity-skimming scam. The following web sites are two licensed loan servicing companies that provide service nationwide:

North American Loan Servicing: www.sellerloans.com/index.htm
PLM Lender Services, Inc.: www.plmweb.com/index.html

Hold All Documents in Escrow When Buying on an Installment Sale Contract

Another step that you must take to protect yourself when buying a pre-foreclosure from an owner with a DVA loan in foreclosure is to have the owner sign all of the necessary title transfer documents, such as a warranty or grant deed, and place them in escrow with a reputable third party such as a title insurance or escrow company or a real estate attorney. You must take this precaution because, if the owner that you are buying the property from decides to renege on your installment sale contract by refusing to transfer the property's title into your name, you would not have to get involved in a costly and time-consuming legal battle in order to get the deed to the property. And once you have the money to satisfy the repayment terms of the installment sale contract, you go to the third party holding the deed in escrow and give the third party a cashier's check made payable to the owner, and you get the signed deed in return, which should be recorded in the public records on the same day the final payment is made.

How to Purchase a Pre-Foreclosure Property Subject to an Existing Loan

To purchase and take title to a pre-foreclosure property subject to an existing mortgage or deed of trust loan, you must insert a *subject to* clause similar to the one that follows into your purchase agreement:

> Subject to that certain mortgage dated August 28, 1997, and executed by David D. Jones, as mortgagor, to Bank of Florida, as mortgagee, in the original amount of one-hundred and twenty-five thousand dollars ($125,000), which mortgage was duly recorded in the office of the Clerk of the Circuit Court of Hillsborough County, State of Florida, in book 790346, on page 45905, of the public records of Hillsborough County, Florida.

Notify Lenders That You Plan to Take Title Subject to Their Loan

If you are leery about the potential risk associated with taking title to a pre-foreclosure property subject to existing loans, which I told you about in Chapter 4, you can do what I occasionally do when I buy a property that I want to hold on to, and ask the lender to modify the loan agreement so that you can formally assume the loan. In most cases, if you are creditworthy and have sufficient income, the lender will approve the loan assumption without changing the terms of the loan. One surefire method of gauging how aggressive lenders are about enforcing the due-on-sale clause contained in their loans is to send a matter-of-fact letter to the president of the bank, informing the bank that you plan to take title to a pre-foreclosure property subject to their loan! I know an investor in Tallahassee, Florida, who claims to have done this numerous times and has never received a response back from any of the lenders and has gone ahead and taken title to the properties, subject to the existing mortgage loans.

Three Potential Sources of Startup Capital

As I briefly told you at the beginning of this chapter, depending on the price range of the pre-foreclosure properties that you plan to pursue, you will need a certain amount of startup capital to pay for loan reinstatement costs, property repairs, closing costs, and the cost of marketing the property for resale. And three of the best sources of startup capital are:

1. Fixed-rate, low-interest lines of unsecured credit.
2. Home equity loans.
3. An investment fund created with family and friends.

Use Fixed-Rate, Low-Interest Lines of Unsecured Credit to Buy Owners' Equity

I use fixed-rate, low-interest lines of unsecured credit to pay loan reinstatement costs, buy owners' equity, and pay for property repairs. *Unsecured lines of credit* are lines of credit that are issued through unsecured credit cards. I currently use two $40,000 lines of unsecured credit, which have fixed interest rates of between 3.4 and 4.5 percent. I am able to obtain these low-rate lines of unsecured credit because I have zero consumer debt and a credit score that is in the top 5 percent. The real beauty in using unsecured lines of credit instead of secured credit lines, such as a home equity line of credit (HELOC), is that you do not have to put your home on the line and pay those exorbitant closing costs that lenders generally charge borrowers for the privilege of doing business with them. In fact, the most that I have ever had to pay when using an unsecured line of credit was a $50 transfer fee. And contrary to what most so-called consumer financial experts may espouse, there is little risk involved when readily available lines of unsecured credit are used in a responsible manner. The fact of the matter is that the escalating debt problems that affect an ever-growing number of credit-challenged Americans are the direct result of a lack of financial self-discipline and poor money management practices on the part of credit card holders and are not caused by the companies that issue credit cards. This is the same kind of convoluted logic that smokers have used to file lawsuits against tobacco companies and that fatsos are using in their claims that fast-food joints are what has caused their obesity and not their own unwillingness to stop stuffing their pusses with super-sized portions of, aptly named, junk food! Pardon my rant, but I am sick and tired of irresponsible people playing the blame game by claiming they have been the victims of some diabolical plot on the part of the XWZ Company to make them broke, fat, stupid, sick, or whatever else ails them.

A Creative Way for Cash-Strapped Investors to Pay Owners for Their Equity

Finally, if you are having a hard time coming up with the cash needed to pay owners for their equity, you can do what I used to do when I was strapped for cash and trade monthly rental payments with owners for their equity. To do this, you would offer to buy a pre-foreclosure property owner's equity for a set number of monthly rental payments. For example, if you wanted to buy an owner's equity for the discounted price of $4,500, you would offer six monthly rental payments of $750 per month. I used to do this by signing a separate promissory note, outside of the closing, for the amount that owners had agreed to sell their equity in the property. Thus, I was able to buy the owner's equity in monthly installments, without having to come up with a lump sum payment on the same day that the deal closed. However, do not, under any circumstances, allow the owner to stay in the property as a tenant after you have closed on the purchase. To do so is an invitation to all kinds of potential problems, such as the very real possibility of owners later going to court and claiming that you somehow bamboozled them out of their home.

CHAPTER 6

How to Get Started Right
Now as a Profitable Pre-Foreclosure
Property Investor

Before you move on to Part Two of this book and learn all about my 14-step process for investing in pre-foreclosure properties, I want to tell you how you can set up shop as a pre-foreclosure investor without having to hock the family jewels to do it. I am a very frugal transplanted Yankee who was born in Vermont and raised in New Hampshire. I pretty much adhere to the use-it-up, make-it-do, wear-it-out, or do-without philosophy that is a way of life for many New Englanders. My wife, Barbara, who was born in Canada, knows how to pinch a penny until it screams! We are not cheap; we just do not like to spend our hard-earned money when we do not have to. For example, in my pre-foreclosure property investment business, I use a Compaq 7550 personal computer that I bought at Sam's Club for under $600. My computer came with a Microsoft 2003 Windows XP operating system. I use Microsoft Word 2003 word processing software that I also bought at Sam's Club for $245. My laser printer is a Hewlett Packard LaserJet 1300, which I purchased at Sam's Club for under $400. I use a four-year-old Qualcom dual-band cell phone that I bought from Sprint PCS for less than $100. My total equipment cost was right around $1,345, which I wrote off as a business expense for tax purposes. My cell phone bill is less than $40 a month, and I spend under $50 a month for a high-speed cable connection to the Internet through Bright House Networks. And, it costs me $25 a month to have my web site on the Internet. My total monthly fixed operating costs are less than $115. Most Americans spend more than that a month on fast-food alone, and all they have to show for their money is a big belly and a cholesterol count that is through the roof. For a grand total of $2,725, I have equipped my office and paid my fixed operating costs for a year. That works out to roughly $227 a month, when broken down over a 12-month period. Granted, this figure covers only fixed operating costs and doesn't include advertising and mailing expenses. But they, too, can be controlled by using sound business principles. I am telling you this so that you do not tie up your available investment capital in overpriced equipment that you really do not need in order to be a profitable pre-foreclosure property investor.

Incorporate Today's Technology into Your Pre-Foreclosure Investment Business

I divide the pre-foreclosure property investment business into BTI—Before the Internet—and ATI—After the Internet. In fact, I consider the Internet to be the great equalizer! I say this because before the Internet became available to the general public, the average individual pre-foreclosure investor had no way to readily access public property ownership records and myriad other essential real estate-related records. Today, anyone with a personal computer and an Internet connection who knows where to look can gain access to the same information that Fortune 500 companies use to make business decisions. Please understand that when I tell you to incorporate today's technology into your pre-foreclosure investment business, I do not mean that you should waste your hard-earned money buying the latest gizmos and gadgets that are on the market. By gizmos and gadgets, I mean handheld wireless computers, global positioning devices, and digital personal assistants. However, I do recommend that every serious pre-foreclosure property investor have a:

1. Late-model personal computer with Microsoft Windows 2000 or newer operating system and Microsoft Word 2000 or newer word processing software.
2. Quality laser printer.
3. Reliable high-speed Internet connection.
4. Reliable cell phone.

Set Up a Home Office for Your Business That Qualifies as a Tax Deduction

For a home office to qualify as a business deduction for federal tax purposes, it must be used regularly and exclusively for business purposes. For example, if you are a part-time real estate investor and a full-time schoolteacher with a home office that you claim as a real estate investment business expense, but you use your office for both your real estate investment business and for grading student papers, your home office deduction would be disallowed if you were ever audited by the Internal Revenue Service (IRS). The IRS would do this because your home office is not being used exclusively for business purposes. The best way to make certain that your home office will pass muster with the IRS is to regularly use the space you are claiming as your home office exclusively as your principal place of business. I comply with the IRS home office use rules by having a home office that is located in a separate building behind our home—approximately 40 steps to walk—and used exclusively for business purposes. For more information on how to deduct your home office as a business expense, read IRS Publication 587, *Business Use of Your Home,* which is available online at www.irs.gov/pub /irs-pdf/p587.pdf.

How to Organize Your Office on Wheels

As a pre-foreclosure investor, you are going to be spending a lot of time in your vehicle conducting drive-by property inspections and driving to appointments with owners. This means that the front seat of your vehicle is going to have to double as a sort of office on wheels. To do this, I use a Cab Commander that's available from the Duluth Trading Company to keep my office on wheels organized. The Cab Commander is what building contractors and law enforcement officers use to keep their front seat offices organized. It comes complete with a heavy duty adjustable strap that fits around car or truck seat headrests and doubles as a shoulder strap that lets you carry it in and out of your vehicle. You can log onto the Duluth Trading Company's web site to check out the Cab Commander at www.duluthtrading.com.

Maintain a Separate Checking Account for Your Real Estate Investment Business

For record keeping and tax purposes, you must maintain a separate checking account for your real estate investment business that you can deposit checks into and pay expenses from. One of the criteria that the IRS uses to determine if a business is legitimate and not a sham is bank accounts. A business that claims expenses, losses, and depreciation on federal tax returns but does not maintain a bank checking account is going to be suspect and have a very hard time trying to document expenses if they are ever questioned or audited by the swell folks at the IRS.

Why It Is Best to Pay All Expenses with Business Checks or Business Credit Cards

The best method for documenting and recording expenses is to pay them with checks written on your real estate investment business checking account or with a credit card issued in the name of your real estate business. This way, you will not have to worry about confusing personal expenses with business expenses. Plus, working out of one checking account will allow you to easily track expenses on a daily basis. The same holds true for using business credit cards to charge business expenses. For the past nine years, my company, Home Equities Corp, has used the American Express Optima Card, now called the Business Management Account, to charge all business expenses on. Every three months, the American Express Company sends me a detailed quarterly expense statement that is broken down into various categories. This helps me to simplify my record keeping and tax preparation.

Maintain Automobile Mileage Records to Document Business-Related Travel

Make certain that you claim all travel expenses related to running your real estate pre-foreclosure business. The IRS requires that taxpayers maintain automobile mileage logs to document business-related mileage that is claimed on federal tax returns as a business expense. For the 2004 tax year, the standard mileage rate that can be deducted from federal taxes for the cost of operating a vehicle is 37.5 cents per mile for all business-related travel.

Maintain Expense Records

You must maintain expense records such as paid invoices, bank statements, cancelled checks, tax returns, and accounting records to document all of the expenses associated with operating your real estate investment business.

Use a Computer Software Accounting Program to Maintain Financial Records

Use a computer software accounting program to maintain your income and expense records. I recommend that you set up a separate account for each property that you own, by street address. My company, Home Equities Corp, uses Quick-Books 2003 financial software to maintain all of its financial records. According to *Small Business Computing Magazine,* two of the most popular off-the-shelf small business accounting software programs are made by:

1. QuickBooks Financial Software.
2. Peachtree Software.

Depreciate All Equipment Used in Your Real Estate Investment Business

For your real estate investment business to earn a maximum profit, you must take full advantage of all of the depreciation allowed under the Internal Revenue Code. To do this, make certain that you claim the maximum depreciation allowed on all of the equipment used in your business to include:

1. Office equipment such as computers, printers, and facsimile machines.
2. Software programs for accounting and word processing.
3. Cellular telephones and telephone answering machines.

Best to Store Photocopies of Records and Documents in Three-Ring Binders

I recommend that you place photocopies of all property-related records and documents inside plastic document protectors and store them in clear three-ring binders instead of in multiple folders in a bulky filing cabinet. I like using clear binders because the property's address can be inserted inside the binder's spine for quick reference.

Store Original Copies of Records and Documents in a Safe Deposit Box

I also recommend that you photocopy or scan onto CD ROM all of your important property-related records and documents, and store all of the original copies in a safe deposit box. This way, you'll have all of your original records and documents in a safe, secure, offsite location where they can be easily located in case of an emergency.

Record Keeping Information
Available Online

The Commerce Clearinghouse Small Business Owners Toolkit is a cornucopia of record keeping information that is available online for free at the following web site: www.toolkit.cch.com.

Internal Revenue Service Publications
Available Online

IRS forms and publications are available online in PDF format at the following Web page: www.irs.gov/formspubs/index.html.

Internal Revenue Service Publications
That Pertain to Running a Business

The following IRS publications pertain to running a real estate investment business:

1. Publication 334, *Tax Guide For Small Business.*
2. Publication 535, *Business Expenses.*
3. Publication 583, *Starting a Business and Keeping Records.*
4. Publication 587, *Business Use of Your Home.*
5. Publication 1779, *Independent Contractor or Employee.*

Use the *U.S. Master Tax Guide* as
Your Tax Reference Guide

I highly recommend that you use the *U.S. Master Tax Guide* as your tax reference guide. It's published annually by the Commerce Clearinghouse and available at the following web site: http://tax.cchgroup.com.

Hire a Properly Licensed Professional to
Prepare Your Tax Returns

Unless you are a certified public accountant, board-certified tax attorney, or an enrolled agent, you should hire a tax professional who is licensed to represent taxpayers before all administrative levels of the IRS to prepare your tax returns. And, yes, I am very well aware of all of the inexpensive off-the-shelf tax preparation software programs that are available today. However, here is an excellent reason why I very strongly recommend that real estate investors never, ever use any of these software programs for preparing their tax returns: Who from the tax preparation software conglomerate is going to represent you in front of the IRS when you're audited because there was an unreported glitch in their software program that flubbed up your tax return? Answer: Absolutely no one! You are on your own when you rely on XYZ tax preparation software to prepare your tax return. This is not the case when you hire a properly licensed tax professional to prepare your tax returns. For example, I have used the same enrolled agent to prepare my state and federal tax returns since 1985, and I have never had a single tax return questioned by anyone. However, the main reason that I continue to use the same tax professional is that part of this tax preparation service is free representation in front of the IRS—without my having to be present—if there are ever any questions about the return or in the event of an audit. It's akin to having a free IRS audit insurance policy!

Why You Should Hire Independent Contractors instead of Hourly Employees

From what I have found out over the past 24 years, it usually makes more sense financially to hire independent contractors and pay them by the job than to hire hourly employees and maintain a payroll. For example, my real estate investment business consists of one person—me. I work alone and have no hourly employees at my beck-and-call. When I need something done, I hire it out to an independent contractor who charges me by the job. This way, I avoid all of the rigmarole that goes along with baby-sitting hourly employees and dealing with the following state and federal government agencies that regulate employers:

1. The U.S. Occupational Safety and Health Administration.
2. The U.S. Department of Labor.
3. The Internal Revenue Service.
4. The Social Security Administration.
5. Department of Labor and Employment Security.

Do Not Form a Separate Business Entity until You Actually Become an Investor

I have never been one to advise so-called newbie investors who have never done a deal to form a separate business entity just to buy pre-foreclosures. The fact is, probably fewer than 10 percent of the people reading this book will ever actually buy a pre-foreclosure property. As far as I am concerned, it is totally asinine for anyone to go to the effort and expense of forming a company solely for the purpose of buying pre-foreclosure properties before they even know if they are cut out to be a pre-foreclosure property investor. However, to those of you reading this book who do go on to become pre-foreclosure investors, I very strongly suggest that you form a separate business entity such as a Subchapter S corporation or limited liability company to buy pre-foreclosure properties through. It is one of the best and least expensive methods available to help reduce your risk and limit your personal liability as a real estate investor. This way, there is a clear distinction between your personal and family assets and the assets held by your corporation or your limited liability company. And, in most cases, any liability incurred by the business entity would be limited to the business entity's assets. However, please be advised that there is not a business entity known to man that will protect its owners and officers from being held liable when it's used to engage in fraudulent or criminal behavior. You can find out the filing requirements and fees for forming a business entity in your state by logging onto your state's secretary of state web site and clicking on the division of corporations or a similar name.

One Sure-Fire Way to Fail as a Pre-Foreclosure Property Investor

As you should have realized by now from reading the first six chapters of this book, pre-foreclosure properties are not something that anyone can just jump into and make a cool million dollars in no time flat. The fact of the matter is that this business is best suited for serious, reasonable, rational, intelligent, reality-based, goal-driven, and action-oriented adults who are well organized and able to quickly respond to property owners in foreclosure. I am a firm believer that proper prior planning is the key to preventing a piddle poor performance in any type of endeavor in life. And investing in pre-foreclosures is no exception! My favorite quotation from the sagacious Abraham Lincoln is: "If I had eight hours to chop down a tree, I would spend six sharpening my ax!" Honest Abe's advice is applicable to both aspiring lumberjacks and wannabe pre-foreclosure investors. As an author, I strive to always tell it to my readers as it really is. I do not believe in sugarcoating the truth. This is why I want you to know right from the get-go that there is one sure-fire way that you can fail as a pre-foreclosure property investor. All you have to do is to totally ignore everything that I have just told you in this chapter by failing to do your homework and not getting your ax razor-sharp. And, as a very wise old sage once said, "Ignorance can be overcome by education, but stupidity lasts forever!"

How to Overcome the Fear of Failure That Stops Most People in Their Tracks

Although I realize that the subject of psychology per se is beyond the scope of this book, I want to briefly go over what I firmly believe is the number one reason why most hard-working Americans die flat broke: fear of failure. Granted, all rational, reasonable, intelligent adults have an innate fear of failure. In fact, most Americans are warned from birth to be careful and watch out for the unforeseen. However, it is how human beings are able to overcome the very real fear of failure that determines whether an individual will be successful in a given endeavor. So, if fear of failure is what you feel is holding you back from becoming a profitable pre-foreclosure property investor, I have a possible solution that just might work. I am usually not a big fan of what I refer to as the rah, rah crowd—so-called motivational speakers—as I believe that lasting motivation is something that comes from within. However, I highly recommend that you listen to the following two audio programs by best-selling author Earl Nightingale: "The Strangest Secret in the World for Succeeding Today" and "Lead The Field," which are available at the Nightingale-Conant web site: www.nightingale.com.

Use the Thomaslucier.com Web Site as the Companion Resource for This Book

Finally, you can use my web site, www.Thomaslucier.com, as the companion resource for this book. My web site has direct links to all of the web site URLs that are listed throughout this book. There are also direct links to real estate news sources and trade publications. You can also log onto the Question & Answer Forum and e-mail me any questions that you may have about the contents of this book and get a response back within 24 hours. No other real estate foreclosure book author offers his or her readers this type of one-on-one personal service!

PART II

MY 14-STEP PROCESS FOR INVESTING IN PRE-FORECLOSURE PROPERTIES

How to Find Property Owners with Loans That Are in Default and Facing Foreclosure

There is an old saying in business: "Nothing happens until someone sells something!" Well, nothing happens in the pre-foreclosure property investment business until a lender notifies a borrower that his or her loan is in a default status and files either a foreclosure lawsuit and a notice of lis pendens or a notice of default and records the foreclosure action in the public records of the county where the property that is being foreclosed on is located. And once this nugget of information is recorded in the public records, it becomes public information that is potentially worth tens of thousands of dollars to the few fortunate people who know where to find it.

The Most Important Advice in This Entire Chapter

You will eventually learn from experience that finding a property owner with a mortgage or deed of trust loan that is in the early stage of foreclosure is actually the easiest step in my 14-step process for investing in pre-foreclosures. However, it has been my experience that in the beginning, finding property owners in foreclosure may prove to be a stumbling block for many novice pre-foreclosure property investors. The problem is that most of the newcomers to this business do not know the correct name of the local government agency where foreclosure lawsuits and notices of lis pendens or notices of default are filed and recorded in the public record. Here is the most important advice in this entire chapter: Go in person to your local county government and do not leave until you speak face-to-face with a public servant who works in the office where mortgage or deed of trust loan foreclosure actions are filed and recorded in the public records of your county. This office may be known in your county as the recorder, prothonotary, circuit court clerk, county court clerk, registrar, or bureau of conveyances. And while you are there, ask the person that you are speaking with if your county's public records can be accessed online. If so, you will be able to download notices of lis pendens or notices of default directly onto your personal computer. If your county's public records are not yet available online, ask if there is any type of foreclosure reporting service that gathers information from your county's public records about property owners in foreclosure. If your county's public records are not available online and there is no foreclosure reporting service in your area, ask for the name of the newspaper in your county where foreclosure notices are published.

The Foreclosure Ball Does Not Get Rolling until a Loan Is in a Default Status

The foreclosure ball does not get rolling until after a lender declares a loan to be in a default status. Most lenders consider any loan with payments that are 90 days or more past due to be in default. But it has been my experience that not all lenders are as aggressive as they probably should be when it comes to declaring that a mortgage or deed of trust loan is in default. This has been especially true with lenders servicing government-backed loans. However, I have found that most lenders servicing conventional loans are much more aggressive about declaring delinquent loans to be in a default status. They usually send delinquent borrowers a notice of their intent to foreclose on a loan within 95 days from the date that the last loan payment was received.

The Type of Information That Is Usually Contained in Foreclosure Notices

Once a lender notifies a borrower that his or her loan is in a default status, the lender then instructs its attorney or trustee to initiate a foreclosure action against the borrower. The attorney or trustee then files a foreclosure lawsuit and notice of lis pendens or a notice of default in the same county where the deed to the property being foreclosed on is recorded. After a notice of lis pendens or a notice of default is filed and recorded in the public records, it becomes public information. Typically, foreclosure notices contain the following information about the borrower, property, and loan being foreclosed on:

1. Date the lawsuit or notice of default was filed and recorded in the public records.

2. Names and addresses of defendant—mortgagor or trustor—whose loan is in default.

3. Names and addresses of the plaintiff—lender, trustee, or beneficiary—foreclosing on the loan.

4. Case or notice of default number.

5. Property's street address.

6. Property's legal description.

7. Property's land use or zoning code.

8. Property's tax assessed value.

9. Original loan amount.

10. Date original loan was made.

11. Date last payment was made.

12. Amount of payments in arrears.

13. Loan balance at the time the foreclosure action was filed.

14. Scheduled date of the public foreclosure auction or trustee's sale.

How a Notice of Lis Pendens Works

The legal term lis pendens is Latin for "a pending lawsuit" and refers to the period of time between when a lawsuit is filed and when the case is actually heard in court. In judicial foreclosure actions, lenders file a lawsuit to foreclose on a mortgage or deed of trust loan that is in default and a notice of lis pendens. A notice of lis pendens like the one on page 70 is recorded in the public records to give the public constructive notice that a lawsuit affecting a property's title has been filed in a state or federal court of competent jurisdiction.

How a Notice of Default Works

In non-judicial foreclosure actions, where lenders do not file a foreclosure lawsuit and notice of lis pendens, they instead file what is called a notice of default. A notice of default like the one on page 71 is a legal notice that is recorded in the public record to give the public constructive notice that a mortgage or deed of trust loan is in default and scheduled to be foreclosed on, usually at a private trustee's sale.

IN THE CIRCUIT COURT OF THE THIRTEENTH JUDICIAL CIRCUIT IN AND FOR HILLSBOROUGH COUNTY, STATE OF FLORIDA
CIVIL DIVISION

CITICORP MORTGAGE CORPORATION
Plaintiff
Vs.

CASE NO. 2004-782
DIVISION "B"

RAYMOND RYON
BARNES INDUSTRIAL PIPING, INC.
ALLEN DEVELOPMENT, INC.
And UNITED STATES OF AMERICA,
Department of the Treasury-Internal Revenue Service
Defendants

_____/

NOTICE OF LIS PENDENS

TO: RAYMOND RYON,
        BARNES INDUSTRIAL PIPING, INC.
        ALLEN DEVELOPMENT, INC.
        And UNITED STATES OF AMERICA,

YOU ARE NOTIFIED of the institution of the action, by Plaintiff against you seeking to foreclose a mortgage on the following property in Hillsborough County, Florida:

Lot 54, Block 18, Hyde Park, as per map or plat thereof as recorded in Plat Book 24 on Page 42 of the Public Records of Hillsborough County, Florida.

DATED THIS ninth day of July 2005.

Robert B. Big, Esquire
1950 Langdon Avenue, Suite 15
Tampa, FL 33629
Florida Bar Number 12345
(555) 123-4567

Sample Notice of Default

IMPORTANT NOTICE

IF YOUR PROPERTY IS IN FORECLOSURE BECAUSE YOU ARE BEHIND IN YOUR PAYMENTS, IT MAY BE SOLD WITHOUT ANY COURT ACTION, and you may have the legal right to bring your account in good standing by paying all of your past due payments plus permitted costs and expenses within the time permitted by law for reinstatement of your account, which is normally five business days prior to the date set for the sale of your property. No sale date may be set until three months from the date this notice of default may be recorded (which date of recordation appears on this notice).

This amount is $4,567.89 as of May 1, 2004, and will increase until your account becomes current. While your property is in foreclosure, you still must pay other obligations (such as insurance and taxes) required by your note and deed of trust or mortgage. If you fail to make future payments on the loan, pay taxes on the property, provide insurance on the property, or pay other obligations as required by the note and deed of trust or mortgage, the beneficiary or mortgagee may insist that you do so in order to reinstate your account in good standing. In addition, the beneficiary or mortgagee may require as a condition to reinstatement that you provide reliable written evidence that you paid all senior liens, property taxes, and hazard insurance premiums.

Upon your written request, the beneficiary or mortgagee will give you a written itemization of the entire amount you must pay. You may not have to pay the entire unpaid portion of your account, even though full payment was demanded, but you must pay all amounts in default at the time payment is made. However, you and your beneficiary or mortgagee may mutually agree in writing prior to the time the notice of sale is posted (which may not be earlier than the end of the three-month period stated above) to, among other things, (1) provide additional time in which to cure the default by transfer of the property or otherwise; or (2) establish a schedule of payments in order to cure your default; or both (1) and (2).

Following the expiration of the time period referred to in the first paragraph of this notice, unless the obligation being foreclosed upon or a separate written agreement between you and your creditor permits a longer period, you have only the legal right to stop the sale of your property by paying the entire amount demanded by your creditor.

To find out the amount you must pay, or to arrange for payment to stop the foreclosure, or if your property is in foreclosure for any other reason, contact:

XYZ Trustee Corporation
3745 Palmer Avenue
Glendale, CA 91201
(555) 123-4567

If you have any questions, you should contact a lawyer or the governmental agency, which may have insured your loan.

Notwithstanding the fact that your property is in foreclosure, you may offer your property for sale, provided the sale is concluded prior to the conclusion of the foreclosure.

REMEMBER, YOU MAY LOSE LEGAL RIGHTS IF YOU DO NOT TAKE PROMPT ACTION.

Use Worksheets to Keep Track of Information in Foreclosure Notices

I suggest that you do as I do and use worksheets like the two samples on pages 73 and 74 to keep track of the information that is contained in foreclosure lawsuits and notices of lis pendens and notices of default.

Nationwide County Recorder Office Information Available Online

The following National Recorders Directory web site has a listing of all county recorder offices nationwide: www.zanatec.com.

Foreclosure Notices Are Required to Be Published in a Newspaper of Record

To give the public constructive notice about a foreclosure action, state foreclosure statutes require lenders to publish legal foreclosure notices in a newspaper that is circulated within the same county where the foreclosure notice is recorded. In most counties, county and circuit courts require that foreclosure notices be published in newspapers the courts have approved as newspapers of record. A newspaper of record is a paper that has countywide circulation and is read by the majority of residents within the county. You can call the office of your local county clerk of the court to obtain the names of the newspapers of record for your county.

Where to Find Court and Commercial Newspapers

The following web site has links to court and commercial newspapers nationwide: www.primetimenewspapers.com/dcr/links.htm.

Recorded Foreclosure Notices Can Be Accessed Online

Depending on your state's public records statute and whether your county's public records are available online, you should be able to access information on recorded

FORM 7.1   Sample Foreclosure Lawsuit Worksheet

Property's street address _____

Tax assessor's parcel or folio number _____

Tax assessed value $_____   Date of last assessment _____

Foreclosure lawsuit case number _____   Date filed _____

Defendant/borrower's name _____   Telephone number _____

Defendant's address _____

Plaintiff/lender's name _____   Telephone number _____

Plaintiff's address _____

Plaintiff's attorney _____   Telephone number _____

Attorney's address _____

Scheduled foreclosure auction sale date _____   Minimum bid $_____

Type of loan in default: FHA ( )   DVA ( )   Conventional ( )   Private ( )

Original loan date _____   Original loan amount $_____

Interest rate _____   Assumable? _____

Monthly loan payment: principal $_____   Interest $_____

Taxes $_____   Insurance $_____   Total payment $_____

Unpaid principal loan balance $_____

Total loan payment in arrears $_____

Total amount of interest, late charges, and legal fees owed $_____

Total amount needed to cure the default and reinstate the loan $_____

Copyright Thomas J. Lucier 2005. To customize this document, download it to your hard drive from Thomas J. Lucier's web site at www.thomaslucier.com/pre-foreclosureforms.html. The document can then be opened, edited, and printed using Microsoft Word or another popular word processing application.

notices of lis pendens and notices of default directly from your county's public records library. For example, here in Tampa, I can log onto the Hillsborough County Clerk of the Circuit Court web site at www.hillsclerk.com and click on the Online Records search icon that goes to the Official Records Index Search Menu. And from there I can do a document search, by calendar date, for recorded notices of lis pendens. For example, on June 10, 2004, I did a document search for all of the notices of lis pendens that had been recorded in Hillsborough County on June 8, 2004, because this was the most recent date that recorded documents were made

FORM 7.2   Sample Notice of Default Worksheet

Property's street address _____

Tax assessor's parcel or folio number _____

Tax assessed value $_____   Date of last assessment _____

Notice of default case number _____   Date filed _____

Trustor's name _____   Telephone number _____

Trustor's address _____

Beneficiary's name _____   Telephone number _____

Beneficiary's address _____

Beneficiary's attorney or trustee _____   Telephone number _____

Trustee's address _____

Scheduled trustee auction sale date _____   Minimum bid $_____

Type of loan in default: FHA ( )   DVA ( )   Conventional ( )   Private ( )

Original loan date _____   Original loan amount $_____

Interest rate _____   Assumable? _____

Monthly loan payment: Principal $_____   Interest $_____

Taxes $_____   Insurance $_____   Total payment $_____

Unpaid principal loan balance $_____

Total loan payment in arrears $_____

Total amount of interest, late charges, and legal fees owed $_____

Total amount needed to cure the default and reinstate the loan $_____

available online. My search returned a listing of 74 notices of lis pendens for various types of civil lawsuits affecting the titles of real property. I can usually tell whether a notice of lis pendens is for a foreclosure action by looking at the parties listed in the notice. For example, if one of the parties is a bank or mortgage lender and the other party is a private individual or two people with the same last name, there is a pretty good chance that it is a mortgage foreclosure lawsuit. Once I have printed out the listing of notices of lis pendens, I then log onto the Hillsborough County Property Appraiser web site at www.hcpafl.org and do a property records search using the owner's name that is listed in the notice of lis pendens. And if I am interested in the property after I have completed my property records search, I then send the property owner a copy of letter number one provided in Chapter 8.

Foreclosure Reporting Services Provide Information Online

Most foreclosure reporting services now provide foreclosure notices online. I highly recommend that you subscribe to an online foreclosure reporting service if there is one available in your area. Subscription rates vary depending on the number of foreclosure filings listed and the frequency of publication. When selecting a foreclosure reporting service, pay special attention to how frequently— daily, twice a week, weekly, biweekly, or monthly—the report will provide listings of foreclosure filings. You want to be certain you will be receiving current or fresh leads and not stale information that is weeks old and outdated. The following is a listing of web sites that provide foreclosure notice information online for various locations nationwide:

Atlanta Foreclosure Report: www.equisystems.com

Record Information Services: www.public-record.com/market/foreclose.htm

Chicago Foreclosure Report: www.chicagoforeclosurereport.com

Foreclosure Access: www.foreclosureaccess.com

The Daily Record: www.mddailyrecord.com

Houston Foreclosure Listing Service: www.foreclosehouston.com

PropertyTrac: www.propertytrac.com

Foreclosure Data NW: www.foreclosuredatanw.com

Foreclosure Reporting Service: www.foreclosure-report.com

Jacksonville Daily Record: www.jaxdailyrecord.com

Daily Business Review: www.dailybusinessreview.com

Information Resource Service: www.irsfl.com

New York Foreclosures: www.newyorkforeclosures.com

REDLOC: www.redloc.com

ForeclosureTrac: www.foreclosuretrac.com

Bates Foreclosure Report: www.brucebates.com

Foreclosure Report: www.foreclosurereport.com

Real Data Corp: www.real-data.com

Midwest Foreclosures: www.midwestforeclosures.com

Foreclosure Listing Service: www.foreclosehouston.com

Foreclosure Disclosure Weekly: www.foreclosuredisclosure.com

RETRAN: www.retran.net

County Records Research: www.countyrecordsresearch.com

How Most Lenders Handle Delinquent Loans

Most lenders consider any mortgage or deed of trust loan with payments that are 30 to 89 days past due to be delinquent. Once a loan becomes delinquent, it is placed on the lender's so-called troubled loan list, and the delinquent borrower is sent a loan breach letter like the one on page 77 by overnight courier or certified mail, demanding that the loan payments be brought current within 30 days. In most cases, when a delinquent borrower fails to comply with a lender's demand letter, the lender continues to send the borrower a series of letters demanding payment until the lender declares the loan to be in a default status by sending the borrower a notice of intent to foreclose on the delinquent loan.

Do Not Overlook Property Owners Who Are One Payment Away from Foreclosure

Do not overlook property owners with delinquent loans who are one payment away from having their lender declare their loan to be in a default status and initiate foreclosure action. The good thing about property owners with delinquent mortgage or deed of trust loans is that the general public has not been made aware of their financial plight, which usually means there is less competition from other pre-foreclosure investors. Case in point: I once bought a property from an owner who had not made a mortgage payment in over nine months. This guy had received 12 different demand letters from his lender, but for whatever reason, the lender had never declared his FHA-insured loan to be in a default status. I bought the property subject to the existing loan and sent the lender the amount that was listed as due and payable in letter number 12. And I never heard a peep out of them about my taking title to the property.

Use Classified Ads to Find Property Owners with Delinquent Loans

The bad thing about property owners with delinquent loans is that they are hard to find. That is the downside of there being no public record of their financial

Sample Loan Breach Letter

May 15, 2004

Mr. John J. Default
3345 Costa Rosa Way
Tampa, FL 33649
Re Loan Number: FL08281950

Dear Mr. Default:

You have fallen behind on your mortgage payments. You must bring the mortgage current within thirty days of the date of this letter by sending the amount shown below to the Bank of Florida in the form of a money order or certified check.

The total amount due as of June 1, 2004 is $5,478.98.

To bring your account current, you must also include with the above payment, any payments or late charges that are due during this thirty-day period. Acceptance of less than the total amount due includes, but is not limited to, the principal and interest and all other outstanding charges and costs. Acceptance of less than the total amount due does not waive our right to demand the entire balance due under the terms of your mortgage agreement.

If you do not bring your loan current within thirty days from the date of this letter, the Bank of Florida will demand the entire balance outstanding under the terms of your mortgage agreement. This amount includes, but is not limited to, the principal and interest and all other outstanding charges and costs. The Bank of Florida will start legal action to foreclose on the mortgage, which will result in the sale of the property. We may also have the right to seek a judgment against you for any deficiency after the home is sold.

You have the right to bring your loan current after legal action has begun. You also have the right to assert in the foreclosure proceedings the nonexistence of the default or any other defense to our legal action and sale of the property.

We want to work with you to resolve the problem and help you bring your account into good standing.

We urge you to contact Sally M. Little at (813) 123-4567. Ms. Little will work with you to try to solve your current difficulty.

Sincerely,

William Z. Banker
Vice President

misfortune. The most efficient method that I know of to find property owners with delinquent loans is to place small classified ads, like the following in daily and weekly newspapers that directly target property owners who are one loan payment away from foreclosure:

Trouble Making House Payments? Call (555) 123-4567 Today for Help!	Behind on House Payments? Call (555) 123-4567 Today for Help!
Can't Afford Your House Payments? Call (555) 123-4567 Today for Help!	One Payment Away from Foreclosure? Call (555) 123-4567 Today for Help!

Questions to Ask Property Owners Calling in Response to Your Delinquent Loan Ad

My experience with these types of classified ads is that they generate a lot of calls from property owners who are looking for someone to lend them money to bring their loan payments current. I very strongly recommend that you never lend any money to property owners, period. However, when you do get property owners calling on your delinquent loan ad who seem like they are ready to throw in the towel and sell their property, you need to ask them the following eight questions:

1. When did you make your last loan payment?
2. How much do you owe your lender in back loan payments, accrued interest, late payment charges, and legal costs?
3. Have any of your creditors filed a judgment lien against you?
4. Have you filed a bankruptcy petition?
5. Has your lender started foreclosing on your loan?
6. How much equity do you think that you have in your property?
7. Are you willing to sell your property before your lender forecloses on your loan and you are evicted?
8. When can we get together to further discuss your situation?

CHAPTER 8

How to Contact Property Owners in Foreclosure

Most would-be pre-foreclosure property investors are under the misconception that property owners with mortgage or deed of trust loans that are in default and facing foreclosure will welcome their offer to help with open arms. Believe me, nothing could be further from the truth! The fact of the matter is that most owners in foreclosure are usually in a very strong state of denial—and not exactly in the mood for casual conversations with complete strangers, spouting insincere gibberish about how they are here to help the property owner in their hour of need. So, how do you go about contacting property owners with loans who are facing foreclosure? I highly recommend that you do as I do, and send a series of well-written letters to owners in foreclosure at the addresses that are listed in the foreclosure notices. Later in this chapter, I give you my reasons why you should never cold-call owners in foreclosure in person or by telephone. As far as I am concerned, when properly used, direct mail is the quickest and most efficient method available for contacting all of the property owners in your county with mortgage or deed of trust loans that are in default and facing foreclosure. A well-organized and professionally run direct mail system will enable you to make contact with property owners in foreclosure as soon as their lender's notice of lis pendens or notice of default is recorded in your county's public records and becomes public information. Furthermore, by mailing follow-up letters at regular intervals, every 10, 14, or 30 days, you will be able to maintain contact with owners in default during their loan's reinstatement period. However, you must keep in mind that the use of direct mail to contact property owners in foreclosure is a numbers game that requires consistent persistence. In order to be successful, you must mail introductory and follow-up letters to all the property owners in foreclosure within your buying areas on a regular basis. For example, you may initially mail letters to 200 property owners and get responses from only five of them. But if you bought one or two properties from the five property owners who did respond to your letters and made a profit of $15,000 to $20,000 or more per deal, your efforts would have been very worthwhile. To effectively use direct mail, you must get property owners in foreclosure to:

1. Open your letters.
2. Meet with you face-to-face.
3. Sell the equity in their property to you at a discount of 50 percent or more.

Most Letters Mailed to Owners in Foreclosure Are Very Poorly Written

Before I go any further, I need to tell you that most of the letters that are mailed to property owners in foreclosure are very poorly written. I know this because I always ask property owners what made them decide to contact me instead of one of my competitors. They usually show me some of the other letters and postcards that they have received and make some snide comment about the writers' sixth-grade writing level. Put yourself in the place of an owner in foreclosure, and ask yourself how you would respond to a letter or postcard that is written on a sixth-grade level? I do not know about you, but after I finished laughing, I would throw it in the trash. The point that I am making here is that if you expect owners in foreclosure to take your letters or postcards seriously, they must be well written! Anything less is a waste of ink, paper, envelopes, and stamps.

Use Direct Mail to Contact Property Owners in Foreclosure

I like using direct mail to contact property owners in foreclosure for the following four reasons:

1. *Direct mail is easy to use.* Once you are organized, direct mail is very easy to use. I use Microsoft Word 2003 word processing software that can merge names and addresses with letters. And I use window envelopes so that I do not have to fiddle around addressing envelopes. All that I have to do to generate a letter to an owner in foreclosure is to sit at my computer and click on the Word file that contains the letter I want to send, and then print it out. Once my letters are printed, they just need to be signed, folded, and inserted into an envelope.

2. *Direct mail is relatively cheap to use.* Direct mail gives me the most bang for my buck. For example, I can mail out 100 letters first-class mail for right around $65. This includes the cost of letterheads, envelopes, and postage, the whole shebang.

3. *Direct mail is quick.* I usually get responses from owners interested in selling within one to two weeks from the date I mailed the letters.

4. *Direct mail is effective.* It allows me to make direct contact with all of the owners in the areas where I buy pre-foreclosures. And unlike when you cold-call on owners in foreclosure, direct mail allows me to contact everyone at the same time.

Use Postal Zip Codes to Target
Potentially Profitable Properties

I am no fan of the so-called shotgun approach that many foreclosure experts advocate, where you mail a letter to every owner in your county who is in foreclosure. I mail letters only to preselected zip codes where desirable—stable, middle-income—neighborhoods are located. By using zip codes, I am able to quickly determine which owners to mail to, and I do not end up wasting money on letterheads, envelopes, and postage. You can get a listing of all the zip codes in your county by logging onto www.addresses.com/zip_code_lookup.php. Please keep in mind that you may earn your profit when you buy, but you do not get paid until you sell. And if you buy a pre-foreclosure property that you cannot resell quickly, you may very well end up breaking even or losing money on the deal.

Letters Are Sent to Owners in Foreclosure
during the Loan's Reinstatement Period

The time to send letters to property owners with mortgage or deed of trust loans in default and facing foreclosure is during their loan's reinstatement period. The loan reinstatement period is the time period between when a lender declares a loan to be in default and the scheduled public foreclosure auction or trustee's sale date. Loan reinstatement periods give borrowers the right to cure their loan default by bringing their loan payments current to include the payment of accrued interest, late payment charges, legal costs, and any additional costs incurred by the lender while the loan was in default. Borrowers in default on DVA, FHA, Freddie Mac, and Fannie Mae conventional loans have a borrower's right-to-reinstate clause in their loan documents that gives them the right to reinstate their loans up to five days prior to the foreclosure or trustee's sale.

Letters Appealing to Emotions and Offering Immediate Relief Get Best Response

Property owners whose loans are in default and facing foreclosure usually act more on emotions such as fear, hostility, and anxiety than they do on logic. Your letters should be written so they offer owners in foreclosure immediate:

1. Debt relief.
2. Cash for their equity.
3. Relief from foreclosure.
4. Relief from having a foreclosure on their credit report.
5. Help in finding another place to live.

Mail Typewritten Letters That Are Individually Addressed and Personally Signed

Rule number one when sending letters to owners in foreclosure is to avoid the mass mailing look. The name of the game in this business is to make each of your letters look as personal as possible. Typewritten letters that are individually addressed and personally signed have a human touch, which gives them a much better chance of being read than impersonal, computer-generated letters. Imagine the effect that your envelope would have if it were addressed to "Dear Property Owner in Foreclosure," and signed with a signature stamp. I once had a property owner show me an envelope that was addressed to "The Owner in Foreclosure" in bright red ink. I guess the nitwit sending the letter wanted to get the owner's attention. The trouble with using this type of tactic is that it achieves the opposite effect of what the letter writer intended. Trust me, when an envelope is addressed this way, it has a tendency to make any owner in foreclosure very angry, because it blabs the owner's financial plight to everyone reading it.

Send Your Letters via First-Class, Stamped Mail

To avoid the mass mailing look, I recommend that you send your letters to owners in foreclosure via first-class mail. This will keep your letters from being confused with bulk rate junk mail that usually ends up unopened and in the trash. I also recommend that you use first-class stamps instead of metered mail. Also, have "ADDRESS SERVICE REQUESTED" imprinted one quarter-of-an inch below your return address so that the post office will give you the property owner's current address if the owner has moved from the property within the past 12 months. I often get e-mails from investors asking me what they should include in their envelope's return address. I tell them to put only their address. I recommend leaving off your name because it arouses curiosity, and most people will open the envelope just to see who it is from. Furthermore, I recommend that you mail your letters on Thursday or Friday, so that property owners receive them on a Saturday. It has been my experience that most property owners in foreclosure seem to be more receptive to opening and reading their mail on the weekend than during the rest of the week.

Send Multiple Follow-Up Letters at Regular Intervals to Maintain Contact

I am a firm believer in sending multiple follow-up letters at regular intervals— every 14 to 30 days—to owners in foreclosure. I do this because it greatly enhances my chances of getting face-to-face meetings with owners. I send five follow-up letters to owners in foreclosure. My first follow-up letter is sent 14 days after I send out my initial letter, and my third letter is sent 14 days after that. However, my last three follow-up letters are sent 60, 30, and 14 days before the owner's scheduled public foreclosure auction sale date. I do this to maximize my chances of having the owner read my letter and give me a call to set up a face-to-face meeting. The trick is to keep your name and telephone number in front of property owners in foreclosure, so that when they finally decide to sell their property, your name will be foremost on their minds. You will find that in most cases, when property owners finally decide they have to sell, they have very little time left and are forced to sell fast. So, if you send out only one letter, that letter will most likely arrive before owners have fully comprehended how little time they have and just how precarious their situation really is. To be effective, one of your letters must arrive at the time the property owner finally decides to sell. For example, in a state like California, which has a three-month loan reinstatement period along with a 20-day trustee's sale advertising period, you may want to send a total of seven letters: one introductory letter and five follow-up letters mailed once every 15 days during the loan reinstatement period and one letter during the trustee sale advertising period. In states with shorter loan reinstatement periods, you should send a follow-up letter once every 10 to 14 days. Each follow-up letter must stress the limited amount of time remaining that the owner has before the property is sold at a public foreclosure auction or trustee's sale.

Each One of the Six Letters to Owners in Foreclosure Repeats the Same Message

I do not believe in beating around the bush with property owners in foreclosure. My letters to owners in foreclosure are very direct and right to the point. And as you will see after reading each one of my six different letters at the end of this chapter, every letter repeats the very same message over and over again. The four points that I convey in my letters to owners in foreclosure are:

1. I want to buy your house today.
2. I will give you a cashier's check within five business days for your house.
3. I will handle all of the details of the sale of your house.
4. I will help you find another place to live.

And, unlike most of the correspondence that most owners in foreclosure are inundated with, owners respond to my letters because I spell out exactly what I am willing to do.

Use Computer Files to Keep Track of Letters to Owners in Foreclosure

I recommend that you do as I do and create separate files in your computer's word processing program to keep track of the letters you send to owners in foreclosure. For example, I use six separate letter files that are set up by date and zip code to keep track of the six letters that I send to property owners in foreclosure in Hillsborough County, Florida. For example, letter file number one is named 915.33629.1. The numbers 915 represent the day the letter was mailed, September 15, 2005. The numbers 33629 represents the zip code in Tampa, Florida, where I mailed the letters. The number 1 denotes that letter number one was mailed. This file contains the names and addresses of all of the property owners in the 33629 zip code that letter number one was mailed to on September 15, 2005. This way, before letter number two is mailed out to the same property owners in the 33629 zip code, I can make all the necessary address changes or deletions, based on the information that I have received from the property owners themselves or the post office. I repeat this same procedure for letters number three through six. In the meantime, using newly recorded notices of lis pendens, I contact another group of property owners in foreclosure, using introductory letter number one, and repeat the procedure for letters number two through six. All I have to do is change the date portion of letter file number one and rename it. To illustrate, the date on letter file number 915.33629.1 would be changed to 101.33629.1 for the first letters mailed on October 1, 2005, to property owners in zip code 33629.

Best to Hire a Professional to Write Your Letters

Who should actually write your letters to owners in foreclosure depends on how effective a writer you are. However, if you don't feel comfortable writing your own letters, I highly recommend that you hire a professional writer who knows how to use the right words that cause property owners in foreclosure to call you to set up a face-to-face meeting. You must hire a writer who knows how to write letters that appeal to the emotions of property owners facing foreclosure. After all, you need to get the owners to respond to your offer of immediate relief. Regardless of who writes your letters, they must be written so that they focus totally on helping property owners solve their immediate problem.

Do Not Make Cold-Calls in Person to Property Owners in Foreclosure

As I told you at the beginning of this chapter, I never, ever make cold-calls on property owners in foreclosure, and I strongly suggest that you do not either! First off, put yourself in the shoes of a property owner in foreclosure and ask yourself this question: Would I be willing to share my very personal financial plight with some unknown stranger banging on my front door? I hate to be a killjoy, but cold-calling in person on property owners in foreclosure has an extremely low success rate. Plus, it is very time-consuming and potentially very dangerous. I am pretty certain that most of you reading this are somewhat familiar with the term *road rage;* well, go knocking on the door of a hostile property owner in foreclosure, and you just might experience a phenomenon known as *foreclosure rage*! Most people on the verge of losing their home and being put out on the street do not act as rational, reasonable, intelligent adults. Rather, they are very angry people, who have no desire to discuss their financial predicament with someone whom they perceive as being nothing more than a greedy opportunist trying to profit from their misfortune. Please keep in mind that most people in foreclosure are scared, stressed out, and in a state of panic! However, if you fail to heed the sage advice that I am dispensing here and you still want to cold-call in person on property owners in foreclosure, please be aware that you may be mistaken for a:

1. Lender's representative or a creditor and be verbally or physically assaulted.
2. Law enforcement officer or a bail bondsmen and be physically assaulted.
3. Prowler and be shot or stabbed.
4. Criminal attempting a robbery and be shot or stabbed.

Do Not Make Cold-Calls by Telephone to Owners in Foreclosure

I feel the same way about making cold-calls by telephone to owners in foreclosure as I do about cold-calling in person. Cold-calling owners almost never works because most owners:

1. Have unlisted telephone numbers.
2. Move out and abandon their property.
3. Refuse to answer their telephone.
4. Refuse to speak on the telephone with strangers about their financial problems.

The first letter that I send to property owners in foreclosure is on page 87. I mail it just as soon as the notice of lis pendens is filed with the clerk of the County Circuit Court and recorded in the public records.

The letter on page 88 is a sample of the second letter that I send to property owners in foreclosure. I mail it approximately 14 days after the first letter is sent.

The letter on page 89 is the third letter that I send to property owners in foreclosure. I mail it approximately 14 days after the second letter is sent.

The letter on page 90 is the fourth letter that I send to property owners in foreclosure. I mail it approximately 60 days before their scheduled public foreclosure auction sale date.

The letter on page 91 is the fifth letter that I send to property owners in foreclosure. I mail it approximately 30 days before their scheduled public foreclosure auction sale date.

The letter on page 92 is the sixth and last letter that I send to property owners in foreclosure. I mail it approximately 14 days before their scheduled public foreclosure auction sale date.

FORM 8.1   Sample First Letter to Property Owners in Foreclosure

Thomas J. Lucier

Post Office Box 21283 • Tampa, FL 33622-1283

Phone (813) 237-6267

E-Mail: tjlucier@tampabay.rr.com

June 4, 2005

Ms. Dee Fault
4569 Debtors Lane
Tampa, FL 33647

Dear Ms. Fault,

As you should already know, your mortgage lender has just filed a lawsuit in Hillsborough County Circuit Court to foreclose on your mortgage loan.

This means that if, for whatever reason, you cannot bring your loan payments current before the scheduled foreclosure sale date, your house will be sold at a public foreclosure auction sale on the third floor of the Hillsborough County Courthouse to the highest bidder, and you will be evicted by the new owner.

If your house is sold this way, you will get absolutely nothing from the sale. The bank holding your mortgage only cares about getting back the money that you owe them. They do not care about what you get.

You could put your house on the market and try to sell it yourself. Or, you could take your chances and list it with a real estate broker. However, right now it takes about four months to sell a house in Hillsborough County.

I specialize in helping people in Hillsborough County who are in foreclosure. And I can help you, too! All that you have to do is to pick up the telephone right now, and call me at (813) 237-6267 to set up an appointment so that I can make you an offer to buy your house today. I will give you a cashier's check for your house within five business days from today and stop the foreclosure and keep it off your credit report. I will also help you find another place to live. And, I will handle all of the details of the sale and deal with your lender and the title company processing all of the paperwork that is necessary to transfer the property's title.

I look forward to hearing from you very soon and to working with you to stop your lender from foreclosing on your house.

Sincerely,

Thomas J. Lucier

FORM 8.2   Sample Second Letter to Property Owners in Foreclosure

Thomas J. Lucier

Post Office Box 21283 • Tampa, FL 33622-1283

Phone (813) 237-6267

E-Mail: tjlucier@tampabay.rr.com

June 18, 2005

Ms. Dee Fault
4569 Debtors Lane
Tampa, FL 33647

Dear Ms. Fault,

You are starting to run out of time, and before you know it, the house that you are living in will be sold at a public foreclosure auction sale on the third floor of the Hillsborough County Courthouse to the highest bidder. And the new owner will call the Hillsborough County Sheriff's Department and have you evicted.

Your mortgage lender does not care about what happens to you after they have foreclosed on your house! All they are interested in doing is getting back the money that you owe them.

As I told you in my last letter, I specialize in helping people in Hillsborough County who are in foreclosure. And I can help you, too! All that you have to do is to pick up the telephone right now, and call me at (813) 237-6267 to set up an appointment so that I can make you an offer to buy your house today. I will give you a cashier's check for your house within five business days from today and stop the foreclosure and keep it off your credit report. I will also help you find another place to live. And, I will handle all of the details of the sale and deal with your lender and the title company processing all of the paperwork that is necessary to transfer the property's title.

I look forward to hearing from you very soon and to working with you to stop your lender from foreclosing on your house.

Sincerely,

Thomas J. Lucier

Copyright Thomas J. Lucier 2005. To customize this document, download it to your hard drive from Thomas J. Lucier's web site at www.thomaslucier.com/pre-foreclosureforms.html. The document can then be opened, edited, and printed using Microsoft Word or another popular word processing application.

FORM 8.3   Sample Third Letter to Property Owners in Foreclosure

---

Thomas J. Lucier
Post Office Box 21283 • Tampa, FL 33622-1283
Phone (813) 237-6267
E-Mail: tjlucier@tampabay.rr.com

July 2, 2005

Ms. Dee Fault
4569 Debtors Lane
Tampa, FL 33647

Dear Ms. Fault,

If you do not bring your mortgage payments current, the house that you are now living in will be sold at a public foreclosure auction sale on the third floor of the Hillsborough County Courthouse to the highest bidder, and you will end up being evicted by the new owner. And to make matters worse, you will not receive one red cent from the foreclosure sale.

All of this will happen if you do not take action now! Whatever you do, please do not act like most people in your situation and go into a deep state of denial and pretend that the foreclosure is not happening to you.

You still have time to put an end to your foreclosure nightmare! I can help you; all you have to do is pick up the telephone right now and call me at (813) 237-6267 to schedule an appointment, so that I can make you an offer to buy your house today! You can have a cashier's check for your house within five business days from today and stop the foreclosure and keep it off your credit report. And I will help you find another place to live, too! I will also handle all of the details of the sale and deal with your lender and the title company handling all of the paperwork that is necessary to transfer the property's title.

I look forward to hearing from you very soon and to working with you to stop your lender from foreclosing on your house.

Sincerely,

Thomas J. Lucier

FORM 8.4   Sample Fourth Letter to Property Owners in Foreclosure

---

Thomas J. Lucier
Post Office Box 21283 • Tampa, FL 33622-1283
Phone (813) 237-6267
E-Mail: tjlucier@tampabay.rr.com

August 15, 2005

Ms. Dee Fault
4569 Debtors Lane
Tampa, FL 33647

Dear Ms. Fault,

Time is running out; in 60 days your house will be sold at a public foreclosure auction sale on the third floor of the Hillsborough County Courthouse to the highest bidder. However, if you take action today, you can avoid having your house sold out from under you and being evicted by the new owner.

Your lender is not the least bit concerned that you will receive absolutely nothing from the foreclosure sale of your house. They will get their money from the sale, and that is all they care about.

Call me today at (813) 237-6267 to set up an appointment so that I can make you an offer to buy your house today. You can have a cashier's check for your house within five business days from today and stop the foreclosure and keep it off your credit report. And I will help you find another place to live, too! I will also handle all of the details of the sale and deal with your lender and the title company processing all of the paperwork that is necessary to transfer the property's title.

Please, for your own peace of mind, do not just sit back and do nothing. Act now while there is still time left! In just five days from today, you can have a cashier's check from me, which will stop the foreclosure nightmare that you are going through.

Pick up the telephone and call me right now at (813) 237-6267 to save your house from foreclosure!

Sincerely,

Thomas J. Lucier

FORM 8.5   Sample Fifth Letter to Property Owners in Foreclosure

---

Thomas J. Lucier
Post Office Box 21283 • Tampa, FL 33622-1283
Phone (813) 237-6267
E-Mail: tjlucier@tampabay.rr.com

September 15, 2005

Ms. Dee Fault
4569 Debtors Lane
Tampa, FL 33647

Dear Ms. Fault,

You are very quickly running out of time; in approximately 30 days the house that you are living in will be sold at a public foreclosure auction sale on the third floor of the Hillsborough County Courthouse to the highest bidder. And the new owner will have you evicted.

By now you should know that your mortgage lender does not care about what happens to you after they have foreclosed on your house! All they care about is getting back the money that you owe them.

And that is exactly why you should pick up the telephone right now and call me at (813) 237-6267 to set up an appointment so that I can make you an offer to buy your house today before it is too late! I will give you a cashier's check for your house within five business days from today and stop the foreclosure and keep it off your credit report. And I will help you find another place to live, too! I will also handle all of the details of the sale and deal with your lender and the title company processing all of the paperwork that is necessary to transfer the property's title.

Whatever you do, do not just sit back and do nothing. Act now while there is still time! Imagine, in just five days from today, you can have a cashier's check from me, which will stop the foreclosure nightmare that you are going through.

Call me today at (813) 123-4567, so that I can stop your lender from foreclosing on your house and leaving you with no money!

Sincerely,

Thomas J. Lucier

FORM 8.6 Sample Sixth Letter to Property Owners in Foreclosure

---

Thomas J. Lucier
Post Office Box 21283 • Tampa, FL 33622-1283
Phone (813) 237-6267
E-Mail: tjlucier@tampabay.rr.com

October 1, 2005

Ms. Dee Fault
4569 Debtors Lane
Tampa, FL 33647

Dear Ms. Fault,

This is my last letter to you. In two weeks, your house will be sold at a public foreclosure auction sale on the third floor of the Hillsborough County Courthouse to the highest bidder. And you will end up being evicted by the new owner.

Are you really prepared to lose your house through foreclosure and then be evicted by the new owner, all within the next couple of weeks? I very seriously doubt it. This type of traumatic experience is both financially and emotionally devastating to most people.

The choice is up to you. You can sit on your hands and do nothing and suffer the embarrassment and financial devastation that comes from having your house foreclosed on, or you can call me today at (813) 237-6267.

Fortunately for you, there is still enough time left for you to act. As I have been telling you all along, I can give you a cashier' s check for your house within five business days. All that you have to do is pick up the telephone right now and call me at (813) 237-6267 to set up an appointment so that I can make you an offer to buy your house today. I can stop the foreclosure sale so that it does not show up on your credit report. I can also help you find another place to live. And, I am also willing to handle all of the details of the sale and deal with your lender and the title company processing all of the paperwork that is necessary to transfer the property' s title.

For the last time, please pick up the telephone and call me right this minute at (813) 237-6267 before your lender forecloses on your house and you are evicted.

Sincerely,

Thomas J. Lucier

CHAPTER 9

How to Get the Lowdown on Loans in Default from Foreclosing Lenders

It has been my observation that most newcomers to this business automatically assume that every owner in foreclosure has tons of equity in their property. However, nothing could be further from the truth. I hate to be a spoilsport, but the fact of the matter is that most residential properties in foreclosure are not worth pursuing. I say this because prior to defaulting on their loans, most owners in foreclosure refinanced their loans in order to suck all of the equity out of their property to pay off their credit card debt. The problem with using equity to pay off credit card debt is that most homeowners do not learn from their past mistakes, and they inevitably go out on another credit card buying binge that eventually forces them to default on their home loans. This is why it is crucial that you first determine if a pre-foreclosure property has enough equity to make it worth pursuing. And the best time to do this is when a property owner in foreclosure responds to your letter. Once this happens, you must set up an appointment with the owner so that you can get the lowdown on the owner's loan directly from the foreclosing lender. A word to the wise: Whatever you do, do not blindly rely on the loan information that is published in foreclosure lawsuits, notices of lis pendens, and notices of default, or what property owners in foreclosure tell you about their loan. I know a beginner investor in Sarasota, Florida, who spent countless hours doing due diligence on a pre-foreclosure property, only to find out at the eleventh hour that the owner had zero equity in the property. This colossal waste of time and effort could have been avoided if the rookie had followed my advice and first verified the property's loan information with the foreclosing lender to determine the:

1. Type of loan that is in default: DVA, FHA, conventional, or private.
2. Unpaid principal loan balance, interest rate, amortization period, and total monthly payment to include principal, interest, taxes, and insurance.
3. Total amount of loan payments, accrued interest, late payment charges, and legal costs that must be paid in order to cure the default and reinstate the loan.

Why Time Is Always of the Essence When Verifying Loan Information

My pet peeve with most owners in foreclosure is that they generally wait until the eleventh hour, usually just a few days before their scheduled public foreclosure auction or trustee sale date, before they finally realize they will not be able to bring their loan payments current in order to cure the default and reinstate their loan. And at this point reality sets in, and pre-foreclosure property owners usually go into a panic mode where they want everything done yesterday. This is where I gently remind owners that their cooperation is the key to my quickly getting their loan information from their lender as soon as is humanly possible. I do this to keep the onus on the owners in foreclosure who created the problem, and not on me, the person who is trying to help them solve their problem. I once had a kooky owner in foreclosure tell me that if I was a real investor, I would give him a written offer on the spot and not be bothered about how much he owed the bank. Needless to say, I politely ended our conversation and went on to my next appointment.

The Fastest Way to Obtain Loan Information from Foreclosing Lenders

As I have told you, there is no time to lollygag in this business. To be successful, you must learn the fastest way to get through each step of the pre-foreclosure property buying process. And the fastest way that I know to obtain loan information from a foreclosing lender is to have the property owner who is being foreclosed on contact his or her lender's loan loss mitigation department and request it. I am telling you this because virtually all lenders require that all loan information requests be made in writing by the mortgagor or trustor who is listed in the loan documents as the borrower. By submitting the request through the borrower, it will expedite the loan information verification process and allow you to make a quicker decision about whether the owner has enough equity in the property to make it worth pursuing further. However, sometimes you will have to go above and beyond the call of duty and do what I have had to do in the past: literally drive a property owner to his or her lender's office to get the loan information that you need. I remember one time when I actually drove an owner in foreclosure to the Bank of America branch office, which had her loan information, and waited in the lobby while she had the branch manager complete her mortgage estoppel letter.

Property Owners with Computers Can Obtain Their Loan Information Online

The very first question that I now ask when meeting with an owner in foreclosure is: Do you have online access to your mortgage loan account information? I ask this question because owners who have computers can usually obtain their mortgage or deed of trust loan information online from their lender. In fact, in the last three pre-foreclosure deals that I have done, the owners were able to access their mortgage loan account information online and print it out for me. However, I still have property owners sign a release of loan information authorization letter, like the sample copy later in this chapter (page 100), so that I can verify all of the information directly with the person in the lender's loan loss mitigation department who is handling the loan.

What to Do during Your Initial Meeting with a Property Owner in Foreclosure

First things first: The sole purpose of your initial meeting with a property owner in foreclosure is to compile as much verifiable information as you can about the loan or loans that are in default before you have the owner contact the foreclosing lender. However, this is not the time to engage the owner in negotiations. Your initial meeting with any owner in foreclosure should be nothing more than a fact-finding mission, during which you review the owner's mortgage or deed of trust loan documents, promissory note, loan payment records, and the latest yearly loan escrow analysis statement that the owner has on hand. The escrow analysis statement will have the loan's unpaid principal balance up to the date of the statement, but you will have to get the current loan balance directly from the foreclosing lender. I suggest that you do as I do, and use an owner interview worksheet like the sample on page 96, to record information when conducting your initial interview with property owners.

And to keep track of the owner's loan information, I recommend that you use a loan worksheet like the sample on page 97.

FORM 9.1   Sample Owner Interview Worksheet

Owner's name _____

Owner's mailing address _____

Home telephone number _____   Work telephone number _____

Property's street address _____

Tax assessed value $_____   Date of last assessment _____

How many months are you behind on your loan payments? _____

How much do you owe in loan payments, late charges, penalties, and legal fees? $_____

Type of loan: ( ) FHA   ( ) VA   ( ) Conventional   ( ) Private

Is the loan assumable? ( ) Yes   ( ) No

Monthly loan payment: Principal $_____   Interest $_____

Taxes $_____   Insurance $_____   Total payment $_____

Unpaid principal loan balance $_____

Are there any liens or judgments against the property? ( ) Yes   ( ) No

For how much? $_____

Do you have a recent written property appraisal? ( ) Yes ( ) No

How much did your property appraise for? $_____

Have you tried selling your property? ( ) Yes ( ) No

How long has your property been for sale? _____

Have you had any written offers yet?   ( ) Yes   ( ) No

If yes, for how much? $_____

When is your property's scheduled foreclosure sale date? _____

FORM 9.2   Sample Loan Worksheet

First lender _____

Loan account number _____

Loan officer _____   Telephone number _____

Property's street address _____

Type of loan: ( ) FHA   ( ) DVA   ( ) Conventional   ( ) Private

Original loan date _____   Original loan amount $_____

Interest rate _____   Assumable? ( ) Yes   ( ) No

Monthly loan payment $_____

Unpaid principal loan balance $_____

Total amount of loan payments in arrears $_____

Total amount of accrued interest, late charges, penalties, and legal fees owed $_____

Total amount needed to cure the default and reinstate the loan $_____

Second lender _____

Loan account number _____

Loan officer _____   Telephone number _____

Type of loan: ( ) Conventional   ( ) Private

Original loan date _____   Original loan amount $_____

Interest rate _____   Assumable? ( ) Yes   ( ) No

Monthly loan payment $_____

Unpaid principal loan balance $_____

Total amount of loan payments in arrears $_____

Total amount of accrued interest, late charges, penalties, and legal fees owed $_____

Total amount needed to cure the default and reinstate the loan $_____

Third lender _____

Loan account number _____

Loan officer _____   Telephone number _____

Type of loan: ( ) Conventional   ( ) Private

Original loan date _____   Original loan amount $_____

Interest rate _____   Assumable? ( ) Yes   ( ) No

Monthly loan payment $_____

Unpaid principal loan balance $_____

Total amount of loan payments in arrears $_____

Total amount of accrued interest, late charges, penalties, and legal fees owed $_____

Total amount needed to cure the default and reinstate the loan $_____

Have the Property Owner Request an Estoppel Letter from the Foreclosing Lender

The only way to legitimately verify loan information from foreclosing lenders is for the lender to provide the owner in default with a mortgage or deed of trust estoppel letter verifying the type of loan, unpaid principal loan balance, interest rate, total monthly payment, and the total amount needed to cure the default and reinstate the loan. The term *estoppel* refers to a legal doctrine that prevents parties from later denying facts that they have previously certified as being true. For example, if a lender sends you an estoppel letter stating that Ms. Dee Fault's mortgage or deed of trust loan has an outstanding principal loan balance of $102,750 at 7 percent interest with a total monthly loan payment of $925 as of May 28, 2005, the lender cannot later claim a loan balance of $122,750 on June 1, 2005. I recommend that before the estoppel letter is sent, you first call the foreclosing lender to get the name of the person in charge of the loan loss mitigation department. The owner will have the name of a real live person to call if he or she does not receive a quick response to the estoppel letter request. Also, do not forget to have the owner or owners sign the estoppel letter before it is sent via facsimile to the person in charge of the loan loss mitigation department. Last, have the owner instruct the lender in the letter to fax or e-mail the estoppel letter directly to you. To request a mortgage or deed of trust estoppel letter from a foreclosing lender, send a letter like the sample on page 99.

Obtain the Borrower's Written Authorization to Release Loan Information

In addition to having property owners send estoppel letters to their lenders, I also recommend that you have owners send their lender a letter of authorization to release loan information, like the sample on page 100, which authorizes the lender to discuss the borrower's loan information with the third party named in the letter. This will enable you to discuss the loan directly with the person in the lender's loan loss mitigation department who is handling the loan.

How to Obtain Loan Information from Private Lenders

It can be a lot more difficult to deal with private lenders foreclosing on loans than with institutional lenders such as banks and mortgage lending companies.

FORM 9.3   Sample Estoppel Letter to Institutional Lenders

May 24, 2005

Ms. Karen Burns
Manager
Loan Loss Mitigation Department
Bank of South Florida
6970 Fowler Avenue
Tampa, FL 33647

Reference mortgage loan number: SFL082819501
Mortgagor: Dee Fault

Dear Ms. Burns,

Please send a facsimile of the following information regarding my mortgage loan to Mr. David D. Jones at (555) 123-4567 or via e-mail to ddjones@hotmail.com.

Principal and interest payment $_____   Original loan amount $_____

Insurance payment $_____   Date of original loan _____

Tax payment $_____   Payment due date _____

Interest rate _____   Escrow impound balance $_____

Total monthly payment $_____   Principal balance $_____

Total amount of loan payment in arrears $_____

Total amount of accrued interest, late charges, penalties, and legal fees owed $_____

Total amount needed to cure the default and reinstate the loan $_____

Thank you in advance for your prompt attention to this matter.

Sincerely,

Dee Fault

FORM 9.4   Sample Borrower's Letter of Authorization to Release Loan Information

May 24, 2005

Ms. Karen Burns
Manager
Loan Loss Mitigation Department
Bank of South Florida
6970 Fowler Avenue
Tampa, FL 33647

Reference mortgage loan number: SFL082819501
Mortgagor: Dee Fault

Dear Ms. Burns,

I, Dee Fault, hereby authorize the Bank of South Florida to discuss and release all of the financial information concerning my mortgage loan, loan number SFL082819501, which is secured by the property located at 3345 Costa Rosa Way, Tampa, FL 33629, to David D. Jones.

Sincerely,

Dee Fault

There are two types of private lenders that you will inevitably come across as a pre-foreclosure property investor: those who are sophisticated and those who are not. And private lenders who are sophisticated usually prefer foreclosure to having a third-party investor buy a property they hold a loan on directly from an owner in foreclosure. In many cases, they would rather get the property back from the owner via a deed-in-lieu-of foreclosure, and then resell it for a larger profit. This is why I told you in Chapter 4 that it is imperative that you carefully read private loan documents to verify if they contain a legally enforceable due-on-sale clause that would prohibit you from buying the property subject to the private loan. However, regardless of whether a private loan has a due-on-sale clause, I always have owners in foreclosure send their private lender an estoppel letter like the following sample to request loan information. The way that I look at it is that you have at least a fifty-fifty chance of the lender agreeing to let you buy the property subject to their private loan. After all, the absolute worst thing that can happen is that the lender will say no.

FORM 9.5　Sample Estoppel Letter to Private Lenders

May 24, 2005

Mr. Jerry J. Martin
97 Pasture Lane
Lutz, FL 33549
Reference: First mortgage loan secured by property at 6723 Vermont Avenue, Tampa, Florida
　　33607.
Mortgagor: Dee Fault

Dear Mr. Martin,

Please send the following information about my first mortgage loan to Mr. David D. Jones by facsimile at (555) 123-4567 or via e-mail to ddjones@hotmail.com:

1.　Principal unpaid loan balance $_____

2.　Annual interest percentage rate _____

3.　Amortization period _____

4.　Prepayment penalty (　) Yes　　(　) No

5.　Monthly principal and interest payment $_____

6.　Amount of loan payments, accrued interest, and late charges in arrears $_____

Thank you for your prompt attention to this matter.

Sincerely,

Dee Fault

CHAPTER 10

How to Perform Due Diligence on Pre-Foreclosure Properties

To avoid being snookered into buying a pre-foreclosure property with so-called hidden liens and other undisclosed title problems, you must make certain that you always perform thorough due diligence on the property's title and owner before you ever plunk down your hard-earned money. Over the past 24 years, my real property research credo has evolved into: Trust no one, assume nothing, verify everything, and be prepared for anything! I have learned the hard way not to automatically assume that all information contained in the official public records about a property is complete, up-to-date, and 100 percent accurate. The only way to obtain reliable, up-to-date information is to go directly to the source of the information, and then verify it. For example, when I want to know the tax-assessed value of a property, I first go online and look up the property's street address on the County Tax Collector's web site. I then call the tax collector's customer service department to verify that the property's tax account number and tax-assessed value that is shown on the web site is accurate. To be successful in this business, you must have the most up-to-date and verifiable information that is available on a pre-foreclosure property and its owner. This is the only way that you will have all of the information that is necessary to make an informed, intelligent buying decision that is based on real-time information and not outdated assumptions. Given today's computer technology, you can quickly perform most of your property due diligence research simply by using your personal computer and an Internet connection, linking you to a myriad web sites that will enable you to quickly access the public records that are currently available online about a property's:

1. Ownership.
2. Liens.
3. Sales history.

4. Tax-assessed value.

5. Neighborhood environmental hazards.

6. Neighborhood crime rate.

7. Neighborhood demographic and economic information.

8. Neighborhood real estate market conditions.

The Definition of Due Diligence

In general legal terms, *due diligence* is defined as: "The care that a reasonable, prudent person exercises in the examination and evaluation of risks affecting a business transaction."

Use the Internet to Perform Preliminary Due Diligence on Pre-Foreclosures

To me, the Internet is one of the greatest inventions of all time, and it ranks right up there with flush toilets, sliced bread, and basketball! And for real estate investors, the Internet is the single best property due diligence research tool available, especially for investors who are located in counties where public records information is available online. If your county's property records are available online, you can quickly find out who owns a property, when it was purchased, how much it cost, and its tax-assessed value. For example, here in Tampa, I can log onto the Hillsborough County Property Appraiser's web site, and armed only with a property's street address, I can almost instantly obtain the owner's name, mailing address, sale price and dates for the latest and prior sales, and the tax-assessed value of the property broken down by land and improvements. I can also get a site map plotting the improvements on the property, along with the tax account or folio number assigned to the parcel. Then, I log on to the Hillsborough County Tax Collector's web site and type in the property's street address or tax folio number to obtain information about the property's tax payment status.

It's Best to Use a Pre-Foreclosure Property Due Diligence Checklist

To make certain that you do not overlook anything, I recommend that you use the following checklist to perform your preliminary due diligence research on pre-foreclosure properties:

1. *Property records search:* Check your county property appraiser or assessor's property records for ownership information about the property.
2. *Property tax records search:* Check your county tax collector's property tax records for tax information about the property.
3. *Comparable sales search:* Check your county's property appraiser or assessor's records for recent sales of comparable properties within the same area during the past six months.
4. *Neighborhood crime search:* Check the crime risk rating for the property's address with local law enforcement agencies.
5. *Flood zone map search:* Check the property's address on local flood maps to determine if it is located in a flood zone.
6. *Hazardous waste search:* Check the property's address for environmental hazards with local, state, and federal environmental protection agencies.
7. *Demographic and economic data search:* Check demographic and economic data for the property's address.
8. *Code violation search:* Check the property's address for code violations with your local code enforcement department.

Where to Find the Names of All Property Owners in Your County

The names of virtually every property owner in your county are available at your county property appraiser or assessor's office on what's known as the *property tax roll.* The property tax roll lists every parcel of land in a given county. Depending on where you live, each parcel is assigned a separate tax identification number, either an assessor's parcel number (APN) or an appraiser's folio number.

Where to Search Property Records Online for Free

One of the really great things about the Internet today is that pre-foreclosure property investors can snoop around online from the comfort and privacy of their home and office and search a slew of property records for absolutely no cost. The following web sites list the county property appraiser and assessor offices that have their property records available online:

Public Record Finder: www.publicrecordfinder.com/property.html
Public Records Sources: www.publicrecordsources.com

Access Central: www.access-central.com

Real Estate Public Records: www.real-estate-public-records.com

Search Systems: www.searchsystems.net

Tax Assessor Database: www.pubweb.acns.nwu.edu/~cap440/assess.html

Public Records Online: www.netronline.com/public_records.htm

National Association of Counties: www.naco.org/counties/counties

Public Records USA: www.factfind.com/public.htm

International Association of Assessing Officers: www.iaao.org/1234.html

Public Records Research System: www.brbpub.com

Six States Do Not Require the Public Disclosure of Real Estate Sales Information

You need to know that in so-called non-disclosure states, only the principals and any real estate licensees involved in a real estate transaction know the sale price. The sale price of real estate transactions is not publicly disclosed in the following six non-disclosure states:

1. Indiana.
2. Kansas.
3. Mississippi.
4. New Mexico.
5. Utah.
6. Wyoming.

Private Companies Maintain Real Property Ownership Records Databases

If you live in a non-disclosure state, you will have to get sales data from a private company that maintains real property ownership records for your county or from real estate licensees who have access to the local multiple listing service records. The following is a listing of web sites of companies that maintain real property ownership record databases:

First American Real Estate Solutions: www.firstamres.com/htm1/home.asp

DataQuick: www.dataquick.com

What to Do If Your County's Property Records Are Not Available Online

If your county's property records are not yet available online, contact your property appraiser or assessor's customer service department to see if they provide property record information over the telephone. In most counties, you can call your property appraiser or assessor's customer service department and give them a property's street address, and they will be able to tell you the parcel or folio number, the owner's name and mailing address, if it is different from the property's, when and how much the property last sold for, and the property's current tax-assessed value. This way, you will not have to trudge down to your property appraiser or assessor's office every time you want to look up ownership information on a pre-foreclosure property.

Do Not Be Bashful about Asking "Public Servants" for Help

I do not know about you, but I am not the least bit bashful about asking the so-called public servants that staff government offices for help! So when you visit your county's office where public records are maintained, explain to the person in charge of the public records library that you are there to do a title search on a particular property. In most cases, a staff member will give you a brief orientation on how to locate a property's title information in the official record books, along with instructions on how to use the microfiche machines to read microfiche files.

How Parcels of Land Are Identified for Tax Purposes

Most counties are divided up into map or plat books. Each map or plat book is given a separate number, and each parcel of land is given a separate tax identification number—an assessor's parcel number (APN), or an appraiser's folio number. The property appraiser or assessor assigns a folio number or assessor's parcel number to each parcel of land in the county. These assessor's parcel numbers or folio numbers are used to compile the yearly property tax assessments, which are usually available online. They are also used to list each parcel owner's name, address, and the assessed value of both the parcel and any improvements. In some counties, lot and block numbers are used along with the subdivision's name.

How to Use Grantor and Grantee Indexes

When a deed is recorded in the public records, it is indexed in both a grantor (seller) index and a grantee (buyer) index. Grantor and grantee indexes are maintained in alphabetical and chronological order. They are generally alphabetized according to last and first names. Let us assume that you are trying to determine a current property owner's name, but you have only the name of the person who last sold the property and the year in which it was sold. To obtain the name of the current owner, you would use the grantor's index book for the year the title was transferred to locate the grantee's name. The grantor's index lists, in alphabetical order, all grantors named in documents recorded during a specific calendar year. And beside each grantor's name is the name of the grantee as named in the document, along with the official record book and page number where a photocopy of the recorded document can be located in the public records. The grantee index is arranged by grantee names and gives the name of the grantee and the official record book and page numbers where a photocopy of the recorded document can be found.

How to Use a Tract Index

In some states, the grantor and grantee index system is supplemented or has been totally replaced by a tract index, which indexes all recorded deeds and liens by their location rather than by the property owner's name. In a tract index, one page is used for either a single parcel of land or a group of parcels called a tract, with all recorded deeds, mortgage and deed of trust loans, liens, judgments, and other documents on the same page. The tract index system is much easier to use than the grantor and grantee system.

Many County Records Are Available Only on Microfiche Files

Prior to the advent of digital files, county or public recorder's offices used only a microfiche and microfilm index system to record and maintain property title documents. Once recorded, documents were placed directly onto microfilm, with each document being assigned a reel and frame number. If your county has not yet made its records available online, microfilm readers are available in most courthouses so that the public may review microfiche files.

How to Locate the Owners of Abandoned Properties in Foreclosure

Every once and awhile, you will come across an abandoned property that is in foreclosure, which belongs to an owner who no longer resides at the post office mailing address that is listed on property title records. I once located the owner of an abandoned pre-foreclosure property who was doing time in the Atlanta Federal Penitentiary. I found him by conducting an inmate search online at the Federal Bureau of Prisons web site at www.bop.gov. When you come across an abandoned property in foreclosure, go to the following sources in the county and state of the property owner's last known address and check the:

1. County voter registration records.
2. City and county public library patron records.
3. City and county business license records.
4. City and county jail inmate records.
5. State fishing and hunting license records.
6. State professional license records.
7. State department of motor vehicles.
8. State bar association membership records.
9. State vital statistics records.
10. State prison inmate records.
11. Federal prison inmate records.
12. Social Security Administration's Death Index.

Documents Must Be Notarized and Recorded to Be Part of the Public Record

All states require that any document must first be acknowledged, that is, witnessed and notarized by a notary public, before it can be recorded in the official public records. When recorded, property title documents are considered part of the public record, that is, information that is available to the general public. Recordation of property title documents gives the public written notice of a party's interest, claim, and right to, or in, a specific property. This is known in legal terms as *constructive* or *legal notice*, which means that anyone who needs to know is responsible for looking in the public records to obtain knowledge of any and all parties claiming an interest or right to any property.

The Two Types of Real Property Liens

Real property liens are legal claims that are placed against a debtor's or lienee's real property by lenders, creditors, and government agencies, which are known as lienors, to secure repayment of a debt. The two types of real property liens are:

1. *Statutory liens:* Statutory or non-consensual liens, such as judgment liens, mechanics' liens, and federal and state tax liens, are placed against the title to real property as a result of legal action by a creditor, lender, or government agency.
2. *Equitable liens:* Equitable or consensual liens, such as mortgage and deed of trust liens, are placed against the title to real property with the owner's consent.

Specific Liens and General Liens

Real property liens are either:

1. *Specific liens:* Attach only to a debtor's specified piece of real property.
2. *General liens:* Sometimes referred to as *name liens,* which attach to all of a debtor's real and personal property located within the county where the lien was recorded.

The Priority of a Lien Is Determined by the Type of Lien and Date It Is Recorded

The priority or seniority of one lien over other recorded liens placed against the title to the same property is determined by the type of lien and the date or chronological order in which it was recorded in the official records. For example, a mortgage or deed of trust that was recorded on May 21, 2004, would have priority over another mortgage or deed of trust recorded on May 24, 2004, against the same property because it would be in a first or senior position over the second mortgage that was recorded against the property. However, in most states, property and special assessment tax liens to include liens placed against real property for unpaid governmental services have priority over previously recorded mortgage or deed of trust liens. Judgment liens, mechanics' liens, and even federal tax liens do not have seniority over previously recorded mortgage or deed of trust liens and are considered to be subordinate or junior liens.

Check the Public Records to Verify That All Recorded Liens Are Uncovered

Whatever you do, do not blindly rely on the lienholder information that is contained in foreclosure lawsuits and notices of lis pendens and notices of default. When researching any pre-foreclosure property's title information, always make certain that you check the public records at the county records library to verify that all recorded liens placed against the property and owner have been uncovered. Check for both voluntary liens and involuntary liens. Voluntary liens are liens that are placed against the title to real property with the owner's consent, such as mortgage or deed of trust loans. Involuntary liens are liens that are placed against the title to real property, as a result of legal action by a creditor, lender, or government agency. However, functions of county and circuit court offices vary from state to state, sometimes even county to county. For this reason, I recommend that you contact your county courthouse to find out exactly who in your county maintains records on real property and judgment liens. The following is a listing of where to look when searching the public records for liens that are attached to real property:

1. *County recorder or prothonotary's office:* Check the grantor and grantee or mortgagor and mortgagee indexes, federal tax lien index, public assistance liens, conditional sales contracts such as contracts for deed, agreements for deed and land sales contracts, notices of lis pendens index, writs of attachment, judgment liens such as mechanics' and materialmen's liens, and property tax liens.

2. *Clerk of the county and circuit court:* Check the defendant's judgment index, state income tax liens, state inheritance tax liens, state franchise tax liens, judgment liens, homeowner's association liens, suits to quiet title, suits for specific performance, estates of deceased persons, guardianships of minors and incompetents, termination of life estates, termination of joint tenancies, and condemnation of lands.

3. *U.S. Court:* Check for federal judgments such as federal tax liens and judgment liens resulting from defaults on government-guaranteed FHA, DVA, SBA, and student loans.

4. *Municipal clerk's records:* Check for liens resulting from unpaid bills for municipal services such as water and sewer services and code enforcement fines.

Fifteen Liens to Check When Researching Pre-Foreclosure Property Titles

The following is a listing and brief description of the 15 most common liens encumbering the titles to pre-foreclosure properties:

1. *Real property tax liens:* Real property tax liens are placed against properties by local taxing authorities and city and county tax collectors when property owners fail to pay their property taxes. This results in the local tax collector placing a tax lien against the property in the amount of delinquent taxes owed, plus interest and penalties. If the tax lien is not paid, usually within a two- to three-year period after the first default, the tax collector then forecloses on the tax lien and sells the property at a tax deed sale. Check with your clerk of the circuit court, tax collector, or county recorder or prothonotary's office.

2. *Federal tax liens:* In order for federal tax liens to attach to the title of real property, the IRS must file a Notice of Federal Tax Lien under Internal Revenue Laws, Form 668, in the designated office of the county or state where the property subject to the lien is located or with the clerk of the U.S. district court for the judicial district in which the property is located. If the IRS fails to properly file a federal tax lien with the applicable office, the federal tax lien doesn't attach to the property's title. However, if a foreclosing lender fails to uncover a federal tax lien, which has been properly filed in the same county where the property being foreclosed on is located, the tax lien remains against the property's title. And the new owner would have to pay off the amount of the tax lien, plus interest and penalties in order to get it removed from the property's title. Check the federal tax lien file index in your county recorder or prothonotary's office or the clerk of the circuit court's office.

3. *Mechanics' liens:* Mechanics' liens are statutory liens that allow mechanics, contractors, materialmen, architects, surveyors, and engineers who have furnished work or materials for the improvement of real property to file a lien against the debtor's real property that's being worked on. The lien generally takes effect as of the date the labor or material was initially furnished. In most states, the lienor must show that the improvement was made

at the request of the owner or the owner's agent. Check with your county recorder or prothonotary's office or the clerk of the circuit court's office.

4. *Judgment liens:* Judgment liens result from lawsuits awarding monetary damages. Once recorded, a lien is placed against both the real and personal property of the debtor until the judgment is paid. Judgment liens usually attach only to property located in the county where the judgment was recorded. In most states, failure to voluntarily repay a judgment lien can result in the creditor getting the court to issue a writ of execution, allowing the county sheriff to seize and sell a sufficient amount of the debtor's property to pay the debt and expenses of the sale. When recorded with the appropriate county office, judgment liens awarded by federal courts attach to both the debtor's real and personal property. Check the defendant's judgment index at your clerk of the circuit court's office or the county recorder or prothonotary's office.

5. *Mortgage and deed of trust liens:* A mortgage or deed of trust lien is a voluntary lien that is created when real property is pledged as security for the repayment of a debt. If the debt secured by the mortgage or deed of trust lien is not repaid, the lender can foreclose on the security instrument—mortgage or deed of trust—and sell the property at public foreclosure auction or trustee's sale. Check the grantor and grantee or mortgagor and mortgagee indexes at your county recorder or prothonotary's office.

6. *State inheritance tax liens:* Most states have an inheritance tax, which is levied against the estates of deceased persons. The amount of inheritance tax owed becomes a lien against the estate. Check your clerk of the circuit court's office or the county recorder or prothonotary's office.

7. *Corporate franchise tax liens:* In states with a corporate franchise tax, corporations are taxed for the right to do business within the state. When corporations fail to pay their franchise tax, the state files a lien against any real property within the state that belongs to the corporation. Check with your clerk of the circuit court's office or the county recorder or prothonotary's office.

8. *Bail bond liens:* A lien is created when real property is pledged as a bail bond in order to allow a person arrested on criminal charges to be released on bail pending trial. Check with the clerk of the circuit court or the county recorder or prothonotary's office.

9. *Code enforcement liens:* A lien is placed against a property's title by local code enforcement boards when a property owner has been fined for failing to comply with code enforcement citations and does not pay the fine. Check with your county recorder or prothonotary's office or the clerk of the circuit court's office.

10. *Municipal liens:* A lien is placed against a property's title by local governments when a property owner fails to pay for municipal services such as water, sewage, and trash removal. Check with your county recorder or prothonotary's office or the clerk of the circuit court's office.

11. *Welfare liens:* A lien is placed against a property's title by state and federal government agencies when a property owner collects welfare payments that he or she is not legally entitled to. Check with your county recorder or prothonotary's office or the clerk of the circuit court's office.

12. *Public defender liens:* A lien is placed against a property's title by federal, state, and local governments when a property owner fails to pay for a court-appointed public defender. Check with your county recorder or prothonotary's office or the clerk of the circuit court's office.

13. *Marital support liens:* A lien is placed against a property's title by state and federal government agencies when a property owner fails to pay court-ordered marital support payments. Check with your county recorder or prothonotary's office or the clerk of the circuit court's office.

14. *Child support liens:* A lien is placed against a property's title by state governments when a property owner fails to make court-ordered child support payments. Check with your county recorder or prothonotary's office or the clerk of the circuit court's office.

15. *Homeowners' association liens:* A lien is placed against a property's title by a homeowners' association when an association member fails to pay homeowners' dues as per the deed to their property. Check with your county recorder or prothonotary's office or the clerk of the circuit court's office.

Most County Recorders Are Slow to Index Recorded Documents

For whatever reason, most county recorders are slow to index or place recorded documents into the public records. This can result in a recorded and valid lien not showing up during a lien search of the public records. I suggest that you ask the manager at your county recorder or prothonotary's office how long the time gap is between when a document is recorded and when it is actually indexed into your county's public records. Because of this time gap, I recommend you check the lis pendens index at your county circuit court clerk's office to see if any additional lawsuits have been filed against the property's title. For your information, the names of the plaintiffs and defendants in the lis pendens index are arranged in alphabetical order.

Common Abbreviations Used in Property Title Documents

The following is a listing of abbreviations commonly used in property title documents:

1. Est.—Estate
2. Et al.—And others
3. Et vir.—And husband
4. Et ux.—And wife
5. Jt.—Joint tenants
6. Qc.—Quit claim deed
7. Lov—Gift transfer
8. Dot.—Deed of Trust
9. Grantor—Seller
10. Lt.—Lot
11. Com prop.—Community property
12. Ten in com.—Tenants In Common
13. Pcl.—Parcel
14. Tr.—Trustee
15. Sec.—Section
16. Blk—Block
17. Pt.—Part
18. Tr—Tract
19. Att.—Attachment
20. Ftl.—Federal tax lien
21. Jl.—Judgment lien
22. Ln.—Lien
23. Ml.—Mechanic's lien
24. Stl.—State tax lien
25. Ttl.—Town tax lien
26. Cm.—Committee deed
27. Cn.—Conservator deed
28. Ex.—Executor deed
29. Gn.—Guardian deed

30. Mtg.—Mortgage
31. Pr Mtg.—Prior mortgage
32. Tcd.—Tax collector deed
33. Td.—Trust deed
34. Wd.—Warranty deed

How Title Companies Index Documents in Their Property Records Databases

Unlike county recorders or prothonotaries, who index recorded property title documents by name, title insurance companies index documents in their property records databases, which are called *title plants,* by the legal description that is printed on the recorded document. Title companies index recorded documents by their legal description because it is faster and cheaper. The problem with indexing documents by their legal description is that documents containing erroneous legal descriptions end up being improperly indexed in the title company's database. For example, a valid mechanic's lien against Robert B. Big that contained an error in the legal description would not show up as a lien on a title search that was done using the title company's database. However, the mechanic's lien would be found in a title search that was conducted using the name of Robert B. Big.

Have Title Searches Done at Your County's Public Records Library

I recommend that you require that your title searches be conducted at the public records library in the county where the title to the pre-foreclosure property is recorded. I am telling you to do this because title company databases are indexed by legal descriptions and not by the names of the parties listed on recorded documents. This means that all of the valid liens recorded against a property's title will not be discovered if a lien contains an incorrect legal description for the property.

The Two Most Common Types of Property Title Searches

The two most common types of property title searches are:

1. *Current owner and encumbrance (O&E) title search:* A current owner title search, sometimes referred to as an *owner and encumbrance title of property*

report, is a search of the public records from the date the property's title was transferred to the current owner to the present time.

2. *Full title search:* A full title search involves an in-depth search of the property's chain of title from the date the current owner took title back to a maximum of 60 years.

Hire an Experienced Title Abstractor to Perform Your Title Searches

It never ceases to amaze me why any pre-foreclosure investor worth his or her salt would rely on a do-it-yourself property title search instead of spending a couple hundred bucks to hire a professional to conduct a thorough title search at the county's public records library. Many investors have gotten into serious trouble because they tried to save time and money by doing only a cursory title search themselves without ever having their search results verified by a professional title researcher. I will never forget the frantic telephone call I received this past January from a novice investor in Brooklyn, New York, who was beside herself because she had completed a do-it-yourself title search that had not uncovered a $19,000 property tax lien. And now she was the proud owner of a pre-foreclosure property that was saddled with a $19,000 lien that was not about to go away overnight. The best advice that I could give her was to hire an attorney who specializes in challenging property tax assessments and have the attorney try to convince the local taxing authority to lower her tax bill. As the rookie investor in Brooklyn learned the hard way, an uncovered, but recorded, mechanic's lien, federal tax lien, third mortgage or deed of trust loan, or property tax lien can come back to haunt you at a later date, usually when you are in the process of trying to resell the property. Please understand that researching property title information can sometimes be very tricky, even if you have experience and know what you are doing. So, do what I always do, and hire an experienced title abstractor to do title searches on pre-foreclosure properties that you are seriously interested in buying. To find an experienced title abstractor in your county, log onto the following web sites:

Abstracters Online: www.abstractersonline.com

Abstractor Connection: www.abstractorconnection.com

Online Crime Statistics Search

Your pre-foreclosure property due diligence should also include a check of the neighborhood crime rate with local law enforcement agencies. The last thing that you want to do is to unwittingly buy a pre-foreclosure property that is located right smack dab in the middle of a gang turf war. The following is a listing of web sites that have nationwide crime statistics available online:

Crime.com: www.crime.com/info/crime_stats/crime_stats.html

Neighborhood crime check: www.apbnews.com/resourcecenter/datacenter /index.html

Online Demographic Information Search

Another thing that you must check out during due diligence is the demographic makeup of the neighborhood where the pre-foreclosure is located. You must do this so that you do not buy property in an area that is on the way down. The following is a listing of online sources of demographic information:

FFIEC Geocoding System: www.ffiec.gov/geocode/default.htm

U.S. Census Bureau FactFinder: www.factfinder.census.gov/servlet /BasicFactsServlet

U.S. Census Bureau Gazetteer: www.census.gov/cgi-bin/gazetteer

U.S. Census Bureau QuickFacts: www.quickfacts.census.gov/qfd/index.html

U.S. Census Bureau zip code statistics: www.census.gov/epcd/www/zipstats .html

Where to Search Online for People

A big part of the time that you will spend performing due diligence on pre-foreclosures will be spent trying to locate property owners and lienholders. The following web sites provide people locator and street address information online:

Internet Address Finder: www.iaf.net

lookupusa: www.lookupusa.com

Switchboard: www.switchboard.com

Skipease: www.skipease.com

Social Security Administration Death Index: www.ancestry.com/search /rectype/vital/ssdi/main.htm

Street Address Information: www.melissadata.com/lookups/index.htm

Reverse Telephone Directory: www.reversephonedirectory.com

Always Do a Google Search of a Pre-Foreclosure Property Owner's Name

Google is my favorite Internet search engine of all time! So, whenever I am doing due diligence research on a pre-foreclosure property, I always log onto www.google.com and enter the property owner's name into the Google search engine. And boy, have I found out some good poop about property owners from my Google searches! I especially remember finding out about one owner who was wanted in three states for embezzlement and insurance fraud. I passed on that property because I did not want to do business with a professional crook who was a fugitive from justice. However, I did report Mr. Smoothie to the appropriate authorities in all three states where he was wanted.

Always Verify the Property's Insurance Claims History before Making an Offer

I do not know about property insurance rates in the state where you live, but here in Florida property and casualty insurance rates have gone through the stratosphere! This is why I always check a pre-foreclosure property's casualty and property insurance claims history before I make a written offer. I do this by having my insurance broker verify the property's insurance claims history through the Comprehensive Loss Underwriting Exchange (C.L.U.E.). C.L.U.E. is an insurance claim history information data exchange that insurance companies use to calculate insurance premiums when underwriting policies. According to the C.L.U.E. web site, their service: "Provides loss history to help insurers qualify applicants and properties for homeowner coverage and helps insurers maximize premiums and minimize expenses." You must do this to determine if the pre-foreclosure property is insurable and if it can be insured at the prevailing market rate for similar properties within the same area. To learn more about the C.L.U.E., log onto the following web site and click on C.L.U.E. report: www.choicepoint.net.

CHAPTER 11

How to Thoroughly Inspect a Pre-Foreclosure Property

Y ou learned in Chapter 6 that one sure-fire way to fail as a pre-foreclosure property investor is to not do your homework. In this business, not doing your homework means failing to perform thorough due diligence on a property and its owner. And part of any pre-foreclosure investor's due diligence must include a thorough inspection of the property. One of the biggest mistakes that any pre-foreclosure investor can make is to buy a property without first having it thoroughly inspected. I had an investor in Tampa call me and brag about the $30,000 killing that she had just made on a pre-foreclosure located in the Hyde Park neighborhood of South Tampa. She went on and on about the great bargain that she had gotten on a two-story wood frame house built in 1949. I congratulated her and asked her if any termite damage had been uncovered when she had the property inspected. She laughed and said: "What inspection? I did not have time to have any inspection done!" I proceeded to tell her that most wood frame structures in Tampa contained some type of termite damage and that if her house had any termite damage, it could very well end up costing her an arm and a leg to get the property repaired and brought up to today's building code. To make a long story short, she later called me and stated that she had wound up spending over $20,000 to repair termite damage on what she initially thought was the deal of the century! The really sad part about this novice investor's tale of woe is that this costly lesson could have been entirely avoided if she had taken the time to have the property thoroughly inspected before she ever made a written offer to purchase the property.

Always Include a Property Inspection Clause in Your Purchase Agreements

In Chapter 17, I give you step-by-step instructions on exactly how you should prepare your purchase agreement when buying pre-foreclosure properties. One of the key buyer protection clauses that must be included in your agreements is the right to conduct a thorough inspection of the property.

Find a Competent Property Inspector

If you lack the construction knowledge and experience that is needed to conduct a thorough property inspection, you should hire a professional building inspector to snoop around and inspect properties for you. A word of caution: Be very careful when hiring a building inspector. The home and building inspection profession has more than its fair share of phonies, fakes, frauds, and scam artists because most states do not have any licensing requirements for home or building inspectors. For example, in Florida, anyone can become a home inspector simply by obtaining a city or county occupational business license. The best advice that I can give you is to use an inspector who is a member of the American Society of Home Inspectors, which has very strict membership requirements. Log on to the American Society of Home Inspectors' web site at www.ashi.org/find to find members who are located in your area.

Watch Out for Unscrupulous Owners Trying to Conceal Major Property Defects

The term *cover and concealment* has been used for over a century by the U.S. Marine Corps to describe how Marines can best avoid enemy detection on the battlefield. However, in the pre-foreclosure property investment business, cover and concealment is used to describe how unscrupulous owners go about masking major property defects. To avoid getting snookered into buying a pre-foreclosure needing costly and time-consuming repairs, you must thoroughly inspect the property for the following:

1. Structural roof damage.
2. Sinking and cracking foundations.
3. Mold contamination.
4. Electrical, fire, and safety hazards.
5. Structural dry rot damage.

6. Water and moisture intrusion.

7. Collapsed water and sewer lines.

8. Signs of termite infestation.

9. Missing roofing material, gutters, and downspouts.

10. Rotting wood.

11. Stripped mechanical systems and missing electrical wiring.

Always Have the Owner Accompany You on Walk-Through Property Inspections

When I am seriously interested in buying a pre-foreclosure property, I always insist that the owner accompany me when I do a walk-through inspection of the property. I want the owners at my side so that I can study their facial expressions and listen to their tone of voice as I ever so gently point out needed repairs. And when I conduct a walk-through inspection, I show up at the property in my old coveralls with my clipboard and inspection checklists, searchlight, high-powered binoculars, mini-tape recorder, digital camera, and ice pick. I use the binoculars to inspect the roof, chimney, fascia, and soffit. The ice pick is used to check wood for dry rot and termite damage. I use the mini-tape recorder to record detailed descriptions of needed repairs. The digital camera is used to take pictures of needed repairs that I later e-mail to contractors for repair estimates. During my inspection, when I notice some obvious structural defect or needed repair, I immediately bring it to the owner's attention with a comment like, "How long has this ceiling been sagging?" Most owners will respond with something like, "Oh, my, this is the first time that I have ever noticed it." Sure it is! In other instances when I find something that needs to be fixed, I will just point and shake my head and make comments to myself, like "hmm" or "oh boy," as I annotate the needed repair on my checklist. But I make sure to never insult the property owner; I just want him or her to know that I see exactly what is being offered for sale. The reason that I conduct my walk-through inspection in this manner is to dampen any expectations the owners may have about getting top dollar for their property. I will never forget the time that I was walking into the master bedroom of a house in Brandon, Florida, and I noticed that the concrete slab floor sloped toward the master bathroom doorway. I walked back to the bedroom door and knelt down and gently rolled a large marble toward the bathroom door, and sure enough, the ball picked up speed and rolled downhill toward the bathroom door. This confirmed what I suspected: The bedroom floor was more than a full bubble out of level. But the best part was that the owner looked at me and with a straight face said: "The floor is a little out of level; so what is the big deal?" I told him that the big deal was that his bedroom was most likely sitting on a sinkhole and that was why the floor was slowly starting to sink! Needless to say, I passed on this pre-foreclosure property.

Make Certain You Check Out the Neighborhood Where the Property Is Located

Please do not do what far too many pre-foreclosure investors do and thoroughly inspect a property but totally forget to check out the neighborhood where the property is located. Instead, check out the neighborhood where a pre-foreclosure property is located between the hours of 8 P.M. and 12 P.M. During your neighborhood inspection, check for excessive noise, cars parked in the street, rowdy parties with drunks wandering around, and any other public nuisance that could adversely affect the property's resale value. You must do this to avoid buying pre-foreclosures in neighborhoods that are placid during the day but become ugly after dark. I also recommend that you drive through neighborhoods after a heavy rainfall to check for drainage and flooding problems.

Be on the Lookout for Indoor Mold When Inspecting Properties

Today, the public perception surrounding indoor mold is such that even the suspicion that a building has just a smidgen of indoor mold is enough to strike fear into the hearts of most prospective buyers and stop them from pursuing the property. The fact of the matter is that probably every residential property in the United States contains a small amount of indoor mold, especially in bathrooms. Personally, I have no qualms whatsoever about buying a property with moderate amounts of indoor mold. In fact, in 2002, I bought a pre-foreclosure property in which all of the walls and ceilings in both bathrooms were black with indoor mold. I had the moldy drywall replaced by a professional and sold the house 30 days later. I am not afraid of pre-foreclosures with indoor mold because I understand what causes it to grow and how to quickly clean it up. I know that mold thrives indoors where there is moisture, still air, and darkness, and that the following three conditions must be present in order for indoor mold to grow:

1. A source of nutrients such as wood, drywall, carpeting, wall, and ceiling tiles.
2. Any source of moisture.
3. An optimum temperature with high humidity.

Indoor Mold Information Available Online

The following web sites have information on indoor mold:

> EPA Mold Resources: www.epa.gov/iaq/pubs/moldresources.html
>
> EPA Sick Building Syndrome: www.epa.gov/iaq/pubs/sbs.html
>
> Mold and Fungi Assessment and Remediation: www.nyc.gov/html/doh/html/epi/moldrpt1.html

How to Prevent and Clean Up Indoor Mold

The Environmental Protection Agency (EPA) has published an excellent guide, "A Brief Guide to Mold, Moisture, and Your Home," on how to prevent and clean up indoor mold growth, available online at www.epa.gov/iaq/molds/moldguide.html.

Inspect Suspicious Properties for Environmental Contamination

To avoid buying a potential toxic waste dump, have suspicious properties inspected for various types of environmental contamination that could make a property uninhabitable and render it worthless. A *suspicious property* is a property that has been used to house businesses such as gas stations, dry cleaners, automobile repair shops, and other businesses that use petroleum products, cleaning solvents, and hazardous chemicals. Even if you do not suspect that a property has any type of environmental contamination, use the environmental audit checklist on page 124 to conduct your own inspection.

Online Environmental Hazardous Waste Search

To perform an online environmental hazardous waste search on a pre-foreclosure property, log onto the following web sites:

> EPA superfund hazardous waste site search: www.epa.gov/superfund/sites/query/basic.htm
>
> Environmental hazards zip code search: www.scorecard.org

FORM 11.1   Phase One Environmental Audit Checklist

1. Examine the property's chain of ownership for the past 50 years.

2. Interview the current and available past owners of the property to determine if any present or past uses of the property would have an adverse effect upon the environment.

3. Review available past city cross-reference street directories to determine how the property was previously used.

4. Review available topographic maps of the property.

5. Review available historical aerial photographs of the property.

6. Review available geological reports affecting the property.

7. Research local, state, and federal government files for records of environmental problems affecting the property.

8. Research local, state, and federal government files for records of environmental problems affecting adjacent properties.

9. Conduct an onsite inspection of the property for obvious signs of past or present environmental problems such as odors, soil staining, stress vegetation, or evidence of dumping or burial.

10. Determine the existence and condition of above-ground storage tanks.

11. Determine the existence and condition of underground storage tanks.

Copyright Thomas J. Lucier 2005. To customize this document, download it to your hard drive from Thomas J. Lucier's web site at www.thomaslucier.com/pre-foreclosureforms.html. The document can then be opened, edited, and printed using Microsoft Word or another popular word processing application.

EPA Enviromapper zip code search: www.epa.gov/cgi-bin/enviro/em/empact/getZipCode.cgi?appl=empact&info=zipcode

HUD environmental maps: www.hud.gov/offices/cio/emaps/index.cfm

Housing Built Before 1978 May Pose Potential Lead-Based Paint Hazards

The Residential Lead-Based Paint Hazard Reduction Act requires that all sale agreements to sell residential property built before 1978 contain a Seller's Lead-Based Paint Disclosure Statement that discloses whether the property has been inspected for lead-based paint hazards and if lead-based paint hazards have been found on the property.

Online Lead-Based Paint Hazard Information

The following is a listing of online sources of lead-based paint hazard information:

> EPA National Lead Information Center: www.epa.gov/lead/nlic.htm
>
> Lead-Based Paint Disclosure Fact Sheet: www.epa.gov/opptintr/lead/fs-discl .pdf
>
> Lessor's Lead-Based Paint Disclosure Statement: www.epa.gov/opptintr/lead /lesr_eng.pdf
>
> HUD Lead-Based Paint Abatement Guidelines: www.lead-info.com /abatementguidelinesexamp.html
>
> EPA Lead information Pamphlet: www.hud.gov/lea/leapame.pdf

Use Inspection Checklists to Conduct Your Pre-Buy Property Inspections

Last, the following pages contain my pre-buy property inspection checklists. My inspection checklists are unique because they all contain a repair cost column. I added this column to allow the inspector to use the same form to do a rough repair cost estimate. My inspection forms allow for a fast but thorough inspection of any property.

FORM 11.2 Exterior Property Checklist

Street address _____

Item	Good	Fair	Bad	Repair Cost
Roof				
Foundation				
Siding				
Windows				
Doors				
Carport				
Garage				
Paint				
Screens				
Soffit and Fascia				
Chimney				
Steps				
Other				

FORM 11.3   Grounds Inspection Checklist

Street address _____

Item	Good	Fair	Bad	Repair Cost
Lawn				
Plants and Shrubs				
Trees				
Driveway				
Sidewalks				
Pot Holes				
Sink Holes				
Drainage				
Streets				
Outside Lighting				
Other				

FORM 11.4   Attic Inspection Checklist

Street address _____

Item	Good	Fair	Bad	Repair Cost
Ventilation				
Insulation				
Floor				
Lighting				
Roof Rafters				
Ceiling Joists				
Wiring				
Air Ducts				
Termite Damage				
Mold				
Other				

FORM 11.5   Garage and Carport Inspection Checklist

Street address _____

Item	Good	Fair	Bad	Repair Cost
Walls				
Floor				
Ceiling				
Doors				
Windows				
Lighting				
Heat				
Air Conditioning				
Paint				
Roof				
Soffit and Fascia				
Mold				
Other				

FORM 11.6   Electrical Inspection Checklist

Street address _____

Item	Good	Fair	Bad	Repair Cost
Riser				
Service Panel				
Capacity				
Circuit Breakers				
Electrical Outlets				
Lighting				
Wiring				
Electrical Meter				
Other				

FORM 11.7   Plumbing Inspection Checklist

Street address _____

Item	Good	Fair	Bad	Repair Cost
Water Supply				
Hot Water Heater				
Toilets				
Sinks				
Tub				
Shower				
Septic System				
Water Pipes				
Drains and Sewer Lines				
Water Pressure				
Plumbing Fixtures				
Water Supply Lines				
Well				
Mold				
Other				

FORM 11.8   Heating and Air Conditioning Inspection Checklist

Street address _____

Item	Good	Fair	Bad	Repair Cost
Natural Gas				
Central Heat and Air				
Oil Furnace				
Window and Wall Units				
Solar Panels				
Vents				
Condenser Unit				
Heat Pump				
Mold				
Other				

FORM 11.9   Kitchen Inspection Checklist

Street address _____

Item	Good	Fair	Bad	Repair Cost
Floor				
Walls				
Ceiling				
Doors				
Windows				
Lighting				
Electrical Outlets				
Sink				
Plumbing				
Cabinets				
Countertops				
Refrigerator				
Oven				
Ceramic Tile				
Paint				
Mold				
Other				

FORM 11.10   Bathroom Inspection Checklist

Street address _____

Item	Good	Fair	Bad	Repair Cost
Floor				
Walls				
Ceiling				
Doors				
Windows				
Lighting				
Electrical Outlets				
Shower				
Toilets				
Tub				
Ceramic Tile				
Sink and Vanity				
Ventilation				
Linen Closet				
Mirrors				
Paint				
Mold				
Other				

FORM 11.11   Dining Room Inspection Checklist

Street address _____

Item	Good	Fair	Bad	Repair Cost
Floor				
Walls				
Ceiling				
Doors				
Windows				
Lighting				
Electrical Outlets				
Paint				
Carpet				
Mold				
Other				

FORM 11.12   Living Room Inspection Checklist

Street address _____

Item	Good	Fair	Bad	Repair Cost
Floor				
Walls				
Ceiling				
Doors				
Windows				
Lighting				
Electrical Outlets				
Paint				
Carpet				
Mold				
Other				

FORM 11.13   Bedroom Inspection Checklist

Street address _____

Item	Good	Fair	Bad	Repair Cost
Floor				
Walls				
Ceiling				
Windows				
Doors				
Lighting				
Electrical Outlets				
Closets				
Carpet				
Paint				
Mold				
Other				

FORM 11.14   Home Office Inspection Checklist

Street address _____

Item	Good	Fair	Bad	Repair Cost
Floor				
Walls				
Ceiling				
Windows				
Doors				
Lighting				
Electrical Outlets				
Storage Closets				
Carpet				
Paint				
Mold				
Other				

How to Accurately Estimate the Current Market Value of a Pre-Foreclosure Property

Accurately estimating a property's current market value is the single most important step within my 14-step process for investing in pre-foreclosures. The number one reason so many beginners strike out in this business is that they overestimate the current market value of the very first pre-foreclosure property they purchase. And this usually marks the beginning of the end of the novice's short career as a pre-foreclosure property investor. I say this because when investors overestimate a pre-foreclosure's current market value, they put themselves behind a financial eight ball that is very hard to get free of. When investors pay too much for a pre-foreclosure, they will usually be really lucky if they end up with a breakeven deal after paying all of the costs associated with reinstating the loan, paying off lienholders, repairing the property, and making loan payments while the property is being marketed for resale. The worst case that I know of where an investor overpaid for a pre-foreclosure involved a rookie investor who lived in an area of northern California that had experienced double-digit appreciation rates during the past few years. This newcomer apparently got caught up in all of the hype that usually surrounds hot real estate markets, estimated a pre-foreclosure property's current market value at $345,000, and went ahead and bought it at that price. However, in reality, the property was worth no more than $310,000 in the condition that it was in at the time it was purchased. The guy ended up reselling the property one year later, with $45,000 in repair and holding costs, for a whopping $355,000! Needless to say, this was his first and last pre-foreclosure deal. The last I heard, he was living in Las Vegas, trying to make a living betting on sporting events.

No *Kelly Blue Book* for Investors to Look Up Used Property Values

Regretfully, there is no *Kelly Blue Book* equivalent for pre-foreclosure investors to use to look up property values. This means that you are going to have to learn for yourself how to accurately estimate the current market value of pre-foreclosure properties. However, thanks to computers and the Internet, in most real estate markets, it is not that difficult to get an accurate estimate of a pre-foreclosure property's current market value. This is especially true for pre-foreclosure investors located in counties where all property ownership, sale, and tax assessment records are available online.

The Definition of Equity

In real estate, *equity* is generally defined as "the difference between a property's appraised value and the amount of any liens recorded against the property's title." For example, the owner of a property with an appraised value of $150,000, who had an existing loan balance of $120,000, would have $30,000 worth of equity in the property ($150,000 appraised value minus $120,000 of debt equals $30,000 equity).

How the Real Estate Appraisal Industry Defines Market Value

The Appraisal Foundation's *Uniform Standards of Professional Appraisal Practice* defines *market value* as: "the most probable price a property should bring in a competitive and open market under all conditions requisite to a fair sale, the buyer and seller each acting prudently and knowledgeable, and assuming the sale price isn't affected by undue stimulus." This definition assumes that the following conditions are met:

1. The buyer and seller are motivated.
2. Each party is well informed and acting in his or her own best interests.
3. A reasonable amount of time is allowed for the property to be exposed on the open market.
4. Payment is made in cash in U.S. dollars or in a comparable financial arrangement.

5. The price represents the normal consideration of the property sold and is unaffected by special or creative financing or sales concessions granted by anyone associated with the sale.

The Difference between a Property's Assessed Value and Its Appraised Value

A lot of people confuse a property's assessed value with its appraised value. However, there is a world of difference between the two. A property's tax-assessed value is the value established by the local taxing authority for a parcel of land and the improvements made on the land for property tax purposes. For example, in Florida, owner-occupied single-family houses are generally assessed at around 70 percent of their fair market value by county property appraisers. On the other hand, a property's appraised value is the estimated value given to a property by a licensed property appraiser, using accepted appraisal methods for the type of property being appraised. For example, the accepted appraisal method to accurately estimate the fair market value for an owner-occupied single-family house is the comparison sales method where a property's value is based on the recent sale of comparable properties within the same area.

Online Sources of Property Appraisal Information

The following web sites have information on property appraisers and the appraisal process:

Appraisal Foundation: www.appraisalfoundation.org

Appraisal Institute: www.appraisalinstitute.org

American Society of Appraisers: www.appraisers.org

Three Common Methods Used by Appraisers to Estimate Property Values

The three methods most commonly used by property appraisers to estimate property values are:

1. *Comparison sales method:* The comparison sales method bases a property's value on the recent sales prices of properties that are within the same area and comparable in size, quality, amenities, and features.

2. *Income method:* The income method is used to estimate the value of an income-producing property based on the net income the property produces.

3. *Replacement cost method:* The replacement cost method is based on what it would cost to replace the improvements on property using similar construction materials and construction methods.

Best to Use the Comparison Sales Method to Estimate a Property's Current Value

I recommend that you use the comparison sales method to help you estimate a pre-foreclosure property's current market value. The comparison sales method of estimating a property's value is based on the recent sale prices of properties within the same area that are comparable in size, amenities, and features. In order to be accurate, sale price adjustments must be made for comparable properties that have been sold at unrealistically low prices or on overly favorable financial terms that are not readily available to the public. For instance, I would not use a property that sold for $10,000 more than any other comparable property because the seller took back part of his or her equity in the form of a seller-financed second mortgage loan. Nor would I include a property that sold for $10,000 below market value because it was sold at a public foreclosure auction or trustee's sale.

Online Sources of Comparable Residential Property Sales Data

Comparable sales data for residential properties is available online at the following web sites:

DataQuick: www.dataquick.com

HomeGain: www.homegain.com

REAL-COMP: www.real-comp.com

HomeRadar: www.homeradar.com

Domania Home Price Check: www.domania.com

Yahoo Real Estate: http://realestate.yahoo.com/re/homevalues

OFHEO House Price Index: www.ofheo.gov/HPI.asp

Home Price Forecasts: www.cswcasa.com/products/redex/home

NAR Existing Single-Family Home Sales: www.realtor.org/Research.nsf/Pages/EHSdata

How to Get Free Building Replacement Cost Estimates

You can usually get a free building replacement cost estimate by calling a local independent insurance broker who represents insurers that specialize in providing property and casualty insurance coverage for residential and commercial buildings. When you call a broker, tell him or her that you want a replacement cost quote. Property replacement costs are calculated by using a replacement cost formula that's based on the property's geographical location and its:

1. Street address.
2. Age.
3. Type of construction.
4. Number of stories.
5. Type of roof.
6. Current use.
7. Heating and cooling system.
8. Square footage.

Online Sources for Construction Replacement Cost Calculators

The following web sites have construction replacement cost calculators online:

Construction Cost Calculator: www.get-a-quote.net

Construction Material Calculators: www.constructionworkcenter.com/calculators.html

Building Cost Calculator: www.nt.receptive.com/rsmeans/calculator

Pursue Only Pre-Foreclosures That Have Relatively Low Debt-to-Value Ratios

The key to consistently making money as a pre-foreclosure property investor is to buy only properties that have a debt to value ratio of at least 80 percent. The term *debt-to-value ratio* refers to the total amount of debt owed against a property in foreclosure versus the property's current market value. For example, a property in foreclosure with $80,000 in total debt to include the principal loan balance, loan payments in arrears, late payment charges, legal costs, and subordinate liens with a current market value of $105,000 would have a debt-to-value ratio of 76 percent ($80,000 in debt divided by $105,000 in current market value equals a debt to value ratio of .7619 or 76 percent). Personally, I never pursue a pre-foreclosure property unless it has a debt-to-value ratio below 75 percent.

Defining a Pre-Foreclosure Property's Current Market Value

I define a pre-foreclosure property's current market value as: the value of the property in its current financial and physical condition after deducting all of the costs associated with curing the default and reinstating the loan, paying off all the subordinate lienholders, and repairing the property to a marketable resale condition.

How to Accurately Estimate a Pre-Foreclosure Property's Current Market Value

As I told you in the beginning of this chapter, your success as an investor is tied directly to how well you are able to accurately estimate a pre-foreclosure property's current market value. And unlike playing the game of horseshoes or working at a job where you toss hand grenades for a living, coming close is not good enough in this business. In order to accurately estimate the current market value of a pre-foreclosure, you must first know the:

1. Loan balance of the existing mortgage or deed of trust loans that are in default.
2. Total amount of loan payments that are in arrears.
3. Total amount of accrued interest, late payment charges, and legal costs that the owner owes.
4. Total amount needed to cure the default and reinstate the loan.
5. Total amount of all judgment liens that are recorded against the property's title.
6. Total cost of all the repairs needed to put the property in a marketable resale condition.
7. Property's market value, based on the sales data of comparable properties that have sold within the same area during the past six months.

I recommend that you use the current market value worksheet on page 145 to make certain that you do not overlook anything when calculating a property's current market value.

FORM 12.1 Sample Current Market Value Worksheet

1. Tax assessed value $_____

2. Appraised value $_____

3. First mortgage or deed of trust loan balance $_____

4. Second mortgage or deed of trust loan balance $_____

5. Amount of loan payments, accrued interest, and late payment charges in arrears $_____

6. Amount of legal fees owed $_____

7. Total amount needed to cure the default and reinstate the loan $_____

8. Amount of liens and judgments liens recorded against the property $_____

9. Amount of property taxes owed $_____

10. Amount of all outstanding city, county, and state fines $_____

11. Total amount owed against the property $_____

12. Property's estimated repair and clean-up costs $_____

13. Property's estimated current market value $_____

14. Cost to purchase the owner's equity at a discount of 50 percent or more $_____

15. Property search, acquisition, and closing costs $_____

16. Estimated equity in property after purchase $_____

Four-Step Method for Estimating a Pre-Foreclosure's Current Market Value

Once I find a pre-foreclosure property that has potential, I log onto the Hillsborough County Property Appraiser's web site and type in the street address of the property. From the property's street address, I obtain the owner's name, mailing address, sale price, and dates for the latest and prior sales and the tax-assessed value of the property broken down by land and improvements. I also get the tax account or folio number assigned to the property. Then I conduct an online search of the entire street that the property is located on for recent sales within the past six months. I also do an online search of adjacent streets for recent comparable sales. Next, I log onto the Hillsborough County Tax Collector's web site and type in the property's street address or tax folio number to obtain property tax information about the property to include any tax exemptions claimed, special tax-district assessments, and the tax payment status. Once I have this information, I call my insurance broker to get the current per square foot replacement cost for residential properties within the same area. I recommend that you do as I do, and use the following four-step method to estimate a pre-foreclosure property's current market value:

Step 1: Log onto your county's property appraiser's or assessor's web site to obtain the tax-assessed value of the pre-foreclosure property under consideration for purchase.

Step 2: Search your county's property tax rolls online for sales during the past six months of three to five properties that are comparable in size, amenities, and condition and located within a one-mile radius of the property under consideration for purchase.

Step 3: Carefully analyze comparable property sales and make price adjustments for differences in amenities, age, and physical condition in order to estimate the property's value.

Step 4: Calculate the per square foot cost of replacing the improvements on the property, using the same building materials and method of construction.

How to Calculate the Amount of Equity That an Owner Has in a Pre-Foreclosure

The main reason you must be able to accurately estimate the current market value of a pre-foreclosure property is so that you will be able to calculate the amount of equity that an owner actually has in the property. And the first step in this calculation is to deduct the total amount that it is going to cost to reinstate the loan, pay off all of the recorded judgment liens, and repair the property to a marketable resale condition. For example, a pre-foreclosure property with a fair market value of $150,000 that has a loan in default that requires $6,775 to reinstate and a federal tax lien that will take $1,375 to pay off, along with an estimated $5,325 in needed repairs, would have a current market value of approximately $136,525 ($150,000 fair market value minus $13,475 in costs equals $136,525 in current market value). Once you have determined the property's current market value, you then deduct the existing loan balance to determine how much equity the owner has in the property. In this case, let us assume that the property being discussed has an existing loan balance of

$120,000. To calculate the owner's equity, you would simply subtract the $120,000 existing loan balance from the property's $136,525 current market value, which equals $16,525. Then, depending upon the property, you would offer to pay the owner 50 cents or less on the dollar for his or her equity, which in this case would be $8,265.50 (50 percent of $16,525 equals $8,265.50). In Chapter 13, I show you how to negotiate with owners in foreclosure so that you can buy their equity for 50 cents or less on the dollar.

CHAPTER 13

How to Negotiate with Property Owners in Foreclosure

In Chapter 9, I told you to treat your initial meeting with a property owner in foreclosure as a loan fact-finding mission and not as a negotiating session. In this chapter, I give you the equivalent of a one-on-one seminar on how to negotiate with property owners in foreclosure. Being able to successfully negotiate with owners in foreclosure is second in importance only to knowing how to accurately estimate a pre-foreclosure property's current market value. The old adage that everything in life is negotiable is also applicable to investing in pre-foreclosure properties. How much you pay for a pre-foreclosure pretty much depends upon how good of a negotiator you are. If you are a savvy negotiator, you can usually buy an owner's equity (i.e., the difference between the outstanding loans and the current value of the property) at a discount of 50 percent or more. However, if you are a poor negotiator, you will probably end up paying too much for your first pre-foreclosure property, and it may be your last. In a worst-case scenario, an investor's inability to negotiate a discounted purchase price for an owner's equity could result in the hapless investor later defaulting on the mortgage or deed of trust loan and finding himself or herself in foreclosure. The main reason so many investors stumble when it comes to negotiations is that they are absolutely clueless about what they are going to say when they actually come face-to-face with an owner in foreclosure. As a result, they freeze up completely. Or, if they do summon up enough courage to speak, they usually end up stammering through a poorly worded conversation punctuated by pregnant pauses. A few last words to the wise: If you want to become an excellent negotiator, you must first become an excellent listener. In this business, it literally pays to listen. Finally, the quickest way that I know of to lose credibility with an owner during negotiations is to say something that turns out not to be true. So please, do not try to bluff your way through negotiations.

Five Rules to Follow When Negotiating with Property Owners in Foreclosure

My negotiating style is very direct and to the point. I know what I want, and I know what I am willing to give to get it. And, I refuse to waste my valuable time in rambling negotiating sessions that never yield any results. To keep everything on track, I follow these five rules when conducting negotiations:

Rule 1: Never negotiate through a third party, such as an attorney, accountant, or real estate broker; always insist that the owner be present during all negotiations.

Rule 2: Do not act in a confrontational manner that will alienate the owner and cause negotiations to come to a screeching halt.

Rule 3: Do not automatically assume that everything you are being told by the owner is 100 percent accurate. Take a see-it-to-believe-it attitude and insist that all claims made about the property are supported by verifiable documentation.

Rule 4: Maintain a professional, no-nonsense demeanor that lets the owner know that you are a serious buyer who does not have time for games, gimmicks, and bullspit!

Rule 5: Always take the path of least resistance by agreeing to mundane negotiating points that do not affect the purchase price of property, but are so important to the owner that they could kill the deal.

What You Need to Know about Most Property Owners in Foreclosure

Let me state right from the get-go that many of the people who end up in foreclosure are not bad people. The fact of the matter is that bad things like foreclosure do happen to good people who experience financial misfortune that is not of their own making and is far beyond their control. For example, I once bought a pre-foreclosure from an owner who had been the victim of a violent crime that left her physically disabled and unable to work. The perpetrator who attacked her was a career criminal who had been released early because of prison overcrowding and had no assets. So all the crime victim received for support was a very meager monthly disability payment from the Social Security Administration, which did not cover her basic living expenses—never mind her mortgage payment. However, in most cases, it has been my experience that more than 51 percent of the property owners with loans that are in default and facing foreclosure made a series of very bad financial decisions, which eventually led them on a downward spiral toward financial ruin. And like far too many Americans today, they would rather play the blame game than acknowledge their own financial mistakes. You must also know that most people who find themselves on the brink of foreclosure usually experience some form of emotional trauma, such as denial, stress, fear, panic, anger, and anxiety. Property owners in this situation also feel powerless, overwhelmed, trapped, and incapable of helping themselves solve their own financial problems. And because of their mental state of mind, most people in foreclosure can be extremely hard to deal with because they usually do not act like rational, reasonable, intelligent adults. In other words, their decision-making process is based almost entirely on emotions, rather than on logic. From my many experiences, I have learned that most people in foreclosure:

1. Blame their financial plight on everyone but themselves.
2. Are very reluctant to discuss their financial situation with strangers.
3. Are extremely hard to communicate with.
4. Very rarely tell the whole truth at one time.
5. Are financially illiterate.
6. Have lousy credit and do not really care about their credit rating.
7. Are greedy and expect you to bail them out and then pay them full retail value for their property.
8. Would rather have their loan foreclosed on than sell their equity at a substantial discount and allow a stranger to profit from their misfortune.

Most Property Owners in Foreclosure Do Not Want to Sell Their Property

It may come as a shock to many of you, but the fact is that most property owners with loans that are in default and facing foreclosure have no real interest in selling their property. Their initial interest is in trying to get the money necessary to cure the default and reinstate their loan so they can keep their property. It is only after owners in foreclosure finally realize that they will not be able to beg, borrow, or steal the amount of money necessary to stop foreclosure that they are willing to consider selling their property. This is why I told you in Chapter 8 to send multiple follow-up letters at regular intervals to owners in foreclosure.

Owners Usually Refuse to Enter into
Serious Negotiations with People They Dislike

As the old saying goes, first impressions are lasting impressions, and this is especially true when you begin negotiating with property owners in foreclosure. The fastest way to fail as a would-be pre-foreclosure property investor is to come across to property owners as an arrogant know-it-all, with the personality of a recent honor graduate of the North Korean Army Charm School. I say this because most property owners in foreclosure will refuse to enter into serious negotiations with people whose attitude or behavior they dislike. Most property owners refuse to let someone they personally dislike take advantage of their financial situation.

Why It Is Next to Impossible to Negotiate with
Owners Who Are in a Nasty Divorce

It should not come as a big surprise that many married couples in foreclosure are going through divorce at the same time. In fact, many of the studies that have been done over the past decade about divorce rates have cited the stress and strain from financial failures as the number one cause for divorce in America. The main obstacle that I could not overcome both times that I have tried to negotiate with owners who were going through divorce was the greedy divorce attorneys representing the husband and the wife. Trust me; there is no bigger deal-killer than two greedy, know-it-all divorce attorneys in Armani suits and alligator shoes, who are billing their clients by the hour. They pose an almost insurmountable obstacle to the sale of any property in foreclosure because they have no incentive to get the divorce finalized. And this is especially true when the husband and wife are involved in a nasty divorce. The only way that I will ever consider speaking with a divorcing couple in foreclosure is if they have filed a no-fault, uncontested divorce petition, and neither party is being represented by an attorney!

Avoid Negotiating with Owners Who Are
Addicted to Drugs and Alcohol

As you get started in this business and begin to meet and negotiate with owners in foreclosure, you will come into situations where some owners do not seem to understand anything that you are telling them during negotiations. However, this lack of comprehension on the part of property owners is not your fault. In most cases, it is the long-term result of brain cell deterioration caused by heavy-duty drug and alcohol abuse. The federal government and many states consider people who are afflicted with an addiction to drugs and alcohol to be disabled. In fact, HUD has classified both drug addiction and alcoholism as disabilities that cannot be discriminated against in rental housing. In other words, a landlord is not supposed to deny rental housing to people solely because they are heroin junkies or booze hounds. I am taking the time to tell you this because buying pre-foreclosures from certifiable addicts can be risky business, fraught with unforeseen problems and complications that just are not worth taking a chance on. And this is exactly why I have twice broken off negotiations when I came to the realization that the person I was speaking with had a brain that was fried extra crispy. All I could think of was my being featured in the lead story on the local Channel 8 six o'clock evening news broadcast about sleazy investors who prey on disabled property owners in foreclosure.

Act in an Honest Ethical Manner When Dealing with Owners in Foreclosure

The best advice that I can give to any pre-foreclosure property investor is to always act in an honest, ethical manner when dealing with property owners in foreclosure. This means that you should always make every effort to try to do what you say you are going to do, when you say you are going to do it, and exactly how you say you are going to do it. You must understand that in this business, even when you do act in an honest, ethical manner, there is still a slight possibility that you could end up as a defendant in a lawsuit, accused of what is known in legal circles as, "unjust enrichment derived from a real estate professional taking unfair advantage of a homeowner in foreclosure." In other words, disgruntled former owners in foreclosure file a lawsuit that claims you screwed them because they agreed to sell their home for less than what they later thought it was worth. The best defense against these types of lawsuits is to have a paper trail full of documents that prove you acted in an honest, ethical manner and with the owner's full knowledge and consent. I am proud to say that I have never had any property owner in any circumstance file any type of complaint against me after I have purchased their property. In fact, I have walked away from deals where I did not feel comfortable about doing business with the owner.

Do Not Show Up for Negotiations with an "I Buy Foreclosures" Sign on Your Vehicle

The fastest way that I know of to be instantly rejected by owners in foreclosure, even before you set foot on their property and open your mouth, is to drive up in a vehicle that is plastered with those tacky-looking magnetic signs that announce to the world that you buy properties from owners in foreclosure. When you do this, you not only expose property owners' financial plight to their neighbors and maybe even family members, which causes them much embarrassment and added stress, but also lose any credibility that you may have had with them. I was once in the middle of serious negotiations with a couple in foreclosure, who had not yet broken the bad news to their teenage daughter, when an obnoxious investor showed up in their driveway, uninvited, in an old white Chevy van with "I Buy Foreclosures" painted in gigantic red letters on both sides and on the front and back. The daughter came running into the kitchen and told us that some guy was parked outside in a junky-looking van and then asked her parents if they were in foreclosure. The husband jumped up and made a mad dash outside and told my competitor, in words that would make a U.S. Marine Corps drill instructor blush, that he had damn well better leave the premises while the leaving was good. But on the flipside, I do not recommend that you show up for negotiations in a high-end automobile, such as a Mercedes Benz, Jaguar, or Lexus, wearing designer clothes and draped in expensive jewelry. Your display of wealth only serves as another reminder to owners in foreclosure, who, for all intents and purposes, are financially destitute, that they are financial failures. And rubbing people's noses in you-know-what is not the way to start off negotiations!

Verify the Identity of the Property Owner before You Begin Negotiations

First things first: To avoid being flimflammed by an identity thief posing as the property owner of record, make certain that the person you are negotiating with is the actual owner and not an imposter. The best way to verify that the person you are meeting with is in fact the property owner is to do what I do when I meet with an owner in foreclosure for the first time: Show your driver's license and ask the owner to do likewise. As I show the owner my Florida driver's license, I matter-of-factly explain that I am doing this because of the rampant spread of identity theft. And if, for whatever reason, the owners refuse to identify who they are by showing me some form of government-issued photo identification, I politely excuse myself and get up and leave. So far, I have met with only one property owner who has refused to show me a photo identification. And that person appeared to me to be incoherent and under the influence of a controlled substance, such as drugs or alcohol, and I suspect that he may not have been who he purported to be.

Always Project the Image of a Savvy Polished Professional Investor

The image that you want to project is that of a savvy polished professional investor. Please understand that when I use the term *polished professional*, I am not referring to the slick-looking bozos and bimbos who make their living by starring in infomercials on late-night television. By polished professional, I mean an individual who is sincere, personable, confident, knowledgeable well spoken, well mannered, well groomed, and in control of his or her emotions, and not like typical beginning investors, who oftentimes come across as confused, uninformed, clueless flakes looking like they just came from a Grateful Dead concert. If you want to be taken seriously by property owners, you must look and act like a capable buyer who is ready, willing, and able to negotiate.

First off, dress conservatively. Property owners in the throes of foreclosure will not be impressed by your exotic wardrobe. I recommend that you do not show up on an owner's front steps wearing short-sleeved shirts adorned with controversial expressions, flashy gold jewelry, low-cut blouses, short shorts, sundresses, sandals, or weird colored hair. The image that you want to project during negotiations is that of a rational, reasonable, professional businessperson. At a minimum, men should be well groomed and wear a pair of dress pants, a dress shirt, a sport coat, and a polished pair of dress shoes. Women should be well groomed and wear conservative clothing and footwear and a minimum of cosmetics.

Apply the KISS (Keep It Simple) Principle When Conducting Negotiations with Owners in Default

Unless you aspire to join the ranks of sleazy politicians, plaintiffs' attorneys, and other forms of lowlife, do not use games, gimmicks, and bullspit as part of your negotiating strategy. In other words, limit the use of tall tales, little white lies, and fibs to describing fishing and hunting exploits, but not what you can do to help property owners in foreclosure. Many owners will immediately cease negotiating with prospective buyers who try to dazzle them with brilliance and baffle them with bullspit technique. The first step in negotiating with owners in foreclosure is to replace the myths, preconceived notions, and bad advice that they have most likely received from well-meaning, but equally ignorant, friends and relatives. The best way to do this is to give owners a succinct, easy-to-understand explanation of the foreclosure process and how you can help them avoid it. Do not go off on a long-winded, full-blown, legal tangent when explaining to an owner in foreclosure how the judicial or non-judicial foreclosure process works. The object of your negotiations is to buy an owner's equity at a discount of 50 percent or more and not to impress him or her with your foreclosure expertise.

Adopt a Negotiating Style Compatible with Your Personality

I recommend that you adopt a negotiating style that is compatible with your personality. In other words, do not try to be what you are not. For example, if you consider yourself to be a mild-mannered, soft-spoken type of person, do not try to assume the role of a pushy, loud-mouth person for the sake of negotiations. Instead, adopt a negotiating style that is compatible with your personality. This way, you can be a successful negotiator without having to change your natural personality. I have found that most mild-mannered, soft-spoken people usually make the best negotiators because they are generally non-confrontational by nature, and most people underestimate them at the bargaining table! For example, I have adopted the negotiating style of a cordial professional who is all business after initial pleasantries have been exchanged. In other words, the property owner knows that I take my business seriously, and that I am not there on a social call.

Play the Role of Problem Solver When Negotiating with Owners in Foreclosure

There are two approaches that you can take as pre-foreclosure property investor. You can take the role of vulture and attempt to use fear and intimidation to try to goad property owners into doing business with you, or you can play the role of problem solver. My approach to the pre-foreclosure property investment business has always been that of a problem solver. I sometimes use the highfalutin' title of "Foreclosure Resolution Specialist" when asked what I do for a living. By *problem solver,* I mean an investor who can analyze a property owner's financial situation and quickly come up with a workable solution that is acceptable to both the investor and the owner. And as a problem solver, I offer a very specialized service that most other people associated with the real estate industry are unable or unwilling to provide. For example, I spent six hours on Mother's Day, 1998, negotiating the purchase of a pre-foreclosure with a woman who woke up that morning and decided that she had to get off the dime and do something that very day about her worsening financial plight. During our six-hour negotiating marathon, I was able to show her a workable plan that would break the financial stranglehold that she was under and allow her to get on with her life. To make a long story short, the property owner was recently divorced with two small children, and she wanted to return to her native country of Germany. I was willing to invest six hours of my life in negotiations because the property had a 10-year-old non-qualifying assumable VA mortgage. To close the deal, I agreed to pay off $2,800 in credit card debt and buy her and the kids airline tickets for a one-way trip to Frankfurt, Germany, via Condor Airlines, which set me back another $850. I ended up paying $3,650 for her equity and another $4,700 to reinstate the loan, for a grand total of $8,350. A week later, I turned around and resold the property for a fast $20,000 profit!

How to Open Face-to-Face Negotiations with Owners in Foreclosure

I take control of the negotiating process as soon as I meet with the owner. And the very first thing that I do is to look the owner right square in the eyes and matter-of-factly explain that I earn my living by investing in pre-foreclosures and that I am in business to make a profit. I also point out that I am in a very stressful and risky business and that I must be fairly compensated. After I am sure that I have made my point crystal clear about not running a non-profit business; I switch gears and launch into my opening statement, which goes something like this:

> *Okay, as I told you, I want to see if I can help you and help myself at the same time. Let me briefly outline how I may be able to help you resolve your current situation. First off, we will inspect your property together. And then I will use the loan information that you gave me during our initial meeting to complete my financial analysis of the property. After I have completed my analysis, we will go over the numbers together, and if we think we can make a deal, I will make you a written offer on the spot that will be contingent upon the property's title status. The contingency clause is included in the event that a title search uncovers any other judgment liens that are recorded against the property's title, but were not disclosed to me during negotiations. And if you agree to my offer and sign our purchase agreement and everything else is exactly as you have said it is, we can close on the sale of your property within five business days or*

less from today. So, if you do not have any questions, let us get started with the walk-through inspection of the property.

And once negotiations get started, I always refer back to the owner's situation. For example, when owners get testy with me, I always tell them that I fully appreciate their present circumstances, but that I am not the person who is responsible for their current situation. Also, whatever you do, never, ever leave an unsigned purchase agreement with an owner to mull over. If you do, you are inviting the owner to use your offer as a negotiating tool when your competitors show up to make their offers. I learned this lesson the hard way in 1992, and it ended up costing me more than $15,000 when one of my competitors swooped down and snapped up a deal by paying the owner $500 more than what I had offered.

You Will Never Know What Owners Will Accept Unless You Ask Them

The old saying that you will never know unless you ask is ever so true when it comes to negotiating with owners in foreclosure. Please keep this sage advice in mind when you are in serious negotiations with owners in foreclosure over the purchase price of their property and are hesitant to make what you consider to be an insulting lowball offer to buy their equity. Go ahead and make your offer; you might be pleasantly surprised by the answer you get. The very worst that the owner can say is no, to which you make a counteroffer. But then, again, you will never know unless you ask, will you?

Stress That It Will Not Cost Owners Any Money to Sell Their Equity

One of the main points that I stress during negotiations is that I promise owners that it will never cost them any money out-of-pocket to sell me their equity. I do this by agreeing to pay all of the costs associated with closing the transaction. However, all closing costs are deducted from the estimated amount of the owner's equity. For example, if the closing costs came to $2,678 and I estimated 50 percent of the owner's equity to be $9,500, I would deduct the closing costs, which would reduce the owner's equity to $6,822. And over the years, this has helped me clinch a lot of deals because all of my competitors insist that owners pay their fair share of the closing costs out of their own pocket. However, most people in foreclosure are turned off by this type of greedy attitude and usually tell anyone who proposes they pay their own closing costs to "go away and stay away!"

Know When It Is Time to Stop Talking

Finally, during every negotiating session, there comes a point when it is time to stop talking. But it's usually right at this very crucial point that most amateurs talk themselves right out of a deal because they simply do not know when to shut up. The time to stop talking is immediately after both you and the owner have had your say. This is the time to put up or shut up! In other words, it is time to either close on the purchase or agree to meet again after the owner has had time to mull things over, but it is definitely not the time to ramble on.

Three Scenarios that Determine How Much to Pay an Owner for Equity

First off, I do not have set prices that are firmly etched in stone that I will pay an owner for his or her equity. Rather, my prices are based strictly on the owner's circumstances, the property's physical condition, and its title status. The amount of money I am willing to pay a pre-foreclosure property owner for his or her equity is determined by the following three factors:

Scenario 1: When the property is owner-occupied, in need of repairs, and has judgment liens attached to its title, I offer the owner debt relief and a relocation allowance to cover the cost of moving and settling into a rental unit.

Scenario 2: When the property is owner-occupied, in good condition, and has no judgment liens attached to its title, I offer the owner debt relief and buy the equity for 50 cents or less on the dollar.

Scenario 3: When the property is vacant, in need of repairs, and has judgment liens attached to its title, I offer the owner debt relief and the opportunity to keep a foreclosure off his or her credit report.

Offer Debt Relief Only to Owners with Vacant Properties in Foreclosure

In many cases, owners in foreclosure have moved out and abandoned their property. They assume, incorrectly, that by moving away from the property, they can leave their financial obligations behind. In cases where pre-foreclosure property is vacant, I offer owners debt relief and the opportunity to keep a foreclosure from appearing on their credit report. An offer of debt relief means that you agree to pay the lender the amount of money that is needed to cure the default and reinstate the loan. I offer to pay the cost of reinstating the loan, paying off all recorded judgment liens, and paying all closing costs. I realize that some of you reading this may be a bit skeptical and think that no owner in his or her right mind would accept such an offer. However, you must understand that most vacant properties in foreclosure have been that way for 6 to 10 months. And in places like Florida, where it tends to be very hot and very humid for eight months out of the year, the inside of a house that has been closed up and without the air conditioning on can end up with a severe case of indoor mold contamination or, worse yet, have its interior demolished by roving gangs of vandals. In addition to the property's physical condition, there is the expense of reinstating a loan that has been in default for 6 to 10 months. In fact, you will find out that 8 out of 10 vacant pre-foreclosure properties do not have enough equity to be bothered with, and that the owners would have to pay you to take them off their hands.

Offer Debt Relief and a Relocation Allowance for Owner-Occupied Properties

One of the main problems that you will run into over and over again in the pre-foreclosure investment business is finding properties with equity that is worth pursuing. And then when you do find a property that is worth chasing, you have to be careful that you do not end up losing your tokus on the deal by paying owners too much for their equity. This is why when I locate a rundown, owner-occupied pre-foreclosure that is in need of repairs and has judgment liens recorded against its title, I offer the owner debt relief, along with a $1,500 to $2,500 cash relocation allowance to cover moving expenses and the cost of settling into a rental unit. To the general public, this may seem stingy, but it really is not when you take the time to correctly calculate all of the costs associated with reinstating the loan, paying off subordinate lienholders, paying the closing costs, and putting the property into a marketable resale condition. And do not forget the holding costs, such as debt service, insurance, lawn care, and a security alarm system, that must be paid for while the property sits vacant. Also, there is always the very real risk that vandals could wreak destructive havoc on the property. In fact, I always provide property owners with an itemized listing of all the expenses that I will incur when I buy their property. I have found that it has a rather sobering effect on property owners who initially think they are being ripped off by a greedy investor.

When to Offer to Buy the Owner's
Equity for 50 Cents or Less on the Dollar

On the very few occasions when I do find a pre-foreclosure property that is in good physical condition that has no other judgment liens recorded against its title, I offer to buy the owner's equity for 50 cents or less on the dollar. I do this because on these types of properties, my out-of-pocket expenses are greatly reduced because I do not have the expense of paying off subordinate lienholders, and there are no costly and time-consuming repairs that need to be completed in order to put the property in a marketable resale condition. This results in my having to pay less in holding costs as the property is ready to put right on the market. I usually start off by offering to buy an owner's equity for 40 cents on the dollar. And if the owner rejects my initial offer, I up the ante to 45 cents and then to 50 cents if my second offer is refused. I generally never offer to pay owners more than 50 cents on the dollar for their equity because there just is not enough equity in most properties to offer any more and still make a reasonable profit. And, I want to make certain that I am well compensated for the stress, time, aggravation, effort, and risk that are a part of every pre-foreclosure deal.

CHAPTER 14

How to Get Subordinate Lienholders to Discount Their Liens by 50 Percent or More

I gave you the lowdown in Chapter 10 on how to perform due diligence to uncover all of the liens and judgment liens that are attached to a pre-foreclosure property's title. Now, in this chapter, I tell you how to avoid the missteps that plague most uninformed neophytes when they attempt to negotiate a discounted lien purchase with subordinate or junior lienholders. To my way of thinking, what really separates the profitable pre-foreclosure investors from the ne'er-do-wells and also-rans is the ability to get subordinate lienholders to discount their liens by 50 percent or more. And when approached the right way, it has been my experience that more than 80 percent of all subordinate lienholders are willing to sell their liens at a discounted price. The fact is, most subordinate lienholders are thrilled to get 50 cents or less on the dollar for their liens. Even the stubborn ones eventually come to the conclusion that half of nothing is nothing, but that half of a dollar is 50 cents. I attribute this high acceptance rate to the fact that very few lienholders have the time, money, or desire to fight senior lienholders in court.

Subordinate Liens Affect Profit Margins in Pre-Foreclosure Property Transactions

You must understand that in this business, your profit margin in a pre-foreclosure property is usually tied directly to how well you are able to negotiate discounts with junior lienholders. In many instances, subordinate liens pose a major obstacle and can end up being a real deal-killer if they cannot be bought for way less than their face value. Believe me, I truly wish that getting a judgment lien removed from a property's title was just a matter of simply saying "abracadabra," and poof, the lien magically disappears, but unfortunately, that is not how things work in this business. And because there is no magical formula for getting rid of subordinate liens, you must take the time and effort to learn the ins and outs of exactly how to:

1. Identify all subordinate lienholders of record who claim to have a valid lien claim against the property's title.
2. Verify the validity of each subordinate lien claim.
3. Contact all subordinate lienholders of record.
4. Negotiate the purchase liens for 50 percent or less of their face value.
5. Contest fraudulent liens in a court of competent jurisdiction.
6. Have all of the subordinate liens that you purchase removed from a property's title.

The Difference between a Judgment Lien and a Consensual Lien

The first thing that you need to know is the difference between a judgment lien that is placed against a judgment debtor's property for failure to repay a debt and a consensual lien, such as a mortgage or deed of trust, which is placed against a property's title with the consent of the owner. A judgment lien is a formal written decree issued by a court of competent jurisdiction that declares a judgment debtor to be indebted to a judgment creditor. An example of a judgment lien is a federal tax lien that is recorded against a property's title by the IRS as a result of the owner's failure to pay delinquent federal income taxes, whereas a consensual lien is a legal claim that a creditor places against the title to real property as security for the repayment of a debt with the owner's approval.

Time Can Be a Double-Edged Sword When Negotiating with Lienholders

The biggest hurdle that you will have to overcome when negotiating with subordinate lienholders is the time factor, which is the scant amount of time that is usually available to locate, contact, and negotiate with lienholders before a property's scheduled foreclosure sale date. But in this business, time can also be a double-edged sword. In other words, time can be your enemy or it can be your ally; it all depends on how you use it. I always try to use the time factor to my advantage during negotiations by focusing on how much time lienholders have before their lien is not worth diddly squat. As you will see from reading my sample letter to subordinate lienholders that is included in this chapter, I emphasize this point throughout the letter. I do this so that the lienholder will be thinking more about the ticking foreclosure time bomb that is soon to go off than about the full balance of what the lienholder is owed.

The Five Most Common Types of Subordinate Liens That Attach to Real Property

The five most common types of subordinate liens that attach to the titles of pre-foreclosure properties are:

1. Second and third mortgage or deed of trust liens.
2. Judgment liens.
3. Mechanics' liens.
4. State and federal welfare, medical, and child support liens.
5. Local, state, and federal tax liens.

States Require That Subordinate Lienholders Be Notified of Foreclosure Actions

All state foreclosure statutes require that all subordinate or junior lienholders of record be notified when a senior lienholder files a foreclosure lawsuit or notice of default to foreclose on a mortgage or deed of trust loan. The subordinate lienholder notification requirement is supposed to protect subordinate lienholders from having their liens extinguished by foreclosure without first having the opportunity to defend their lien. However, often because of a flawed title search, not all subordinate lienholders are given proper notice by the foreclosing lender. I once had a title search on a pre-foreclosure uncover a $15,000 second mortgage loan where the lender was not listed as a defendant in the foreclosure lawsuit. In this instance, the lender turned out to be the previous owner, who had taken back a purchase money second mortgage. I eventually had to pass on the property because the private lender refused to budge from her asking price, which was the entire unpaid balance of the loan. I later heard that she had turned the tables on the foreclosing lender and filed a countersuit against the bank on the grounds that they were grossly negligent for failing to provide her with proper notice of their foreclosure action, as required by law.

Subordinate Lienholders Are Named as Defendants in Foreclosure Lawsuits

When a lender files a foreclosure lawsuit, all subordinate lienholders of record are named as defendants in the complaint and notice of lis pendens and served with a copy of the foreclosure lawsuit. You can obtain the names and addresses of subordinate lienholders of record who are named as defendants in a foreclosure lawsuit simply by going to the office of the clerk of your county's circuit court and requesting the foreclosure case file. When a foreclosure lawsuit is filed, the clerk of the court where foreclosure lawsuits are heard assigns it a case number, such as 2005-156, which means that this is the 156th case filed in this particular court during the year 2005. Most court clerks' offices have public reading rooms where people can sit and read documents that have been filed with the court.

Trustees Required to Send Subordinate Lienholders Copies of Notice of Default

Most state foreclosure statutes require trustees foreclosing on deeds of trust to send a copy of the notice of default to each subordinate lienholder of record. This is required because the names of subordinate lienholders are not listed on notices of default. The three parties that are listed on a notice of default are the borrower-trustor, beneficiary-lender, and the trustee that is foreclosing on the deed of trust.

All Subordinate Lienholders Are Not Always Notified of Foreclosure Actions

As I told you in Chapter 10, my credo when researching pre-foreclosure properties is: Trust no one, assume nothing, verify everything, and be prepared for anything! And this is why I am telling you here and now to never automatically assume that all subordinate lienholders of record have been notified about a foreclosure action by the senior lienholder foreclosing on a mortgage or deed of trust loan. Because if you do and a senior lienholder fails to uncover all subordinate liens of record prior to filing a foreclosure lawsuit or notice of default, you could be in for a very expensive surprise after you have plunked down your hard-earned money and bought the property. To illustrate my point, let us suppose that you ignored my advice in Chapter 10 and failed to perform your own due diligence and bought a pre-foreclosure property without having a title search done. And because you assumed that all of the subordinate liens recorded against the property's title had been uncovered by the foreclosing lender, you went ahead and bought the property for what you thought at the time was a bargain-basement price. However, when you were in the process of reselling the property, you received the surprise of your life when a search of the property's title revealed a $15,000 mechanic's lien that the foreclosing lender had somehow overlooked. Now what you had thought was the bargain of a lifetime has turned into a breakeven deal, at best. All of this could have easily been avoided by spending $125 to $175 for a title search by a competent title abstractor.

You Must Become Familiar with Your State's Lien Law

I very highly recommend that you take the time and effort to become familiar with your state's lien law. In particular, you must know:

1. How long judgment liens stay attached to real property titles.
2. How long judgment liens can be renewed for.
3. Which parties are authorized to file a mechanic's lien.
4. How long a mechanic's lien stays attached to real property titles.
5. How long a mechanic's lien can be renewed for.

Unlicensed Contractors Have No Lien Rights in Most States

Most state construction lien laws prohibit unlicensed contractors and repairmen from filing any type of lien. For example, if unlicensed contractors or repairmen worked on a property and, for whatever reason, they did not get paid, they could not legally record a mechanic's lien against the property's title. However, if they did file a lien, they would not be able to enforce it in court. I once had to file a contest of lien lawsuit against a fly-by-night unlicensed pool contractor who had illegally placed a bogus $40,000 mechanic's lien for labor and materials against a pre-foreclosure that I had bought. What tipped me off that there might be some type of contractor shenanigans going on was the fact that the house had been appraised a year earlier for $95,000. And sure enough, when I checked, there was no record of this clown holding any type of construction contractor license anywhere in the entire state of Florida. I filed my lawsuit, and a professional process server served the man with a complaint and summons. And guess what, the lowlife never answered my suit within the allotted 60 days, and I had the lien expunged from the property's title.

Most Local, State, and Federal Government Agencies Will Not Discount Their Liens

First off, you cannot just waltz down to your county tax collector's office and ask for a discount on a property's delinquent tax bill. Trust me, that tactic will get you absolutely nowhere. The fact of the matter is that most local, state, and federal government agencies will not discount their liens below the amount that is owed. However, under certain circumstances, I have been able to negotiate discounts on federal tax liens and city and county code enforcement liens.

How to Have a Federal Tax Lien Removed from a Property's Title

As you work in this business, you will find that many pre-foreclosure properties have federal tax liens recorded against their titles. I have bought over a dozen pre-foreclosures that had federal tax liens recorded against their titles. In each case, I contacted the IRS on the owner's behalf and negotiated discounted payoffs of the tax liens, which ranged from 60 to 80 cents on the dollar. I did this by writing detailed hardship letters to the IRS that explained each property owner/ taxpayer's financial plight and impending foreclosure. The IRS agents that I negotiated with accepted my offers because they realized that all of the owners were insolvent and had very little or no chance of ever paying their liens off in full. IRS publication number 783, "Certificate of Discharge of Property from Federal Tax Lien," provides step-by-step instructions on how to go about having a federal tax lien removed from the title of a pre-foreclosure property and is available at http://www.irs.gov/pub/irs-pdf/p783.pdf.

How to Contact the Internal Revenue Service on a Property Owner's Behalf

As I just told you, when I find a pre-foreclosure property that has a federal tax lien, I always contact on the owner's behalf the IRS office that has jurisdiction over the county where the property's title is recorded. I do this by having the owner in foreclosure complete and sign IRS Form 8821, "Tax Information Authorization," which authorizes me to receive the owner's tax records directly from the IRS office that recorded the federal tax lien. This way, I can verify the lien directly with the IRS and then go about negotiating a discounted payoff with the agent handling the case. To obtain a copy of IRS Form 8821, log onto www.irs.gov/pub/irs-pdf/f8821.pdf.

Internal Revenue Service Office Locations Nationwide

To have a federal tax lien removed from the title of a pre-foreclosure property, the property owner will have to first contact the IRS office that has jurisdiction over the county where the lien is recorded. For a listing of IRS office locations nationwide, log onto www.irs.gov/localcontacts/#stateLinks.

Do Not Pursue Pre-Foreclosures That Belong to Owners in Bankruptcy

I do not mess around with pre-foreclosure properties where the owner has filed a bankruptcy petition in order to get the local federal bankruptcy court to issue an order to stay or stop the foreclosure action. The main reason I do not pursue pre-foreclosure properties that belong to owners in bankruptcy is that the property is under the control of a court-appointed trustee who must approve the sale of the property. I know an investor in Tulsa, Oklahoma, who had to wait over six months to get a bankruptcy trustee to approve the sale of a pre-foreclosure property. And that is exactly why I never buy property through any third-party representative, such as court-appointed bankruptcy trustees!

Where to Research Federal Bankruptcy Cases Online

Nowadays, thanks to the Internet, you can research federal bankruptcy cases online. The Public Access to Court Electronic Records (PACER) is an electronic public access service that allows users to obtain case and docket information from federal bankruptcy courts. Each federal bankruptcy district court maintains its own case information. To learn more about PACER, log onto its web site at www.pacer.psc.uscourts.gov.

You Must Verify All Judgment or Name Liens to Determine Their Validity

A judgment lien that is recorded and indexed in the public records under the name of a judgment debtor and not under the legal description of real property is often referred to as a *name lien*. You must verify all judgment liens because the name of a judgment debtor that is listed in a lien document may be the exact same name as a borrower in foreclosure, but it belongs to a different person altogether. First off, if the judgment lien document has the judgment debtor's Social Security account number or driver's license number listed on it, you can use that to verify the judgment debtor's full legal name. Or, if there is a legal description listed in a judgment lien, you can compare it to the legal description that is listed on the deed of the property in foreclosure. If a judgment lien document lists only a street address where the judgment creditor believed that the judgment debtor named in the lien lived at the time the lien was recorded, you can compare the street address to the street address of the property in foreclosure. Finally, because it can get pretty dicey when trying to determine the validity of judgment liens, I highly recommend that you follow the advice that I gave you in Chapter 10, and hire a competent title search professional to do your title searches on pre-foreclosure properties.

In Most States, Recording a Fraudulent Lien Constitutes Slander of Title

In most states, recording a fraudulent lien against the title to real property is considered slander of title and a civil offense. For example, let us suppose that another investor, who is a competitor of yours, records a bogus lien against the title of a pre-foreclosure property that you have under agreement for the sole purpose of creating a cloud on the property's title. In most states, this would be considered slander of title and grounds for a civil lawsuit. For instance, the Florida Statutes state that willfully exaggerated liens or liens prepared in a grossly negligent manner may be deemed fraudulent and unenforceable. In addition, people who are convicted of recording fraudulent liens in Florida may also be liable to the owner for damages, court costs, and attorneys' fees and end up with a third-degree felony on their record for life.

How to Contest the Validity of a Judgment Lien

I recommend that you contest any judgment lien that you suspect is fraudulent. For example, in Florida, a lien's validity can be contested by filing a notice of contest of lien (like the sample copy on page 170) in a court of competent juris- diction. Once a notice is filed, a lienholder has 60 days from the date the notice is served to file a counterlawsuit to enforce the lien. And if a lienholder fails to respond to the notice of contest of lien within the 60-day period or fails to prove the lien's validity in court, the judge presiding over the case will issue an order removing the lien from the property's title.

What to Do When a Lienholder Is No Longer in Business

Here in Florida, it is not uncommon to find subordinate liens that were filed by individuals and companies that are no longer in business and nowhere to be found. And when you find a pre-foreclosure that is worth pursuing but has a lien against its title, which is owned by an entity that is no longer in business, your only option is to file what is known as a *lawsuit to quiet title*. In a lawsuit to quiet title, you as the plaintiff would name the not-to-be-found business entity as the defendant. Once the lawsuit is filed, you would be required to publish public no- tices of your action in your county's legal newspaper of record to give the public constructive notice. The public notice is required because the defendant cannot be found in order to be personally served with the complaint and summons. This way, maybe a member of the public knows the whereabouts of the long-lost party named in the lawsuit and informs the party of the pending lawsuit. However, the drawback with filing this type of lawsuit is that it can be costly and time con- suming. In fact, the few times I have even contemplated filing a lawsuit to quiet title, I quickly changed my mind after I had done a rough cost estimate and real- ized I would have lost my butt on the deal.

What to Do When You Find a Loan That Is Owned by a Bank That No Longer Exists

In theory, what is supposed to happen when one bank gobbles up another is that all of the assets of the soon-to-be-defunct bank that is being taken over are as- signed to the entity that is acquiring the bank. However, in some cases the

Sample Florida Notice of Contest of Lien

STATE OF FLORIDA

COUNTY OF HILLSBOROUGH

Emma S. Crook
6900 Sleazy Street
Tampa, FL 33647

You are notified that the undersigned contests the claim of lien filed by you on July 3, 2004, and recorded in Official Records Book 4567, Page 123, of the public records of Hillsborough County, Florida, and that the time within which you may file suit to enforce your lien is limited to 60 days from the date of service of this notice.

Dated on this tenth day of June, 2005.

_____

David D. Jones
Plaintiff

STATE OF FLORIDA

COUNTY OF HILLSBOROUGH

I hereby certify that a true and correct copy of the foregoing Notice of Contest of Lien has been mailed to the lienor, Emma S. Crook, at the address shown above by First Class United States Mail on this tenth day of June, 2005.

CLERK OF THE CIRCUIT COURT

By: _____

As Deputy Clerk

paperwork is sloppy, and some loans fall through the crack. In other words, the loans are not assigned and remain the property of a bank that no longer exists. The first thing that you must do when you come up against this problem is to contact the equivalent of your state's department of banking. For example, in Florida, you would contact the Florida Department of Financial Services. And if your state's banking department cannot help you solve your problem, call the Federal Deposit Insurance Corporation (FDIC) at (800) 378-9581, and ask to speak with the department that handles loans owned by banks that are no longer in operation. The FDIC web site is at www.fdic.gov.

Use a Worksheet to Compile Information about Each Subordinate Lienholder

I recommend that you use a subordinate lienholder worksheet, like the one on pages 172–173, to compile information on each subordinate lienholder.

Contact Subordinate Lienholders by Letter

Once you have identified all of the subordinate lienholders of record, send each one a letter like the one on pages 174–175, by U.S. Postal Service Priority Mail, Delivery Confirmation, offering to buy their lien at a discounted price of 50 percent or more. I used to send my letters via FedEx, but their shipping rates are far more than the U.S. Postal Service.

What to Say to Lienholders during Negotiations

The last thing that you want to do during negotiations with lienholders is to come across like some fast-talking telemarketer trying to unload an overpriced water softener on some poor sap. My style of speech is straightforward, short, sweet, and right to the point. And that is exactly why I have nothing but disdain for how-to books that are peppered with long, drawn-out scripts full of disingenuous babble that was written by some verbose blowhard. For starters, I can count on one hand the number of times that I have had an actual face-to-face negotiation with a junior lienholder. Most lienholders are usually not located within the same county where the pre-foreclosure property is situated. And

FORM 14.1   Sample Subordinate Lienholder Worksheet

First lienholder's name _____

Mailing address _____

Telephone number _____

Facsimile _____

E-mail address _____

Type of lien _____

Amount of lien _____

Date lien recorded _____

Date lienholder contacted _____

Comments _____

_____

_____

_____

_____

Second lienholder's name _____

Mailing address _____

Telephone number _____

Facsimile _____

E-mail address _____

Type of lien _____

Amount of lien _____

Date lien recorded _____

Date lienholder contacted _____

Comments _____

_____

_____

_____

_____

Third lienholder's name _____

Mailing address _____

Telephone number _____

Facsimile _____

E-mail address _____

Type of lien _____

Amount of lien _____

Date lien recorded _____

Date lienholder contacted _____

Comments _____

_____

_____

_____

_____

second, there is almost never enough time to go traipsing all over town to meet and sit down with each lienholder. After all, isn't this what cell phones, e-mail, and facsimile machines are for? The main point that you must always stress during any form of negotiations with subordinate lienholders is that if the property in foreclosure is sold at a public foreclosure auction or trustee's sale, their lien will be wiped out, and they will end up with absolutely nothing. During your discussions with lienholders, you must explain to them why it is in their best financial interest to sell you their lien today at a discounted price, rather than have their lien extinguished by a foreclosure action. As far as I am concerned, your main goal during negotiations should always be to push a lienholder's panic and greed buttons, so that they get up off their duff and sell you their lien at a discount of 50 percent or more. In other words, use their fear of losing everything to scare them into selling you their lien!

FORM 14.2   Sample Letter to Subordinate Lienholders

May 29, 2005

Mr. Ralph R. Rowdy
6178 Bowler Avenue
Brandon, FL 33508

Dear Mr. Rowdy:

I am writing to you in regard to your $1,346.89 judgment lien, which is recorded against the title to Mr. Robert F. Default's property that is located at 3345 Costa Rosa Way, Tampa, FL 33649.

You should have already been notified that the Bank of Florida has filed a foreclosure lawsuit against Mr. Robert F. Default, in Hillsborough County Circuit Court, to foreclose their mortgage loan, which is secured by the property located at 3345 Costa Rosa Way, Tampa, FL 33649.

The public foreclosure auction sale is scheduled for September 10, 2005, at 11 A.M., on the third floor of the Hillsborough County Courthouse.

I am sure you already know that if Mr. Default is unable to bring his mortgage payments current and the Bank of Florida does foreclose on his loan, your judgment lien will be extinguished and you will receive nothing in the process.

I am currently in negotiations with Mr. Default to possibly purchase his property before the Bank of Florida forecloses on their mortgage loan and all subordinate liens, like yours, are wiped out.

However, the only way that I will be able to purchase Mr. Default's property and stop the Bank of Florida from foreclosing on their loan and snuffing out your lien in the process is if judgment lienholders, such as yourself, are willing to sell their liens to me at a 60 percent discount.

Please let me know at your earliest convenience if you are willing to accept my offer to purchase your judgment lien for $538.76.

I can send the satisfaction of lien form along with instructions and a cashier's check for $538.76 to you by overnight mail.

Please call me at (555) 123-4567 or e-mail me at davidjones@hotmail.com if you have any questions.

I look forward to hearing from you soon and to working with you to come to a mutually beneficial resolution to your situation.

Sincerely,

David D. Jones

What to Do When a Lienholder Balks at Your Initial Offer

Every once in a while, you will come across a lienholder who will hold out for top dollar. When this happens, you have five options. You can:

1. Make a counteroffer to buy the lien for 10 percent more than your initial offer.
2. Keep making counteroffers until one is accepted.
3. Give in and pay the full amount of the lien.
4. Buy the property with the lien still attached to its title.
5. Throw in the towel and not buy the property.

The Most Important Advice in This Entire Chapter

First things first, whatever you do, do not pay off any subordinate lienholders until after the title to the property has been transferred into your name and recorded in the public records. And when you do pay off subordinate lienholders, have them sign a satisfaction or release of lien or judgment that is in a recordable form in the presence of a notary public. *Recordable form* means that the document meets the standards set by your state's recording statute to be recorded in the official public records. I learned the hard way just how important this seemingly minor point is when the Hillsborough County Clerk of the Circuit Court's office refused to record a satisfaction of lien because of a minor technicality that rendered it not recordable. The worst part was that the three people who had to sign a recordable satisfaction of lien in the presence of a notary public all lived in Miami. It took me $50 worth of long-distance telephone calls and over a month before I finally got the mess straightened out. Once that is done, record the satisfaction of lien in the public records of the county where the property's deed is recorded. A sample satisfaction of judgment form is shown on page 177.

Sample Florida Satisfaction of Judgment

STATE OF FLORIDA

COUNTY OF HILLSBOROUGH

KNOW ALL MEN BY THESE PRESENTS that Ralph R. Rowdy, plaintiff, hereby acknowledges receipt of the sum of $1,346.89 plus costs in the amount of $22.50 as payment and satisfaction in full of that certain judgment rendered in circuit court in and for Hillsborough County, Florida, on the tenth day of July 2003, wherein Ralph R. Rowdy was plaintiff and Robert F. Default was defendant; said judgment being entered in the public records in the office of the Clerk of the Court in and for Hillsborough County, Florida, in Official Record book 3724, page 469, and the said Ralph R. Rowdy hereby acknowledges full payment and satisfaction and hereby authorizes the said Clerk to enter this satisfaction of record.

Dated on this sixteenth day of August, 2005.

_____

Plaintiff's Signature

STATE OF FLORIDA

COUNTY OF HILLSBOROUGH

The foregoing instrument was acknowledged before me on the sixteenth day of August, 2005 by Ralph R. Rowdy, who has produced a Florida Driver's License as identification and who did not take an oath.

CLERK OF THE CIRCUIT COURT

By: _____

As Deputy Clerk

CHAPTER 15

How to Negotiate with Foreclosing Lenders and Their Attorneys and Trustees

In Chapter 9, I taught you how to go about getting the skinny on loans that are in default from foreclosing lenders. Now, in this chapter, you are going to use what you learned about negotiations in Chapter 13 and apply the same fundamentals to negotiating with foreclosing lenders and their attorneys and trustees. In most cases, once a lender declares a loan to be in default, the loan is turned over to a special department, or even a separate company, that specializes in what is called *loan loss mitigation*. And today, there is a whole industry that specializes in loan loss mitigation that handles everything from filing foreclosure lawsuits and notices of default, to protecting lender-owned properties from vandalism. In addition to loan loss mitigation departments, foreclosing lenders use attorneys and trustees to deal with property owners during the foreclosure process. *Default management* is the term that is used to describe what trustees do when they process deed of trust loans that are in foreclosure. And you can use the same techniques that are outlined in this chapter to negotiate with trustees who are servicing deed of trust loans that are in foreclosure. Your main objective whenever you are negotiating with a lender's attorney or trustee should always be to get them to pass your proposal on to the person at the lending organization who has the authority to say yes. Understand that, ultimately, a lender's decision on whether to accept your proposal boils down to whether the lender feels that it is in its best financial interest to do so. However, the criteria that lenders base their decisions on often change from day to day and, often, depend on factors such as the lender's debt to assets ratio, number of nonperforming loans, other real estate owned, and local real estate market conditions that the average investor has absolutely no control over. And sometimes it may seem like a lender's decisions are influenced by arbitrary things, such as the time of day, the day of the month, the phase of the moon, or whether the lender is having a bad hair day.

What You Need to Know about Loan Loss Mitigation

In today's kinder, gentler world of mortgage lending, the buzzword is *loan loss mitigation,* which is the complete opposite to a few years ago when lenders were pushing their loan servicing departments to start immediate foreclosure proceedings against borrowers who defaulted on their mortgage or deed of trust loans. This change of heart has led to lenders creating loan loss mitigation departments, whose primary mission is to maximize the net amount that a lender recovers from a nonperforming mortgage or deed of trust loan, without having to resort to foreclosure. To accomplish this, lenders have instructed their loan loss mitigation minions to pursue alternatives to foreclosure, including forbearance plans, loan modifications, restructuring of loan payments, short payoff sales, and deeds-in-lieu-of foreclosure. The following is a listing of the various names that lenders give to the department that handles loans in default:

1. Loan loss mitigation department.
2. Default management department.
3. Loan workout department.
4. Loan resolution department.
5. Nonperforming assets department.
6. Foreclosure department.
7. Collections department.
8. Special loans department.

How to Deal with Uncooperative People in Loan Loss Mitigation Departments

You will learn that sometimes in this business, things do not always go the way they should because of uncooperative people who couldn't care less about doing their jobs. And a prime example of this can be found in some of the people who make up the staffs of loan loss mitigation departments, who are not the least bit interested in helping borrowers get their loans reinstated. These uncooperative troglodytes have nasty personalities, which make them best suited for work as prison guards. Case in point: After I was blown off twice by the same snotty loan loss mitigation clerk, I had the property owner hand-carry a letter of authorization to the president of the bank that was foreclosing on the loan. The letter spelled out exactly what the president was expected to do to rectify the problem. The bank president must have had a nice little chat with Miss Congeniality about the finer points of customer service because, from that point on, she was very well mannered and gave me 100 percent cooperation. The lesson that I learned from this little episode is to always send the top dog at the lending organization that is doing the foreclosing copies of all the correspondence that I send to their loan loss mitigation department. This way, the swell folks working in the loan mitigation department know that the head honcho just might be looking over their shoulder while they are working with you.

How to Contact the HUD Nationwide Loan Loss Mitigation Department

The HUD nationwide loan loss mitigation department is located at their National Servicing Center, which can be contacted by telephone at (888) 297-8685 or by e-mail at hsg-lossmit@hud.gov. You will need the FHA case number and the lender's loan account number when calling them about a loan that is in foreclosure. Their mailing address is as follows:

Department of Housing and Urban Development

National Servicing Center

301 Northwest 6th Street, Suite 200

Oklahoma City, OK 73102

Negotiating with Lenders' Loan Loss Mitigation Departments

As I told you in Chapter 9, when I first meet with owners in foreclosure to get information on their loan from the foreclosing lender, I always have them sign a letter authorizing the lender to release loan information directly to me. This way, when I call the loan loss mitigation specialist who is handling the owner's loan, I identify myself as Thomas J. Lucier, a private individual who has written authorization from the owner to discuss the current status of this loan. At this point, the person on the other end of the telephone should be able to quickly verify my claim by simply looking in the loan file and seeing the owner's signed letter of authorization. However, unlike many investors who often mistakenly take an adversarial approach when trying to negotiate with lenders' loan loss mitigation departments, I turn the tables on them and offer solutions on how I can help them get a nonperforming loan back on the books and generating revenue so they can quickly close out the loan file. I start off my conversation by telling the person with whom I am speaking that I am an experienced professional pre-foreclosure property investor who makes his living buying properties from owners in foreclosure. I also explain that I am creditworthy and have the financial resources on hand to cure the default and reinstate the loan and that I promise not to waste their valuable time with games, gimmicks, and bullspit. I then ask the person my version of the $64,000 question: "What are you guys willing to do to help me buy this property today?" The response that I initially receive is that of stunned silence. And then they ask me, "Just what do you mean?" At this point, I launch into my patented spiel about how I am prepared to buy the property today, but that I need the lender's help to make it happen. I tell the person that I am speaking with that I need to talk with a decision maker who has the authority to allow me to take over the loan without violating the due-on-sale clause. To add a sense of urgency to our conversation, I also mention that the owner is considering filing a Chapter 7 bankruptcy petition if the lender cannot work out a deal with me. The person that I am speaking with usually puts me on hold while he or she asks coworkers what to do. What generally happens is that a short while later, a different person comes on the line and asks me how he or she can help. And this goes on until I am either satisfied that I am speaking with the person who is in the position to help me or I get the name of a decision maker who is located somewhere else. Once I connect with the right person, I give him or her my sales pitch. To date, I am batting right around 700. In other words, 7 out of 10 lenders allow me to assume what were previously non-assumable loans, once I cure the default and reinstate the loan.

Why Attorneys and Trustees Have No Real Incentive to Work with Investors

First off, you must understand that an attorney or trustee who is representing a lender or beneficiary in a foreclosure lawsuit against a property owner with a loan that is in default and facing foreclosure has little or no incentive to work with an investor wanting to purchase a property in foreclosure. Most attorneys and trustees representing foreclosing lenders give short shrift to investors because lenders pay them only to file foreclosure actions. And the way that most attorneys and trustees look at it, working with investors is not in their job description and thus not what lenders are paying them to do. This is especially true with law firms that specialize in filing foreclosure lawsuits for large lenders, which are known in the trade as "foreclosure mills" because they are staffed by attorneys and legal assistants who do nothing but crank out foreclosure lawsuits all day long, the same way that a paper mill produces paper. Foreclosure mills are notorious for putting callers into voicemail hell or, worse yet, passing telephone calls from person to person and office to office, without callers ever getting straight answers to their questions. The best way to avoid dealing with foreclosure mills is to have the owner in foreclosure call the person in the lender's loan loss mitigation department who signed the last letter the owner received. Once the owner gets this person on the telephone, have the owner explain that he or she has a potential buyer with good credit and the cash needed to reinstate the loan, who wants to speak with him or her about getting the financial mess straightened out. At this point, you want to get on the phone and explain that you are a serious buyer, but that you first need to see how much it is going to cost you to bail the owner out and that you are sick and tired of getting the runaround from the lender's attorney. The person on the phone will usually ask you to hold on while he or she calls the attorney to find out how much the owner owes the lender to date. Once he or she tells you the total cost of reinstating the loan, ask the loan loss representative to mail the property owner a loan reinstatement packet via overnight courier.

How to Avoid Getting Ripped Off by Attorneys Charging Excessive Legal Fees

In this business, it is not uncommon for lenders' attorneys to pad their legal bills and charge property owners in foreclosure excessive legal fees when they reinstate their loans. This all too common practice of overcharging owners who reinstate their loans is not only unethical and immoral but also a potential dealkiller for pre-foreclosure property investors. The most egregious example of a foreclosing lender's attorney attempting this form of legalized extortion that I have run into involved a pre-foreclosure in Valrico, Florida, in which a nationwide bank was trying to extort $2,500 in legal fees from the owner. However, when the lender refused the owner's request for an itemized hourly billing statement from their attorney, showing how many hours were spent performing legal tasks, I decided to play my version of hardball with them. I did some quick legal research and found out that the standard fee that HUD pays an attorney in

Florida to complete a judicial foreclosure action from start to finish is $1,000. And this greedy attorney was trying to hit the owner up for $2,500 for doing just a title search and filing a foreclosure lawsuit and notice of lis pendens! I wrote a very starchy letter to the lender and their sleazy attorney, which the owner signed, that told both of them exactly why they were not entitled to more than $700 in legal fees for the legal work that had been performed. I also went on to explain in the letter that the owner was ready, willing, and able to file a lawsuit against the lender under four separate sections of the Florida Statutes. Plus, I had the owner file a formal written complaint against the attorney with the Florida Bar. Two days later, the owner received a revised loan reinstatement packet from the lender, with a cover letter explaining that, upon further review, the bank had concluded that the $2,500 legal fee was indeed incorrect and that the correct amount was $675. Upon receiving this bit of great news, I jumped for joy and clicked my heels and then called my attorney and set up a closing for 11 A.M. on the following day. For your information, a state-by-state schedule of the standard attorney fees that HUD pays attorneys to perform various actions, associated judicial, and non-judicial foreclosure proceedings is provided at www.hudclips.org/sub_nonhud/html/pdfforms/98-26att.pdf.

CHAPTER 16

How to Do a Short Payoff Sale on Properties with Little or No Equity

Over the past couple of years, it seems like everyone and their brother has jumped onto the short payoff sale bandwagon. To hear the short sale promoters tell it, you would think that short payoff sales were one of the greatest real estate acquisition techniques of all time. The problem with all of this hype is that it has fueled unrealistic expectations on the part of would-be short sale investors, who have been led to believe that every lender in America will approve a short payoff sale at the drop of a hat. I hate to be a party pooper, but that is unadulterated malarkey! The fact of the matter is that there are very few bona fide short sale opportunities in most real estate markets nationwide. And this is especially true in today's robust housing market. In my foreclosure market, which includes most of Hillsborough County, Florida, there are very few short payoff sale opportunities. In fact, I can count the number of short payoff sales that I have done on one hand. Please do not get me wrong; you definitely can make money from short payoff sales. However, it has been my experience that a short payoff sale transaction is much harder to complete than a typical pre-foreclosure property purchase. And that is why in this chapter I also give you complete step-by-step instructions on exactly how the short payoff of a mortgage or deed of trust loan actually works. You will then have the knowledge that is needed to take advantage of any short sale opportunities that may become available.

Short Payoff Sales Provide an Opportunity for Investors to Create Instant Equity

The type of property owners who are the best short sale candidates are the ones who are upside down in their property and have little or no equity. In other words, they owe more on their property than what it is currently worth. However, the only way for an investor to create any equity in a property like this is to help delinquent borrowers to convince their lender that it is in the lender's best interest to accept less than the balance that is owed on their mortgage or deed of trust loan. The difference between the amount that a lender agrees to accept from a borrower to pay off a loan and the property's fair market value becomes instant equity to the investor buying the property. The largest amount of so-called instant equity that I have been able to create so far from a short payoff sale has been $25,000, and I earned every penny of it! I had to deal with a totally helpless homeowner, who was an emotional basket case, and an incompetent loan loss mitigation specialist, who had a demeanor that was better suited for work as a prison guard.

The Definition of a Short Payoff Sale

A *short payoff sale* is generally defined by loan loss mitigation professionals as:

> *A sale in which a lender allows the property securing a mortgage or deed of trust loan to be sold for less than the existing loan balance, due to factors such as the borrower's financial circumstances, the property's physical condition, and local real estate market conditions.*

The Four Parties That Are Usually Involved in a Short Sale Transaction

The four parties that are usually involved in a short payoff sale transaction are the:

1. Property owner facing the prospect of having his or her loan foreclosed on.
2. Investor buying the property that is securing the loan.
3. Third party servicing the loan.
4. Investor who owns the loan.

Short Sale Requests Are Processed by Lenders' Loan Loss Mitigation Departments

To reiterate what I just told you in Chapter 15, once a borrower begins to miss loan payments, the so-called nonperforming loan is usually turned over to the lender's loan loss mitigation department. Most lenders also use their loan loss mitigation departments to process borrowers' short payoff sale requests. So, you can follow the same advice that I just gave you in Chapter 15 when negotiating short payoff sales with lenders.

Short Payoff Sales Are Lenders' Last Resort before Proceeding with Foreclosure

In spite of what almost all the short sale pros may espouse, most lenders will approve a short payoff sale only as a last resort, when foreclosure is not economically feasible because the borrower is insolvent, and:

1. The property was purchased or refinanced at the top of a seller's market at an overinflated price and has since had a substantial drop in value.

2. The property was refinanced at 125 percent of its value, which was based on an overinflated property appraisal report.

3. The property is located in an area where property values have dropped due to a dramatic change in local economic conditions.

4. The property's value has decreased to an amount that is below the loan balance due to local and national economic conditions that are beyond the borrower's control.

5. The property's as-is condition has deteriorated to the point where it is not financially feasible for the lender to put it into a marketable resale condition.

6. The proposed purchase price is more than the lender would be able to sell the property for after foreclosing on the loan.

7. Any sales commission the lender must pay is less than what the lender would have to pay to sell the property after foreclosing on the loan.

Most Lenders Have a Stringent Hardship Test That Borrowers Must Pass

Contrary to what the short sale seminar promoters would lead you to believe, most lenders have a very stringent hardship test that borrowers must pass in order to have the short payoff of their loan approved. In most cases, the borrower must be experiencing one or more of the following financial hardships:

1. The borrower or an immediate member of the borrower's family has experienced a catastrophic illness that has wreaked havoc on his or her personal finances.

2. The borrower's spouse has died or divorced, and the borrower has insufficient income to pay the loan payment.

3. The borrower's employer has transferred the borrower out of the area, and he or she is unable to sell or rent the property.

4. The borrower has been called away to active duty military service for an extended period and lacks the monthly income to pay the loan.

5. The borrower has suffered a disabling injury that precludes him or her from ever working again.

6. The borrower is unemployed and has no realistic expectations of finding employment in the foreseeable future due to local economic conditions that are beyond his or her control.

7. The borrower has become financially insolvent, and there is no realistic expectation that his or her financial condition will improve within the foreseeable future.

8. The borrower has been incarcerated and no longer has the income to pay the loan payment.

Twelve Factors Lenders Consider during the Short Payoff Sale Approval Process

When deciding whether to approve a short payoff sale, lenders consider the following 12 factors:

1. The number of nonperforming loans that the lender has in his or her portfolio.

2. The lender's overall financial condition.

3. The financial condition of the third-party investor who owns the loan.

4. The loss mitigation policy of the third-party investor who owns the loan.

5. The loss mitigation authority of the lender servicing the loan.

6. The loss mitigation policy and procedures of the government agency insuring or guaranteeing the loan.

7. The borrower's overall financial condition.

8. The property's as-is value.

9. The cost to put the property into resale condition.

10. The property's as-repaired value.

11. The cost of securing and maintaining the property while it is being marketed for resale.

12. The cost of marketing and selling the property.

How Private Mortgage Insurance Can Affect a Short Payoff Sale

Private mortgage insurance (PMI) is purchased by institutional lenders—and paid for by borrowers—to insure against a lender's loss in the event that a loan is foreclosed on. Institutional lenders require borrowers to pay premiums for private mortgage insurance coverage because conventional residential loans have a high loan to value (LTV) ratio, which does not give lenders enough of an equity cushion to compensate them when a loan is foreclosed on. This way, if the lender recoups less than the balance owed from the proceeds of a public foreclosure auction or trustee's sale, the private mortgage insurance company must pay a claim up to the amount of the coverage. Once a lender declares a loan that is covered by private mortgage insurance to be in default, the insurer could:

1. Advance the borrower the funds needed to cure the default and reinstate the loan.

2. Purchase the loan from the lender and modify the repayment terms to match the borrower's current income.

3. Approve the short sale and reimburse the lender for the lender's loss up to the amount of the coverage.

Final Short Sale Approval Must Come from the Investor Owning the Loan

Here is another very important point that most of the short sale experts gloss over: In almost all cases, the lender or loss mitigation company that is servicing a loan is not authorized to approve a short payoff sale because final approval for a short payoff sale usually must come from the investor who actually owns the loan. And often, it can take 30 days or longer for an investor like Fannie Mae or Freddie Mac to approve a short payoff sale. One time I was working on a short sale with a property owner who had to wait 87 days before she heard back from her lender about her short sale proposal. And guess what? After all that time had passed, the lender balked at my short sale offer and foreclosed on the loan. The property sat vacant for over a year, while it was used as a hangout by neighborhood kids.

How to Quickly Determine the Feasibility of Attempting a Short Payoff Sale

It has been my experience that less than 5 percent of all properties in foreclosure qualify for a short payoff sale. Thus, before you invest the time and effort that is necessary to put a credible short payoff sale package together, you must first know the:

1. Total amount of all liens recorded against the property's title.
2. Lender's loan loss mitigation policy.
3. Borrower's current financial condition.
4. Type of loan in default.
5. Current status of the loan in default.
6. Property's as-is market value.
7. Property's as-repaired value.
8. Local economic and real estate market conditions.

Obtain the Borrower's Written Authorization to Release Loan Information

Once you have determined that an owner's financial situation and a property's physical condition have a better than average chance of meeting a lender's short payoff sale approval criteria, you must have the borrower sign a letter of authorization to release loan information, like the sample letter in Chapter 9 that authorizes the lender to discuss the borrower's loan information with the third party named in the letter.

Investors Need Cash to Finance Short Payoff Sale Transactions

One key point about short payoff sales that is often overlooked by rambunctious rookies is the simple fact that all short sales are cash sales, which means investors must have the cash on hand to finance the transaction. And most lenders require the buyer to submit a verifiable proof of funds letter stating the source of the funds needed to finance the purchase of the property at the same time they submit their offer to purchase. Another major drawback is that 99 percent of all lenders will not sign a purchase agreement that contains an assignment clause.

All Lenders Require That Short Payoff
Sales Be Arm's Length Transactions

Another key point about short payoff sales is that virtually all lenders require that all sales be arm's length transactions. The term *arm's length transaction* means that a family member, relative, or close friend of a property owner in default cannot be a party to a short payoff sale transaction. In other words, Uncle Elmo cannot negotiate the short payoff of a loan in order to buy his nephew Joey's house. Please note that if Elmo does buy Joey's house and the lender later discovers that they are related, there is an excellent chance that the lender will file a lawsuit to have the sale rescinded. A word to the wise: Do not do short sale transactions with family members, relatives, and close friends.

Two Main Reasons That Property Owners
Will Not Agree to a Short Payoff Sale

Initially, you will find that most of the property owners you approach about doing a short sale are pretty much open to the idea. However, you will also find that most people quickly change their mind when they learn that:

1. Lenders do not allow property owners to receive any of the proceeds from a short payoff sale. They figure that borrowers with loans that are facing foreclosure should not be rewarded for being financially irresponsible.
2. The amount of debt that is cancelled by the short payoff of a mortgage or deed of trust loan is subject to federal income tax as ordinary earned income. However, cancelled debt is not taxable when the borrower is bankrupt or deemed insolvent by the IRS.

Offer to Pay Property Owners a
Separate Relocation Allowance

Over the years, I have heard numerous people come up with a number of cockamamie ways to bribe property owners to become involved in a short payoff sale. I have heard everything from offering to buy their household appliances and furniture, to paying for a one-way trip and a two-night stay at Disney World, to buying their old clunker of a car. However, to me, the very idea of paying a bribe to anyone for anything is just downright repulsive. Plus, when you pay a bribe to a property owner to induce them to participate in a short sale, there is a very good chance that the lender will get wind of it and put the kibosh on the sale and then come after both of you for conspiring to defraud, or whatever else the law allows. To avoid all of this rigmarole, just do what I do, and make a separate written offer to pay the property owner a relocation allowance on the day that the short payoff sale closes. My relocation allowance covers the cost of renting a medium-size truck and gas for an in-town move, the first month's rent and security deposit for a medium-priced apartment, and the deposits needed to have water, electric, and gas utilities turned on. For example, on the last short payoff sale that I closed on, all of my competitors offered to give the property owner between $500 and $800 for her old washer and dryer. I came along and offered her a $1,600 relocation allowance, which she accepted on the spot.

Tell the Property Owner about the Tax Consequences of a Short Payoff Sale

I am a firm believer in always acting in an honest, ethical manner during any type of business transaction. In fact, I always try to go above and beyond the call of duty when I am involved in a real estate transaction with owners in foreclosure. When discussing a potential short payoff sale, I always tell the property owner upfront that the amount of debt that the lender cancels will be taxed as ordinary income, unless the borrower is bankrupt or insolvent. I also give the owner copies of IRS Publication 544, "Sales and Other Dispositions of Assets," and Publication 908, "Bankruptcy Tax Guide."

A Loan Sold Short Is Cancelled Debt and Subject to Federal Income Tax

Under the Internal Revenue Code, a mortgage or deed of trust loan that is sold short, or discounted by $600 or more, is considered a cancelled debt that is subject to federal income tax as ordinary earned income. When a lender accepts a short payoff on a mortgage or deed of trust loan for $600 or more, the lender must report the sale to the IRS on Form 1099C, Cancellation of Debt. IRS publication 544, "Sales and Other Dispositions of Assets," available at http://www.irs .gov/pub/irs-pdf/p544.pdf, explains in detail how cancelled debt is taxed.

How the Internal Revenue Service Defines Insolvency

The IRS defines *insolvency* as follows: "You are insolvent when, and to the extent, your liabilities exceed the fair market value of your assets."

Most Lenders Use a Broker's Price Opinion to Determine a Property's Value

The term *broker's price opinion* (BPO) refers to the appraisal format that real estate licensees use to appraise property for lenders. Most major lenders have their own broker's price opinion forms that they require real estate licensees to use. However, most lenders will not order a broker's price opinion or property appraisal report until after they have received a complete short payoff sale package to include all of the documentation that is required to support the borrower's financial condition. Lenders order brokers' price opinions or appraisal reports to determine a property's:

1. As-is value.
2. As-repaired value.

Include a Short Payoff Sale Proposal Letter in the Short Sale Package

I highly recommend that you always include a short payoff sale proposal letter, like the sample on page 193, in the borrower's short payoff sale package that is submitted to lenders.

Include a HUD 1 Settlement Statement in the Short Payoff Sale Package

Most lenders generally require buyers to submit a net sheet as part of their short payoff sale package. Lenders use net sheets to calculate how much money they will net from the proceeds of a proposed short sale. A word of caution: When calculating a net sheet, make certain that the seller's net proceeds from the sale are zero because lenders will not approve a short sale from which borrowers will profit.

FORM 16.1   Sample Short Payoff Sale Proposal Letter

May 18, 2005

Ms. Sally S. Short
Manager
Loan Loss Mitigation Department
Bank of Florida
4467 Rich Avenue
Clearwater, FL 33227

Reference Loan Number: FL 08281950, Robert D. Default, Mortgagor, 3345 Costa Rosa
Way, Tampa, Florida 33649

Dear Ms. Short:

Please find enclosed the short payoff sale package for loan number FL 08281950, Robert D. Default, mortgagor, 3345 Costa Rosa Way, Tampa, Florida 33649.

My proposed purchase price of $90,000 is based upon the following facts:

1. Based on the recent sale of comparable properties within the same area, the as-is sale price for the property is between $88,000 and $92,000 (see the attached listing of comparable property addresses).

2. Based on repair cost estimates from three licensed home repair contractors, it will cost between $18,000 and $25,000 to repair the property to a marketable resale condition (see the attached repair cost estimates).

3. The borrower is insolvent.

4. Property values within the area surrounding the subject property have declined by over 20 percent in the past two years.

Please note that I have the funds on hand to close on the purchase of the property within 24 hours' notice.

Please call me at (555) 123-4567 or e-mail me at davidjones@hotmail.com if you have any questions.

Sincerely,

David D. Jones

HUD 1 Settlement Statement Available Online

You can fill out a HUD 1 Settlement Statement online at my web site at: www.thomaslucier.com/HUD1SettlementStatement.pdf.

Use a Checklist When Preparing a Short Payoff Sale Package

To stay organized, I recommend that you use a checklist when assisting a property owner in the preparation of a short payoff sale package. Your checklist should include the following items:

1. Buyer's letter of short payoff sale proposal.
2. Borrower's signed letter of authorization for the lender to release financial information about the loan in default to the buyer.
3. Borrower's completed and signed short payoff sale application.
4. Borrower's hardship letter.
5. Borrower's financial statement.
6. Borrower's payroll checkstubs from employer.
7. Borrower's financial history.
8. Borrower's unemployment compensation insurance coverage payment history.
9. Borrower's state and federal income tax returns for the past two years.
10. Borrower's bank statements for the past six months.
11. Copies of the borrower's consumer credit files from Equifax, Experian, and Trans Union credit reporting agencies.
12. Summary of any medical illnesses, to include treatment costs for any illnesses that the borrower may be currently suffering from.
13. Copies of any divorce decree showing borrower's financial obligations for child support or alimony payments.
14. Completed and signed purchase agreement.
15. A listing of comparable sales of similar properties within the same area.
16. HUD 1 Settlement Statement.
17. Itemized listing of repairs and the cost of putting the property into a marketable resale condition.
18. Pictures of the property's as-is condition.

Fifteen Steps Necessary to Complete a Typical Short Payoff Sale Transaction

Here are the 15 steps that an investor must take to complete a typical short payoff sale transaction:

Step 1: The buyer contacts a property owner in foreclosure and determines that the borrower's financial situation and the property's physical condition make it a potential short payoff sale candidate.

Step 2: The borrower gives the investor written authorization to contact the loan loss mitigation department currently servicing the loan.

Step 3: The buyer contacts the loan loss mitigation department listed on the latest correspondence that the borrower has received from the lender to obtain the name, e-mail address, and telephone and facsimile numbers of the person in charge.

Step 4: The buyer sends the person in charge of the loan loss mitigation department a facsimile of the borrower's authorization to release loan information letter.

Step 5: The buyer calls the person in charge of the loan loss mitigation department to discuss the current status of the borrower's loan and to request a short payoff sale package for the borrower.

Step 6: The borrower receives the short payoff sale package along with the lender's instruction on how to complete it.

Step 7: The borrower obtains all of the documentation that the lender requires to support his or her financial hardship.

Step 8: The buyer obtains the repair cost estimates from three licensed home improvement contractors.

Step 9: The buyer obtains the addresses and sale prices of similar properties located in the same area that have sold within the past six months, along with the addresses and asking prices of properties that are currently for sale.

Step 10: The buyer returns the short payoff sale package to the lender via courier. The package includes a signed purchase agreement to buy the property for 40 percent less than what is owed the lender.

Step 11: The lender reviews the short payoff sale package and orders a broker's price opinion or property appraisal report to determine the property's as-is and as-repaired values.

Step 12: The lender makes a decision to accept or refuse the short payoff based on the property's value and physical condition.

Step 13: The lender refuses the buyer's initial short payoff offer based on the BPO.

Step 14: The buyer makes the lender a counteroffer that is either accepted or refused.

Step 15: The buyer closes on the short payoff transaction 30 days after the offer was accepted.

Federal Housing Administration Short Sales Are Called Pre-Foreclosure Sales

Short payoff sales are known in HUD or the Federal Housing Administration as pre-foreclosure sales. Pre-foreclosure sales of FHA-insured loans are covered in HUD Mortgagee Letter 00-05, dated January 19, 2000. The only lenders authorized to approve a short payoff or pre-foreclosure sale of an FHA-insured loan are loss mitigation lenders that have been approved by HUD. To be eligible for a pre-foreclosure sale, the:

1. Property securing the loan in default must be owner-occupied.
2. Loan must be at least 90 days in arrears.
3. Borrower must have a bona fide financial hardship.
4. Borrower must receive counseling from a HUD-approved agency.

Federal Housing Administration Short Payoff Sale Information Available Online

Federal Housing Administration (FHA) pre-foreclosure sale information is available online at www.hudclips.org/sub_nonhud/htm1/pdfforms/00-05.doc.

Toll-Free Telephone Number for the FHA National Loan Servicing Center

The toll-free telephone number for the FHA National Loan Servicing Center is (888) 297-8685.

Department of Veterans Affairs Short Payoff Sales Are Called Compromise Sales

The Department of Veterans Affairs (DVA) calls short payoff sales *compromise sales*. A compromise sale of a DVA-guaranteed loan is approved when the DVA considers a loan default to be insoluble. The DVA will consider a default insoluble when a review of the borrower's financial circumstances indicates that the borrower lacks the ability to prevent foreclosure of the loan and at the same time provide for the welfare of his or her family.

Department of Veterans Affairs Compromise Sale Information Available Online

DVA compromise sale information is available online at www.vba-roanoke .com/rlc/forms/Compromise%20Sale%20Program.pdf.

Department of Veterans Affairs Regional Loan Centers

The following is a listing of DVA regional loan centers and the states they serve:

Atlanta, GA
(888) 768-2132
Georgia, North Carolina, South Carolina, Tennessee

Cleveland, OH
(800) 729-5772
Delaware, Indiana, Michigan, New Jersey, Ohio, Pennsylvania

Denver, CO
(888) 349-7541
Alaska, Colorado, Idaho, Montana, New Mexico, Oregon, Utah, Washington, Wyoming

Houston, TX
(888) 232-2571
Arkansas, Louisiana, Oklahoma, Texas

Manchester, NH
(603) 666-7502
Connecticut, Maine, Massachusetts, New Hampshire, New York, Rhode Island, Vermont

Phoenix, AZ
(888) 869-0194
Arizona, California, Nevada

Roanoke, VA
(800) 933-5499
District of Columbia, Kentucky, Maryland, Virginia, West Virginia

St. Paul, MN
(800) 827-0611
Illinois, Iowa, Kansas, Minnesota, Missouri, Nebraska, North Dakota, South Dakota, Wisconsin

St. Petersburg, FL
(888) 611-5915, × 7500
Alabama, Florida, Mississippi

Hawaii
(808) 433-0480

Puerto Rico
(787) 772-7313

CHAPTER 17

How to Prepare Your Purchase Agreements

First things first: Please, whatever you do, do not, I repeat, do not use any of those ubiquitous purchase agreements that are available for free at various Internet web sites. I am telling you this because many people falsely assume that a purchase agreement that is available for free on the Internet is perfectly legal in their state. In fact, I know a newbie investor in California who used a free purchase agreement that he downloaded from one of those no-money-down web sites to make an offer on a pre-foreclosure property. However, the novice forgot to include a notice of cancellation in the agreement, as required by California law. Well, the homeowner in foreclosure had a relative who just happened to be a California licensed real estate broker. And the broker flipped her lid when she read the rookie's purchase agreement and saw that it did not include the required cancellation notice. The wannabe investor ended up paying the homeowner what amounted to a $1,500 bribe to keep from being sued. The fact of the matter is that this clueless neophyte never seemed to grasp the very basic concept that real estate contract law varies from state to state. I cannot overemphasize the financial consequences that a poorly written purchase agreement can have, especially when put under the scrutiny of a judge presiding over a lawsuit filed by a disgruntled former homeowner, accusing you of taking unfair advantage of his or her financial plight while the loan was in foreclosure. You must understand that unlike conventional real estate transactions that are conducted between willing sellers and willing buyers, pre-foreclosure property sales are almost always conducted between reluctant sellers and rambunctious buyers, who are often sloppy and careless when it comes to preparing their purchase agreements. In this business, the combination of a reluctant seller and a rambunctious buyer using a flawed purchase agreement is a potential lawsuit waiting to happen. This is why when buying pre-foreclosure properties, you need to prepare your purchase agreements so that they:

1. Conform to your state's foreclosure and real estate sales statutes.
2. Do not include any provisions that could be deemed unconscionable in a court of law.
3. Are valid and legally enforceable in a court of competent jurisdiction.
4. Fully protect your position as buyer in a pre-foreclosure property transaction.

Fourteen Key Provisions That Must Be Included in Your Purchase Agreements

The following 14 key provisions must be included in your purchase agreement to clearly define the terms and conditions of the agreement and the rights and responsibilities of both the buyer and the seller:

1. *Parties to the agreement:* Designate all parties to the purchase agreement as buyer and seller and include their legal status as to whether they are a single individual, husband and wife, or a business entity such as a corporation or limited liability company.

2. *Earnest money deposit:* State that if the buyer fails to perform this agreement within the time herein specified, the full amount of earnest money deposit made by the buyer shall be forfeited as liquidated damages, and such forfeiture shall jeopardize the seller's right to sue for specific performance.

3. *Legal description of property:* Use the exact legal description that is written on the recorded deed of the property in the purchase agreement.

4. *Purchase price:* State the firm purchase price of the property.

5. *Terms of purchase:* Specify exactly how the purchase of the property is going to be financed.

6. *Marketable title:* Specify that the buyer must be able to obtain an owner's title insurance policy commitment letter from a title insurer in order to close on the purchase of the property.

7. *Assignment of the purchase agreement:* Include a clause that the buyer has the right to assign or sell the purchase agreement to a third party.

8. *Default by buyer:* Specify that the earnest money paid is the sole and exclusive remedy in the event that the buyer fails to close on the purchase of the property.

9. *Default by seller:* State that the buyer shall have the right of specific performance in the event the seller defaults on the agreement by refusing to sell the property.

10. *Eminent domain:* Specify that the buyer shall be entitled to a full refund of the earnest money deposit paid, plus any accrued interest, in the event the property is condemned by eminent domain prior to the closing date.

11. *Buyer's right of entry:* State that the buyer or the buyer's assigns have the right, upon giving the owner 24 hours' notice, to enter the property and inspect, repair, market, and show it to third parties prior to the closing date.

12. *Risk of loss:* Specify that the buyer is entitled to a full refund of the earnest money deposit paid, plus accrued interest, in the event the property is damaged or destroyed by fire, storm, or earthquake prior to the closing date.

13. *Right to examine records:* State that the buyer has the right to examine all of the financial and tax records associated with the property prior to the closing date.

14. *Seller must vacate property:* Require that the seller completely vacate the property and grounds prior to the closing date.

Three Contingency Clauses That Must Be Included in All Purchase Agreements

I am not one for loading up real estate purchase agreements with a slew of what is known derisively in the business as *weasel clauses*. To me, weasel clauses are something that risk-adverse fanatics overuse to try to cover their assets under every conceivable situation that could happen during the completion of a real estate transaction. However, I do very highly recommend that you include the following three contingency clauses in each and every purchase agreement that you sign with an owner in foreclosure:

1. Buyer must approve of the property's title status and marketability before this transaction can be closed.

2. Buyer must approve of the status of the property's existing loans before this transaction can be closed.

3. Seller must completely vacate the property and grounds before this transaction can be closed.

Do Not Use the Same Purchase Agreements That Real Estate Licensees Use

A word of warning: Never use the same real estate purchase agreements that are used by real estate licensees in your state to document the purchase of a pre-foreclosure property. I say this because virtually all of the real estate agreements used by real estate licensees are written to protect the licensees' sales commissions and the legal rights and interests of the sellers who have listed their property through real estate brokers. In addition to not being buyer-friendly, these agreements are also not investor-friendly, because they are geared toward traditional real estate transactions with conventional terms.

Hire an Experienced Board-Certified Real Estate Attorney in Good Standing

Let me state for the record that, on the whole, I have nothing but total disdain and contempt for the majority of Americans who are members of state bar associations and engage in the so-called practice of law! And, in my humble opinion, legal practitioners, as a group, are nothing more than a giant festering carbuncle on the buttocks of American society. Okay, now that I have had the opportunity to vent my disgust and displeasure with most of the swell guys and gals who make up the legal profession, it is now time for you to learn how to avoid being bamboozled by some incompetent $300-an-hour attorney in an Armani suit and alligator shoes masquerading as a real estate attorney. I highly recommend that you proceed with caution when selecting a real estate attorney. You must hire an honest, competent, board-certified real estate attorney in good standing, who has experience with foreclosure actions in your state. Once hired, your attorney's job is to advise you on the proper preparation of your purchase agreement. A word of warning: Please do not ignore the very sage advice that I am dispensing here and use the services of an attorney specializing in divorce law to advise you on your state's foreclosure statute. If you expect to receive expert advice on real estate law, you must hire the services of an experienced, board-certified real estate attorney in good standing who:

1. Specializes in the daily practice of real estate law.
2. Is well versed on how the foreclosure process works in your state.
3. Has ample experience preparing purchase agreements.
4. Is affiliated with a reputable title insurance underwriter.
5. Is licensed to sell title insurance in your state.

The Standard Qualifications for an Attorney to Be Certified in Real Estate Law

The basic qualifications for attorneys to be certified in real estate law are pretty standard nationwide. For example, the Florida Bar requires that all attorneys certified in real estate law must have practiced law for at least five years, with 40 percent or more of their time spent in the practice of real estate law during the three years immediately preceding their application for certification. In addition, attorneys applying for certification must have passed a peer review, completed 45 hours of continuing legal education within the three years immediately preceding their application, and passed a written examination.

The Standard Definition of an Attorney in Good Standing

In most states, an *attorney in good standing* is defined as:

> *Those persons licensed to practice law who have paid annual state bar association membership dues for the current year and who are not retired, resigned, delinquent, inactive, or suspended members of the state bar association.*

How to Find a Board-Certified Real Estate Attorney in Your State

The best way to find a qualified, board-certified real estate attorney in your area is to contact your local bar association lawyer referral service or your state's bar association lawyer referral service. Once you have the names of board-certified real estate attorneys in your area, you will need to do an online search of your state's bar association membership rolls to verify that each attorney is licensed to practice law in your state and to check whether any of the attorneys have been disciplined or had their license revoked for misconduct. And once you do find an honest, competent, board-certified attorney who is willing to work with you, treat him or her fairly, and stick with him or her throughout your investment career.

Online Attorney Locator Services

The following three web sites provide online lawyer locator services that allow you to search for an attorney by specialty and location:

Martindale Hubbell Lawyer Locator: www.martindale.com/locator/home.html

Findlaw: www.findlaw.com/14firms

Lawyers: www.lawyers.com

Make Certain Your Purchase Agreement
Does Not Violate Your State's Statutes

When buying homes from homeowners with mortgage or deed of trust loans that are in default and facing foreclosure, you must make certain that your purchase agreement does not violate any provisions in your state's foreclosure and real estate sales contract statutes. For example, some states, most notably California, have home equity sales contract statutes, which allow homeowners in default the right to rescind or cancel a home equity purchase agreement, usually within five business days, excluding weekends and holidays, after the purchase agreement was signed. Such statutes were enacted by state legislatures to give financially distressed homeowners a respite from the high-pressure buying tactics used by some predatory pre-foreclosure investors. The sample purchase agreement on pages 205–206 is for instructional and informational purposes only. I highly recommend that you seek the assistance of a board-certified real estate attorney who is licensed to practice law in your state to help you prepare a purchase agreement to buy properties from owners in foreclosure.

Equity Purchase Agreement Notices
Required by California Civil Codes

California Civil Codes require that the notices on page 207 be included in all equity purchase agreements to buy owner-occupied homes in foreclosure.

Make Certain That All of Your Purchase
Agreements Are Properly Witnessed

Each state has its own requirement as to the number of witnesses that are needed to attest the signatures on documents affecting real property. For example, in Florida, two witnesses are required to attest the signatures on real property title transfer documents. You can have the world's greatest purchase agreement, but if the signatures of both the buyer and seller are not properly witnessed, the agreement may end up being good for only two things: wrapping garbage in and lining birdcages. I am telling you this because purchase agreements that are not properly witnessed may not be enforceable in a court of law. For example, unscrupulous owners may try to renege on your deal when they get what they perceive to be a better offer for their property after they have signed a purchase agreement with you. When this does happen, you can bet your bottom dollar that the sleazy seller

<u>**FORM 17.1** **Sample Real Estate Purchase Agreement**</u>

This agreement made this tenth day of August 2005 between David D. Jones, a single man, known hereinafter as the Buyer, and Donald S. Reed, a single man, known hereinafter as the Seller.

Seller agrees to convey, transfer, assign, sell, and deliver to Buyer all of Seller's rights, title, and interest in and to the following property known as 7272 West Lyman Road, Tampa, Florida 33609, and legally described as: Lot 34, Block 17 of the Elliot and Harrison Subdivision, according to map or plat thereof, as recorded in Plat Book 37, Page 79, of the public records of Hillsborough County, Florida.

Seller agrees to sell to Buyer and Buyer agrees to buy from Seller under the following terms:

Purchase Price. . . . . $130,000.

Earnest money deposit held in escrow by John B. Good, Attorney at Law, in the amount of . . . . $1,000.

Subject to that certain mortgage dated August 28, 1997, and executed by Donald S. Reed, a single man, as mortgagor, to the Bank of South Florida, as mortgagee, in the original amount of one-hundred and twenty-five thousand dollars, $125,000, which mortgage was duly recorded in the office of the Clerk of the Circuit Court of Hillsborough County, State of Florida, in book 790346, on page 45905, of the public records of Hillsborough County, Florida.

Loan payments, accrued interest, and late payment charges in arrears . . . . $6,900.

Balance to close transaction payable in United States currency by cashier's check drawn on a local bank, subject to prorations or adjustments . . . . $5,900.

Any net differences between the approximate balance of the existing encumbrances shown above and the actual balance at closing, to include all unpaid loan payments, accrued interest, late charges, legal costs, taxes, liens, judgments, assessments, and fines, shall be adjusted to the purchase price at closing.

In the event that all or any portion of the property shall be damaged or destroyed by fire or other casualty before closing, Buyer shall have the right to terminate this purchase agreement by providing Seller with a termination notice and will be entitled to an immediate refund of the deposit.

Buyer shall pay no consideration for the assignment of any escrow-impound funds held by the lender.

Title to the property shall be conveyed from Seller to Buyer by warranty deed at the closing.

Buyer must approve of the property's title status and marketability before this transaction can be closed.

Buyer must approve of the status of the property's existing loans before this transaction can be closed.

(continued)

FORM 17.1 (Continued)

Seller must completely vacate the property and grounds before this transaction can be closed.

Buyer may assign Buyer's rights, title, and interest in and to this purchase agreement to a third party.

The closing of this transaction shall take place at the office of John B. Good, 4409 Himes Avenue, Tampa, Florida 33679, on or before August 28, 2005.

Seller accepts the foregoing offer and agrees to sell the herein described property to Buyer for the purchase price and on the terms and conditions herein specified.

All provisions of the Agreement shall extend to, bind, and inure to the benefit of heirs, executors, personal representatives, successors, and assigns of Seller and Buyer.

Seller and Buyer or Buyer's assigns authorize Mr. John B. Good, Attorney at Law, to act as Escrow Agent and hold the earnest money deposit and close this transaction in accordance with the terms of this Agreement.

IN WITNESS WHEREOF, Seller and Buyer have set their hands the date aforesaid

Donald S. Reed	David D. Jones
Seller	Buyer
Robert B. Big	Sally M. Little
Witness	Witness

Copyright Thomas J. Lucier 2005. To customize this document, download it to your hard drive from Thomas J. Lucier's web site at www.thomaslucier.com/pre-foreclosureforms.html. The document can then be opened, edited, and printed using Microsoft Word or another popular word processing application.

will be going over your agreement with a fine-tooth comb in search for any way to weasel out of it. And an agreement with flawed signatures would play right into the weasel's hands.

Have the Owner Complete and Sign a Property Disclosure Statement

Finally, at the same time you and the owner are signing your purchase agreement, also have the owner complete and sign a property disclosure statement that is approved for use in your state. At a minimum, the disclosure statement should ask the following 10 questions:

Question 1: Are there any hazardous substances at, on, under, or about the property? The term *hazardous substances* shall mean and include those

---

FORM 17.2   Notice Required by California Law

Until your right to cancel this contract has ended, (name) or anyone working for (name), CANNOT ask you to sign or have you sign any deed or any other document.

The contract required by this section shall survive delivery of any instrument of conveyance of the residence in foreclosure and shall have no effect on persons other than the parties to the contract.

You may cancel this contract for the sale of your house without any penalty or obligation at any time before (date and time of day).

Notice of Cancellation

(Enter date contract signed)

You may cancel this contract for the sale of your house, without any penalty or obligation, at any time before (date and time of day).

To cancel this transaction, personally deliver a signed and dated copy of this cancellation notice, or send a telegram to (name of purchaser), at (street address of purchaser's place of business) no later than (date and time of day).

I hereby cancel this transaction (date).

_____

(Seller's Signature)

---

elements or compounds that are contained in the list of hazardous substances and toxic pollutants adopted by the U.S. Environmental Protection Agency or under any hazardous substance laws.

Question 2: Have any documents ever been filed in the public records that adversely affect the title to the property?

Question 3: Are there any liens against the property for unpaid bills owed to architects, surveyors, engineers, mechanics, laborers, and materialmen?

Question 4: Are there any actions, proceedings, judgments, bankruptcies, liens, or executions recorded among the public records or pending in the courts that would affect the title to the property?

Question 5: Are there any unpaid taxes or claims of lien or other matters that could constitute a lien or encumbrance against the property or any of the improvements on it?

Question 6: Have any improvements been placed on the property in violation of applicable building codes and zoning regulations?

Question 7: Are there ongoing legal disputes concerning the location of the boundary lines of the property?

Question 8: Is any person or entity other than the owner presently entitled to the right to possession or is in possession of the property?

Question 9: Has the title or ownership of the property ever been disputed in a court of law?

Question 10: Are there any unrecorded mortgages or deed of trust loans and promissory notes for which the property has been pledged as collateral?

CHAPTER 18

How to Close on the Purchase of a Pre-Foreclosure Property

Throughout this book, I have given you detailed step-by-step instructions and practical no-nonsense advice on how to become a professional pre-foreclosure property investor and go about the business of buying properties directly from owners in foreclosure. Now, in this chapter, you are going to learn what to do when you actually put your newfound knowledge to practical use and are ready to close on the purchase of a pre-foreclosure property. The biggest factor working against any investor trying to close on the purchase of a pre-foreclosure is time. And because the foreclosure process is a sort of ticking time bomb, which is set to go off on the day the property is scheduled to be sold at a public foreclosure auction or trustee's sale, investors are always in a constant race against time. In this business, if you are unable, for whatever reason, to close on a deal, all of your efforts leading up to the closing will have been a colossal waste of time and money. Personally, I am willing to do whatever it takes within legal and ethical bounds to get a deal done. In fact, on my first pre-foreclosure deal, which I told you about in Chapter 1, I picked up both of the owners after they called to say their old clunker of an automobile would not start, and all three of us drove through a violent thunderstorm in monsoon-like conditions to get to the title company so that I could close on the purchase of their property.

Expect the Unexpected When Closing on a Pre-Foreclosure Property

As I told you in Chapter 10, my credo when conducting business as a pre-foreclosure property investor is: Trust no one, assume nothing, verify everything, and be prepared for anything! I guess you could say that my investment credo is the civilian equivalent of the U.S. Army Infantry credo of: Adapt, overcome, and improvise. In most business endeavors, there is always a mismatch between perception, theory, and reality. In other words, there is the way in which business functions are perceived to work by the general public; then there is the way that business functions are supposed to work in theory; and finally, there is the way that business functions work in reality. And the name of the game, when it comes to closing on a pre-foreclosure property, is: Expect the unexpected. This is because you never know what can happen prior to actually sitting down at the closing table and completing the deal. To illustrate this point, not too long ago, I received a frantic call from my attorney's legal secretary to let me know that she had just received a telephone call from their title abstractor, who had just completed a last-minute check of the lis pendens index that morning and found that a lawsuit had been filed against the owner of a property in foreclosure that I was scheduled to close on the following day. The person who filed the lawsuit was a roofer who had done roof repairs on the property six months earlier but had been paid with a $1,500 worthless check, which he had never bothered reporting to the local state attorney's office. Evidently, the roofer had just gotten wind of the pending foreclosure and decided that this was his last chance to get the owner to make good on his rubber check. I contacted the roofer later that afternoon and negotiated a $500 payoff on the bounced check. Trust me, this kind of stuff happens all of the time in this business, so be prepared for the unexpected, and be ready to take the bull by the horns and do what you have to do, within financial reason, to close the deal.

The Most Important Advice in This Entire Chapter

If you do not get anything else from this chapter, please make certain that you at least get this much: To avoid being ripped off by dishonest property owners in foreclosure, you must never do any of the following until after you have closed on the purchase and the property's title has been transferred into your name or the name of a business entity such as a corporation or limited liability company that you own the controlling interest in:

1. Pay any lender to reinstate a loan and personally send the payment directly to the lender via courier service.
2. Pay off any judgment lien.
3. Pay property owners for their equity until after they have removed all of their possessions from the property and grounds.

Title and Escrow Agents Are Nothing More Than Third-Party Facilitators

The primary role of title and escrow agents is nothing more than to act as impartial third-party facilitators in real estate transactions. However, there is a common misconception among the real estate buying and selling public that title or escrow agents always look out for the best interests of all parties involved in a transaction. This may be what the trade associations want everyone to believe, but it is nothing but pure bunkum! I hate to be a spoilsport, but title and escrow agents are trained to act in the best interest of their companies and the title insurer. They have no fiduciary obligation to the principal parties involved in any type of real estate transaction. In other words, when you are a principal in a real estate transaction in which a title or escrow agent is acting as the closing agent, there is no one but you looking out for your best interests. The only thing that the title or escrow agent is concerned about is that all the closing documents are signed and that the proceeds from the sale are disbursed. Nothing more! The fact is that title and escrow agents are legally prohibited from:

1. Providing legal, accounting, and financial advice.
2. Acting as a negotiator between the parties involved in a transaction.
3. Acting as a mediator between the parties involved in a transaction.

Most Title and Escrow Companies Are Not Investor-Friendly

My idea of an investor-friendly title or escrow company is a company that is staffed with knowledgeable professionals who are ready, willing, and able to do whatever it takes, within legal and ethical bounds, to close any type of real estate transaction. And, I can tell you from my personal experiences that I have found most title and escrow companies are not exactly what I would call investor-friendly. The reason for the cold-shoulder treatment is probably that most title insurance and escrow companies are generally leery of doing business with anyone they perceive as being unconventional. By the very nature of their business, title and escrow companies are generally suspicious of any type of real estate transaction that involves more than a typical, run-of-the-mill, easy-to-close residential sale with a buyer and seller and two real estate agents. But when you buy a pre-foreclosure property directly from an owner in foreclosure, it is what title insurers and escrow companies refer to as a transaction between principals, and there is no third party, such as a real estate broker, involved in the transaction. The average title or escrow agent does not understand how un-conventional transactions are structured. And like most people, they fear what they fail to understand. This fear factor that most title and escrow companies seem to have about real estate investors fosters an atmosphere of mistrust that is not conducive to a good working relationship. Those of you who have received shoddy treatment at the hands of title insurance and escrow agents know exactly what I am talking about!

Use a Board-Certified Real Estate Attorney to Close All Your Transactions

For the reasons that I have previously stated in this chapter about how most title insurance and escrow companies usually treat real estate investors, I strongly recommend that you follow my advice and hire an honest, competent, board-certified real estate attorney to act as your legal counsel and closing agent in all real estate transactions. This way, you will have someone working for you who:

1. Has a working knowledge of real property statutory regulations and case law.
2. Is experienced in solving complex legal problems related to real estate transactions.
3. Understands the mechanics of how lien, judgment liens, and foreclosure actions work.
4. Has a fiduciary obligation to act in his or her client's best interest.

What You Need to Know about the Real Estate Settlement Procedures Act

The Real Estate Settlement Procedures Act, better known by the acronym RESPA, is a federal consumer statute that was enacted into law in 1974 to supposedly protect the property-buying public from being ripped off by the so-called real estate industry, which consists of title insurers, escrow companies, mortgage and deed of trust lenders, mortgage brokers, real estate agents, and attorneys who perform real estate settlements or closings. HUD is responsible for enforcing RESPA nationwide. And according to HUD, the purposes of RESPA are: "To help consumers become better shoppers for settlement services and to eliminate kickbacks and referral fees that unnecessarily increase the costs of certain settlement services."

To learn more about RESPA, log onto www.hud.gov/offices/hsg/sfh/res /respa_hm.cfm.

Review Your HUD 1 Settlement Statement on the Day before the Closing

Under RESPA, the buyer and seller are allowed to review their HUD 1 Settlement Statement 24 hours in advance of the scheduled closing date. The last time that I ever used a title insurance company to act as my closing agent, I found a bogus $250 document preparation fee tacked onto my HUD 1, even though the title insurer did not prepare any title transfer documents. The title agent who made the calculations tried to explain the $250 overcharge as an "honest mistake." Sure it was!

You can review and fill out a HUD 1 Settlement Statement online at my web site: www.thomaslucier.com/HUD1SettlementStatement.pdf.

Double-Check all Closing, Loan, and Title Transfer Documents for Mistakes

Whatever you do, do not automatically assume that all of the information that is contained in closing, loan, and property title transfer documents is accurate and up-to-date. And prior to sitting down at the closing table, take the time to double-check all of the documents used to close on the purchase of a pre-foreclosure for:

1. Mistakes made in computing prorations.
2. Mistakes made in transposing numbers and letters.
3. Mistakes made in spelling and typing.

Prorate the Property Taxes Using the 365-Day Method

The 365-day method of proration is based on the assumption that every year has 365 days. For example, if the annual property tax bill for a pre-foreclosure property is $2,200 and the seller owned the property for 270 days, the seller's prorated portion of the tax would be $1,627.40 ($2,200 ÷ 365 days = $6.027 per day × 270 days = $1,627.40). However, if the property taxes for the current year can't be ascertained, stipulate in the closing statement that any tax proration based on an estimate shall be readjusted upon receipt of the tax bill.

Have All Utility Meters Read on the Day before the Closing

On the day before the closing, have all of the meters read by the public and private utility companies providing services that the property owner is responsible for paying. You must notify utility service providers that the property is under new ownership so that you don't get billed for utility services that were provided to the previous owner.

Do a Final Walk-Around Inspection of the Property on the Day of the Closing

On the day of the closing, I recommend that you do as I do and conduct a final walk-around inspection to double-check for any last-minute changes that may have occurred to the property that could have an adverse effect upon its value. To do your quickie inspection, use the following property inspection checklist:

FORM 18.1   Sample Walk-Around Property Inspection Checklist

1. Are there any condemnation notices posted on the property? (   ) Yes   (   ) No

2. Are there bodies of standing water on the property that cannot drain? (   ) Yes   (   ) No

3. Are there any visible signs that the property is infested with termites or rodents?
    (   ) Yes   (   ) No

4. Are there any visible signs of environmental hazards on the property? (   ) Yes   (   ) No

5. Are there any code violation notices posted on the property? (   ) Yes   (   ) No

---

Use a Buyer's Closing Checklist to Avoid Overlooking Anything at the Closing

I suggest that you do as I do and use a buyer's closing checklist like the following sample to avoid overlooking any aspect of closing on a pre-foreclosure property, which could result in costly mistakes and which is usually not uncovered until after the seller is long gone and not to be found.

FORM 18.2   Sample Buyer's Closing Checklist

1. Review the title insurance policy.

2. Review the survey of the property.

3. Verify the property's legal description.

4. Verify the property's zoning designation.

5. Check with government agencies for building, fire, safety, and health code violations.

6. Review the hazard insurance policy.

7. Review the termite inspection report.

8. Verify the property's tax payment status.

9. Compute the mortgage interest proration.

10. Compute the real property tax proration.

11. Check with government agencies for environmental hazard citations.

12. Review the bill of sale for personal property.

13. Review the deed.

14. Review the promissory note.

15. Review the mortgage.

16. Review the loan assumption documents.

17. Review the closing statement.

18. Verify that a current certificate of occupancy has been issued for the property.

Record the Deed and Mail All of the Checks to Lenders and Lienholders

Finally, to reiterate what I told you earlier in this chapter, never pay off any lenders or subordinate lienholders until after the property's title has been transferred into your name or the name of your business. The reason for waiting until after the deal closes is that shady property owners could refuse to close on the sale of their property, and you would be out any money that you had prematurely paid to lienholders. I have a foolproof method for paying off subordinate lienholders, which I have successfully used for years. First, I require that all of my closings take place at 11 A.M. sharp, and I never, ever have a closing scheduled on Monday or Friday. I insist on 11 A.M. so that there will be enough time left in the day to straighten out any delays or screw-ups that might occur. I also do this so that I have enough time to personally go to the Hillsborough County Clerk of the Court's Office and have my deed recorded. Once the deed is recorded, I go straight to the main Tampa Post Office at Tampa International Airport, and I personally mail cashier's checks directly to the lender and all subordinate lienholders via U.S. Express Mail. This way, I have firsthand knowledge that everything has been properly taken care of!

CHAPTER 19

How to Fix Up
Pre-Foreclosures for Maximum
Curb Appeal and Resale Value

Unlike most real estate book authors, who cringe at the very thought of getting a blister on their pinky finger, I am a trained journeyman carpenter who still does most of his own property repairs. I am also capable of doing journeyman-level electrical, painting, plumbing, drywall, masonry, and stucco repairs. However, I realize that most of the people reading this book do not have the skills and tools that are necessary to complete professional quality do-it-yourself property repairs. So take it from a seasoned professional, if you are contemplating doing a pre-foreclosure property fix-up yourself, first ask yourself this very important question: Do I possess the knowledge, skill, and experience necessary to do a top-notch, professional-quality job? And please be brutally honest with yourself when answering this all-important question. I have seen a ton of money wasted by so-called weekend handymen who did not possess the skill levels necessary to achieve a first-class job and had to call in a professional, at great expense, to bail them out and redo their handiwork. I still have a very vivid memory of the time that I pulled into the driveway of a pre-foreclosure property, which belonged to a part-time investor who happened to be an attorney, and saw nothing but a sea of white dust coming from the opened garage door. This wannabe handyman was using his new Craftsman table saw to cut drywall. The guy was covered from head to toe in gypsum powder. I took pity on him and showed the amateur how the pros cut drywall using a T square and a utility knife. The lesson that everyone should learn from the attorney's drywall mishap is that if you try your hand at drywall repairs, you just might end up with a butchered-looking drywall patch job and a garage and house coated in powder-fine drywall dust. In other words, know what you do not know about property repairs, and never attempt to fix stuff that you know absolutely nothing about, regardless of how many times you have seen Norm fix it on reruns of "This Old House!" The often-heard refrain of "Do not try this at home" should be the motto to all amateurs who get the urge to attempt some type of home repair. Finally, understand that you are not fixing up the property to win the most spiffy-looking house award in the neighborhood. And whatever you do, do not get carried away when fixing up a pre-foreclosure property and throw money away on foolish things like putting up expensive vertical blinds, installing expensive floor coverings, such as shag carpeting, or adding exotic touches like mirroring the master bedroom ceiling. Your goal during the fix-up of a pre-foreclosure property should simply be to put the property in a marketable condition for resale by:

1. Giving the property and grounds an industrial-strength cleaning.
2. Applying a cosmetic facelift to the exterior of the property and grounds.
3. Applying a cosmetic facelift to the interior.

Seven Key Elements That Must Be Included in Your Property Fix-Up Plan

The trick to having a fast property fix-up that is on schedule and within budget is to be well organized. To do this, you must make certain to include the following seven key elements in your property fix-up plan:

1. *Budget:* Establish a bottom-line budget before you start the job.
2. *Total job cost estimate:* Estimate to within 5 percent how much the total fix-up is going to cost.
3. *Labor:* If you do not have the knowledge, experience, and time to do a first-class professional-looking job, hire competent tradesmen and contractors to do it for you.
4. *Job supervision:* If you do not have the knowledge and time to supervise the job yourself, hire a competent professional to do it for you.
5. *Quality control:* Have all of the completed work inspected to make certain that it has been done in a professional manner and in accordance with acceptable construction methods and building codes.
6. *Work schedule:* Set a coordinated work schedule to complete the entire job.
7. *Completion date:* Put completion dates in all your contracts and hold everyone accountable.

Avoid Being Ripped Off by
Unscrupulous Repairmen and Contractors

Here are three ways that you can avoid being ripped off by the many unscrupulous repairmen, tradesmen, and contractors who make a living taking real estate investors to the cleaners on a regular basis:

1. Hire only properly licensed and insured repairmen, tradesmen, and contractors.
2. Require written estimates for all jobs.
3. Require that everyone who provides labor and materials on your job sign your state's version of a waiver and release of lien upon final payment form.

Hire Only Properly Licensed and
Insured Repairmen and Contractors

To avoid being duped into hiring one of the numerous unlicensed and uninsured crooks masquerading as legitimate repairmen and contractors, you must follow these eight steps to weed out the phonies, fakes, and frauds from the real McCoy:

Step 1: Require that all repairmen and contractors provide copies of their license or certificate of competency, occupational license, workers' compensation insurance certificate, workers' compensation exemption certificate for sole employees, general liability insurance certificate, and automobile liability insurance certificate.

Step 2: Require that all repairmen and contractors provide four verifiable customer references.

Step 3: Contact all of the customer references provided, and ask them if they would hire the repairman or contractor again.

Step 4: Conduct an online search of your state's contractor license database to verify that the contractor has a valid license.

Step 5: Contact all of the insurers listed on the insurance certificates to verify that the policies are valid and in effect.

Step 6: Contact your local city and county building departments to check for a history of complaints against the repairman or contractor.

Step 7: Contact your local Better Business Bureau to check for a history of complaints against the repairman or contractor.

Step 8: Log onto your state attorney general's consumer investigations web page to check to see whether the repairman or contractor is under investigation.

Find Competent Professional
Tradesmen to Work on Your Properties

It has been my experience that the best sources of competent building trades professionals are retired tradesmen. Here in Florida, there are a lot of retired tradesmen who are always looking for part-time employment. And for the most part, these people do top-quality work at fair prices that are a fraction of what a contractor would charge. In addition to hiring retired tradesmen, you can also visit construction job sites and ask tradesmen if they are interested in what is commonly called *side work*. Once you find tradesmen who want to work for you, ask them for references from people that they have done work for in the past. Also, try to see previous examples of their work. Keep in mind that a little investigative work on your part can help you avoid becoming the next victim of some fly-by-night huckster posing as a Jack-of-all-trades.

Require That Tradesmen Submit
Written Estimates for All Jobs

Another way to protect yourself against being ripped off by one of the numerous flimflam artists who seem to permeate the construction industry in America is to require that tradesmen submit written estimates for all jobs that include the following information:

1. Detailed description of the scope of all work to be performed on the job to include clean up.
2. Detailed work schedule with commencement and completion dates.
3. Specifications for all building materials to be used on the job.
4. Listing of all building permits required to perform the job.
5. Detailed payment schedule outlining the amount and time when payments are to be made.
6. Warranties covering workmanship and building materials used on the job.

What You Need to Know about Your State's Construction Lien Law

You need to know that under most state construction lien laws, anyone who provides a service, labor, or materials for the improvement of real property has a right to file a lien against the property's title for non-payment. Furthermore, if you do pay a contractor for a job and the contractor fails to pay the subcontractors who supplied the labor and the materialmen who supplied the materials, you are still financially responsible for paying them even though you have paid the contractor in full. In other words, you could end up paying for a job twice if you do not have legal proof that everyone was paid in full. The only way to avoid having this happen to you is to require that everyone who supplies services, labor, and materials on your job sign your state's version of a waiver and release of lien upon final payment form when they receive payment. This way, you will have legal proof that everyone connected to your property fix-up has been paid in full.

I recently received an e-mail from an investor in Pensacola, Florida, who did not do what I am telling you to do here and got ripped off to the tune of $13,000 for a kitchen remodeling job by an unscrupulous contractor who took the money and ran without paying the subcontractors and building material suppliers who provided the labor and materials to complete the job. This guy ended up paying twice for a $6,500 kitchen remodeling job because the unpaid subcontractors and building suppliers had placed mechanics' liens against the title of a pre-foreclosure property they had worked on. And the only way that the hapless investor had to get the liens removed from the property's title was to pay them off in full.

Free Job Cost Estimating CD-ROM Available at Home Depot Stores

Home Depot has a free job estimating CD-ROM called "The Worksite CD," which has a listing of building materials, along with estimating software designed specifically for construction professionals, by the Craftsman Book Company. The "Worksite CD" allows you to create accurate estimates that can be automatically converted to orders and sent to your local Home Depot via the Internet. Plus, it exports invoices to QuickBooks accounting software programs. You can pick up a copy of the latest version of "The Worksite CD" at the contractor help desk at any Home Depot store.

Building and Repair Cost Calculators Online

The following web sites have building and repair cost calculators online that you can use to get a ballpark figure on what various repairs in your area should cost:

Construction Cost Calculator: www.get-a-quote.net

Construction Material Calculators: www.constructionworkcenter.com /calculators.html

Building Cost Calculator: www.nt.receptive.com/rsmeans/calculator

Give the Property an Industrial-Strength Cleaning

My number one priority when fixing up any pre-foreclosure property is to always complete the exterior facelift first. This way, the property looks enticing from the curb and helps to lure potential buyers inside for a further look. And the first step in an exterior facelift is to thoroughly clean the property's exterior to include the roof and all walkways and parking areas. You can apply an industrial-strength cleaning to any type of property by using a pressure washer with a minimum capacity of 3500 PSI at 3.5 GPM. Pressure washing will remove all dirt, grime, soot, oils, and other pollutants from all exterior surfaces. I recommend that you hire the services of a competent professional pressure washing service that uses state-of-the-art equipment and the proper chemicals. The main objective in having your property's exterior thoroughly washed is to be able to see what is beneath the last five years of dirt, filth, and grime. It always amazes me what a professional pressure washing can do for a property's appearance. Plus, pressure washing eliminates a lot of labor-intensive work such as scraping paint. In most cases, the only things necessary prior to applying the finishing coat of exterior paint will be caulking and priming the surfaces. And, a thorough pressure washing will expose any rotted wood and other building materials needing replacement.

Eliminate Smelly Indoor Odors from the Property

The best odor eliminator that I have found to get rid of smelly indoor odors is the NI-712 Orange Odor Eliminator, which is manufactured by Neutron Industries.

It comes in a refillable spray container and has a very strong and long-lasting orange citrus scent. Log onto www.neutronindustries.com to learn more about the odor eliminators that Neutron Industries makes.

The Most Important Advice in This Entire Chapter

Here is the most important advice in this chapter: A properly applied paint job using a quality grade of paint will be well worth the money spent when fixing up a pre-foreclosure property. It never ceases to amaze me how a quality paint job can drastically upgrade the appearance and resale value of any property. However, the combination of cheap paint applied by an inexperienced painter will always result in an amateurish-looking paint job that sticks out like a sore thumb, while a professional-looking paint job will literally add thousands of dollars to a property's resale value. You will learn that in this business, there is no greater return on investment than the increased value a property receives from a top-quality, professional-looking exterior and interior paint job. I use Behr brands of exterior and interior paint. Behr paint costs more than most other brands, but it covers well with just one coat and is very durable.

Choose Color Schemes That Enhance Your Property's Curb Appeal

It is extremely important that you choose an exterior paint color scheme that will enhance your property's curb appeal. I use a three-color exterior paint scheme that my wife, Barbara, came up with in 1995. It incorporates three tropical colors that people generally associate with Florida. For example, I paint the body of the building one color, the fascia and exterior doors a different color, and the drip edge around the roof and window shutters another color. Go to paint-related web sites online, or visit your local paint store for suggestions on the exterior color schemes that will best accentuate your property's character and charm. The interior walls and ceilings should be painted in light neutral colors, using quality interior flat latex paint. The interior trim and doors should be painted with latex semi-gloss enamel paint. For example, I use a two-color interior color scheme: flat white paint on walls and ceilings and antique white semi-gloss on trim and doors. Last, do not do like an investor I know in Orlando, Florida, who had an entire house carpeted before the interior walls, ceilings, trim, and doors were painted. The poor woman ended up spending a small fortune to have her newly installed carpet professionally cleaned to get the paint spots taken out. And all of this grief and unnecessary expense could have been avoided if she had had the good sense to know that the installation of floor coverings should always be left for last!

Apply Textured Coatings to Rough Interior Wall and Ceiling Surfaces

You can avoid the cost of replacing interior walls and ceilings that have rough surfaces by applying a textured coating to them. A professional-looking texture job will greatly enhance the appearance of your problem walls and ceilings. In most cases, the best and least expensive texture to use is premixed joint compound. Joint compound will bond to most wall and ceiling surfaces such as drywall, lath, and plaster. And, premixed joint compound is less expensive and easier to apply than conventional plaster mixes.

Use a Professional Carpet Cleaning Service to Clean the Carpets

I use only professional carpet cleaning services that use Von Schrader carpet cleaners. I like Von Schrader's equipment because they use a patented extraction system that cleans and extracts soil in only one pass. This eliminates the danger of overwetting a carpet, which can cause mildew, shrinkage, or browning. Plus, Von Schrader carpet cleaners use low moisture foam that usually lets carpets dry in one hour or less. If you don't own or know how to properly operate a professional quality carpet cleaner, I recommend that you hire a reputable carpet cleaning service to professionally clean your carpets. But watch out when hiring a carpet cleaning service. Carpet cleaners are notorious for using bait and switch advertising tactics. So before you hire any carpet cleaning service, insist that you get a written estimate to clean all the carpeted rooms in the property.

Install Low-Nap Commercial Grade Carpet on 7/16-Inch Rebond Carpet Pad

In instances where having the carpets cleaned by a professional carpet cleaning service would not remove the dirt, grime, odor, and stains in carpets, I recommend that you do as I do and replace the worn carpets in pre-foreclosures with low-nap commercial grade carpet in earth tone or brown colors, which is laid on 7/16ths-inch Rebond carpet padding. Commercial grade carpet is less expensive than the residential grade of carpet that is installed in most homes today. I have found that low-nap carpet also wears better and lasts longer than residential carpet and is easy to clean. Installing commercial grade carpet on 7/16ths-inch Rebond pad instead of gluing it to the floor provides a cushion between the carpet and floor and makes it easy to walk on. Most people do not even know that it is commercial grade carpet because it has a pad underneath. Log onto the following Carpet and Rug Institute web site for information on the selection and care of carpet: www.carpet-rug.com.

My Property Fix-Up Motto Has Always Been Clean, Repair, or Replace as Needed

Being a parsimonious Yankee from New Hampshire, my pre-foreclosure property fix-up motto has always been clean, repair, or replace as needed. In other words, first try cleaning it, and if that does not do the trick, try repairing, and if that fails to work, replace it with a pre-owned replacement from a reputable source. The following is a listing of items that must be cleaned, patched, repaired, or replaced when fixing up a pre-foreclosure property:

1. *Walkways and parking areas:* Clean, repair, patch, and seal all walkways and parking areas as needed.

2. *Mailboxes:* Clean, repair, or replace all mailboxes as needed.

3. *Exterior doors:* Clean, repair, or replace all exterior doors, hardware, and locksets as needed.

4. *Windows:* Clean, repair, or replace window frames, glass, and locks as needed.

5. *Exterior lighting:* Clean, repair, or replace all exterior light fixtures and bulbs as needed.

6. *Interior doors:* Clean, repair, or replace all interior doors, hardware, and locksets as needed.

7. *Kitchen cabinets:* Clean, repair, or replace all cabinet doors, hardware, and countertops as needed.

8. *Interior lighting:* Clean, repair, or replace all interior light fixtures and bulbs as needed.

9. *Plumbing fixtures:* Clean, repair, or replace all sinks, tubs, showers, faucets, commodes, and vanities as needed.

10. *Heating and cooling systems:* Clean, repair, or replace all heating and cooling systems as needed.

11. *Floor coverings:* Clean, repair, or replace all carpets and floor coverings as needed.

12. *Exterior and interior paint:* Clean, prepare, and paint all exterior and interior surfaces.

13. *Landscaping:* Prune, cut, trim, and mow the property's landscaping and lawn as needed.

14. *Gutters and downspouts:* Clean, repair, or replace all gutters and downspouts as needed.

15. *Roofs:* Clean, repair, or replace as needed.

Always Conduct a Walk-Through Inspection before Making the Final Payment

A word to the wise: Before you shell out any of your hard-earned cash and make any final payments to tradesmen and contractors, first do a walk-through inspection of the property to determine if all work has been satisfactorily completed up to local building codes. In doing your walk-through, check the quality of the materials and workmanship. Make lists of all the discrepancies you find during your walk-through inspection and give them to each applicable contractor or tradesman to correct. In doing this, be fair and realistic, but do not let anyone take unfair advantage of you. When making your final payments, be certain you get a release of lien form signed by all contractors or tradesmen, which states that they have been paid in full for all labor and materials used on your property.

Keep Track of Your Property Repair Expenses on a Daily Basis

The best way to avoid getting carried away during a property fix-up and end up with a huge cost overrun on the job is to keep track of your repair costs on a daily basis. And the easiest way to do this is by maintaining a daily repair cost worksheet, like the sample on page 227, to record both material and labor costs.

FORM 19.1   Sample Daily Repair Cost Worksheet

Date	Material Costs	Labor Costs	Miscellaneous	Total Cost

CHAPTER 20

How to Package, Market, and Resell Pre-Foreclosures for Maximum Profit

In the past 19 chapters, I have given you the inside scoop on the finer points of just how the pre-foreclosure property investment business actually works and what you need to know and do in order to be a successful investor. In this final chapter, I give you the lowdown on how to quickly resell pre-foreclosures for maximum profit. Granted, you make your profit upfront when you buy a pre-foreclosure property well below market value, but you do not get paid until you turn around and resell it for a profit. And it should come as no great surprise to most people that there is a direct correlation between how well a property is marketed and how fast it sells. The fact of the matter is that properties that are properly packaged and advertised to a targeted segment of potential buyers almost always sell much faster than properties that are advertised willy-nilly. For example, when I have a pre-foreclosure property for sale near MacDill Air Force Base in South Tampa, I target potential buyers who are in any way connected to the military. I do this by placing classified ads in the base newspaper, the *MacDill Thunderbolt,* and the *Tampa Tribune.* I also have the property listed with the MacDill base housing office. I e-mail copies of my property fact sheet to all of the military recruitment offices in Hillsborough County to alert military recruiters about my house for sale, which is close to the base. In addition, I place small ads in Veterans of Foreign Wars (VFW) and American Legion Hall newsletters to let their members know about the property I have for sale. As you can see, the focal point of my advertising is toward active duty military members, civilian employees, and military retirees who have a need to live in close proximity to the base. I am constantly amazed at the number of investors whose idea of marketing a property consists of placing a crude-looking for-sale sign on their property and then waiting by the telephone for the thundering herd of would-be buyers to call them. I am also somewhat perplexed by investors who, for whatever reason, allow themselves to be duped into signing four- to six-month-long exclusive right-to-sell listing agreements with real estate brokers—especially when an investor's decision to do so was based solely on unsupported claims the broker made about how fast he or she could sell the property. I do not know about you, but I sure as heck do not want to take a hands-off marketing approach and rely on homemade for-sale signs or lethargic real estate brokers to resell my property. The fact is that investors in today's competitive real estate market must take an active, hands-on, proactive marketing approach in order to quickly resell pre-foreclosure properties—within 30 to 60 days—for maximum profit. However, in order to do this, you must first know how to:

1. Calculate the resale value of a pre-foreclosure property.
2. Gauge local real estate market and economic conditions.
3. Package pre-foreclosure properties to highlight their best features.
4. Use an outgoing message on your telephone answering machine to advertise property.
5. Advertise pre-foreclosure properties on the Internet to prospective buyers worldwide.
6. Have real estate brokers help you sell your property without ever signing a listing agreement.
7. Send property fact sheets to potential buyers by e-mail.
8. Establish a network of potential buyers.
9. Assign or sell your purchase agreements to third parties.

How to Calculate the Resale Value of a Pre-Foreclosure Property

The first step in packaging a pre-foreclosure property for resale is to determine its value, based on the sale of comparable properties within the same area. To do this, use the same step-by-step instructions that I outlined in Chapter 12 to calculate a pre-foreclosure property's current market value. Next, contact three residential real estate agents who farm or work the neighborhood where the property is located, and have them give you listing presentations to see what they think your property's resale value is. And then compare the resale value that each real estate agent gave you with the resale value that you came up with. Once you have done this, you should have a pretty good idea as to what the property's resale value is. However, any pre-foreclosure property that you are reselling that requires the buyer to obtain a mortgage or deed of trust loan in order to finance the purchase must be appraised by a licensed property appraiser. This must be done because no lender will make a loan without first knowing the property's appraised value. And most lenders accept appraisal reports only from certain appraisers whom they have deemed as being honest, competent professionals. A word of caution: Never order a property appraisal until the buyer has shown you a loan pre-approval letter written on the lender's stationery and signed a purchase agreement to buy the property. Last, when calculating a pre-foreclosure property's resale value, do not get greedy and try to suck every last dime out of the deal. Instead, price your property at least 5 percent below its estimated fair market value. By doing this, potential buyers will perceive your asking price to be somewhat of a bargain when compared to what other sellers in your area are asking for their properties. Finally, when you calculate a property's resale price, be sure to include the cost of:

1. Searching for the property.
2. Acquiring the property.
3. Putting the property into a marketable resale condition.
4. Marketing the property for resale.
5. Your time spent on the transaction.

Compile a Property Information Sheet Listing All of Your Property's Features

The first step in preparing to market a pre-foreclosure for resale is to do what I always do and compile a comprehensive property information sheet that lists all the property's features. Your property information sheet should contain the following information:

1. Your name, web site address, e-mail address, and telephone number.
2. The street address of the property being sold.
3. The asking price, sale terms, and existing loan information.
4. The year the property was built along with the type of construction and architectural style.
5. The square footage of living space and the number of bedrooms and bathrooms.
6. Descriptions of the living room, dining room, family room, den, carport, utility room, garage, basement, and any other rooms.

7. The type of heating and air conditioning system.

8. Descriptions of any fenced-in yard, sprinkler system, security system, swimming pool, spa, patio, deck, landscaping, and other special features that are part of the property.

Package Pre-Foreclosure Properties to Highlight Their Best Features

Keep in mind that how much you are able to resell your pre-foreclosure property for is tied directly to how well you are able to package the property. *Packaging a property* means to present the property to buyers in a way that fully highlights its best features. Make sure you fully highlight the following four features when preparing your pre-foreclosure property package:

1. Property's geographical location to include any special features or benefits about the area and neighborhood.

2. Size and shape of the property to include any unique architectural features.

3. Nearby sources of public transportation, employment, shopping, schools, recreation, and healthcare facilities.

4. Special features and amenities about the property and grounds, including lush landscaping, large shade trees, fenced yard, and home office.

Use the Internet to Market Your Properties Globally

The key to quickly reselling your pre-foreclosure properties is to market them to the largest possible number of potential buyers. In today's wired world, this includes the global audience of potential buyers that are available online via the World Wide Web. The fact is, American real estate attracts investors from around the globe. For example, here in Central Florida, people from the United Kingdom, Germany, the Netherlands, Canada, and Spain are continually investing in residential and commercial real estate. And best of all, most European investors are cash buyers, who do not have to play the mortgage loan disqualification game with lenders in order to finance the purchase. As far as I am concerned, it is absolutely imperative that you use the Internet to tap into the global real estate marketplace and expose your pre-foreclosure properties to prospective buyers worldwide by using:

1. Property for sale web pages.
2. Property for sale ads online.
3. Property e-mail fact sheets.

Create a Property for Sale Web Page to Advertise Your Properties Online

If you have a web site, all you will have to do is to create a property for sale web page to advertise your pre-foreclosure properties for sale online. To see an example of a property for sale web page, log onto my web site, www.tampahomeforsale .com, and click on the Property for Sale button. And make certain that you include a buyer e-mail notification form on your web page. One of the most efficient ways to compile a listing of potential buyers is to have visitors to your web site complete a buyer e-mail notification form to submit their name and e-mail address so they can be notified by e-mail when you have a pre-foreclosure property for sale. I recommend that you include the following information on your property for sale web page:

1. Interior and exterior photographs of the property.
2. Property location map.
3. Driving directions to the property.
4. Property site plan.
5. Property features.
6. Property's sale price and terms.
7. Information on how to set up an appointment to view the property.

Mapping Information Available Online

The following is a listing of web sites that provide online location maps and driving directions, which you can use on your property for sale web page:

MapQuest: www.mapquest.com

MapBlast: www.mapblast.com

Maptech: www.mapserver.maptech.com

Expedia: www.expedia.com

Topozone: www.tpozone.com

Yahoo Maps: www.maps.yahoo.com

Maps: www.maps.com

Use URL Forwarding for Property for Sale Domain Names

If you already have a web site, for an annual fee of around $50, you can have your property for sale domain name forwarded to a specific web page on your existing web site. For example, when you use URL forwarding, or domain redirection, you can link your property for sale domain name directly to a property for sale web page on your existing web site. This way, you avoid the cost and aggravation of building an entirely new web site for your property for sale domain name. For example, if you were reselling pre-foreclosure properties in Glendale, California, you could register the domain name, www.glendalehomesforsale.com, to market your properties to potential buyers worldwide via the Internet. And whenever this domain name is typed into an Internet search engine, the URL would automatically be forwarded to an existing web site, which is called the destination domain.

What to Include in Your Pre-Foreclosure Property for Sale E-Mail Fact Sheet

When notifying potential buyers via e-mail about a pre-foreclosure property that you have for sale, send them a property fact sheet that includes the following information:

1. Property address.
2. Description of the property.
3. Sale price and terms.
4. Location map of the property.
5. Driving directions to the property.

Place Classified Ads in Local Newspapers

In addition to using property for sale web pages, online advertising, and e-mail property fact sheets to market your pre-foreclosure properties, I recommend that you place classified ads, like the following sample, in local daily and weekly newspapers. Include your web site address, e-mail address, and telephone number in the body of the ad:

> Homes for Sale
> www.glendalehomesforsale.com
> Sales@glendalehomesforsale.com
> (555) 123-4567

Best to Include Buyer Qualifications in Your Classified Ad Copy

For me, the buyer qualification process begins when I write my classified ad copy. I always include qualifiers such as the down payment and total monthly mortgage payment in the ad's headline and body copy. For example, if I had a pre-foreclosure property for sale that required a $5,000 down payment and the monthly income to pay $880 a month in loan payments and I was willing to provide seller financing to buyers with good credit, my ad would read as follows:

> $5,000 Moves You In!
> Seller Will Finance with Good Credit
> Only $880 Total Monthly Payment
> Call (555) 123-4567 for Details

Potential buyers reading the ad will be able to quickly determine three things. They need $5,000 for the down payment, a good credit rating to get seller financing, and the monthly income necessary to make an $880 monthly loan payment. In most cases, people who do not meet any of these three qualifications will not pester you with phone calls.

Always Place a Professional-Looking For-Sale Sign on the Property

Another marketing tool that you always want to use to advertise your pre-foreclosures is a professional-looking for-sale sign, placed in a strategic location on the property. The sign by itself may not sell the property, but it will let passersby know that the property is for sale. I use four-foot by four-foot signs that are made from ¾ inch marine-grade plywood and attached to four- by four-inch by eight-foot pressure-treated posts. My signs have a white background, and the numbers and letters are painted in red and black colors by a professional sign painter. My signs are made of marine-grade plywood because it is very durable and does not delaminate after it becomes wet. And my signs have my web site address, e-mail address, and telephone number prominently displayed like the following sample sign.

```
Home For Sale
www.tampahomeforsale.com
Sales@tampahomeforsale.com
(813) 237-6267
```

Record an Outgoing Message for Buyers on Your Telephone Answering Machine

In conjunction with your property for sale web page, online advertising, classified advertising, and for-sale sign, record a detailed outgoing message on your telephone answering machine, which explains in detail the property's features, location, sale price, sale terms, and directions to the property. The sample on page 236 is an outgoing telephone message that I have successfully used to sell pre-foreclosure properties.

Work with Real Estate Brokers without Signing a Listing Agreement

If you want local real estate brokers to show their clients your pre-foreclosure properties without your ever having to sign an exclusive listing agreement, have the brokers sign a participating broker agreement like the sample on page 237. Under a properly written participating broker agreement, you would pay only a sales commission if a broker's registered prospect bought the property. In the meantime, you avoid having your property tied up by an exclusive listing agreement.

Local Real Estate Market and Economic Conditions Affect Real Estate Sales

It should be a no-brainer that local real estate market and economic conditions have a direct effect on real estate sales. For example, in real estate markets that

---

FORM 20.1   Sample Outgoing Sales Message

You have reached the sales office of Home Equities Corp. Thank you for calling about the home we have for sale that is located at 4429 Park Drive in Tampa, Florida, and advertised in today's *Tampa Tribune*. 4429 Park Drive is approximately three blocks south of Kern Boulevard and two blocks easy of Bay View Drive. This charming home is of concrete block construction and only eight years young. It has three bedrooms and two bathrooms, with a total living space of 1400 square feet. This quaint home comes complete with a frost-free refrigerator, range, ceiling fans, blinds and drapes, wall-to-wall carpeting, central heat and air, and an oversized two-car garage. The lot is 70 feet wide by 120 feet deep. And the backyard is fenced in and has a large utility shed. This home is priced at $125,000 for a fast sale as is; its sale price is below the sale prices of comparable homes in the neighborhood that have recently been sold. Please note that the sellers are unable to provide any type of owner financing at this time and that whoever buys this home must be able to obtain a mortgage loan in the $125,000 price range in order to finance the purchase. This home is being shown by appointment only to serious homebuyers who have been pre-approved by a Florida licensed mortgage lender for a mortgage loan in the $125,000 price range. Please call back at (555) 123-4567, and leave a message if you would like to set up an appointment to view this lovely home after you have driven by it.

---

are so-called buyer's markets, there are more properties for sale than qualified buyers to buy them. This problem brings us back to the simplest concept of Economics 101, supply and demand. The supply, the number of properties for sale, is greater than the demand, the number of qualified buyers ready, willing, and able to buy. When supply is greater than demand, two things generally happen: Sales prices decrease, and the amount of time it takes to sell a property increases. To illustrate, under what would be considered normal market conditions, a fast sale is generally considered to be any sale taking less than 60 days. However, during uncertain economic conditions, a fast sale could be considered any sale taking less than 120 days. Another factor that contributes to slower sales during uncertain economic conditions is buyers' reluctance or unwillingness to commit to large purchases, such as real estate. What happens is that a wait-and-see attitude prevails among many qualified buyers, who may actually be in the market to buy, but who are reluctant to invest because of real or perceived fears they have about the Future of the economy.

FORM 20.2   Sample Participating Broker Agreement

This agreement is made this nineteenth day of August 2005 between David D. Jones, known hereinafter as the Seller, and Douglas Avery, known hereinafter as the Broker. Broker holds a valid real estate broker's license, license number 568976, issued by the state of Florida.

Seller agrees to pay the Broker a brokerage commission, equal to three percent of the purchase price and payable at the time of the closing, when the Broker's prospect purchases the Seller's property, under the following conditions:

1. Participating Broker must register the Broker's prospects with the Seller by mailing, on Broker's company stationery, the Broker's prospect's name, signed by the Broker and the Broker's prospect. If the Broker fails to register prospects with the Seller as set forth, no commission will be paid to the Broker. No oral registrations of the Broker's prospects with the Seller will be accepted.

2. Participating Broker may serve only as a broker representing prospects and not as a principal, lender, or other financial participant in the purchase of the Seller's property. No commission shall be paid to any Broker participating as a buyer of the Seller's property.

3. Neither participating Broker nor any principal thereof, licensed salesperson associated therewith, nor any employee or licensee thereof, is or will be a principal or financial participant with or lender to any buyer of Seller's property.

IN WITNESS WHEREOF, Seller and Broker have set their hands the date aforesaid

Seller   Broker
David D. Jones   Douglas Avery

Copyright Thomas J. Lucier 2005. To customize this document, download it to your hard drive from Thomas J. Lucier's web site at www.thomaslucier.com/pre-foreclosureforms.html. The document can then be opened, edited, and printed using Microsoft Word or another popular word processing application.

Qualified Buyers Are Hard to Find in Most Real Estate Markets Nationwide

I hate to be a real estate killjoy, but in most real estate markets nationwide, it is not that easy to find qualified buyers. *Qualified buyers* are financially responsible adults who are gainfully employed and have the income, down payment, creditworthiness, and debt-to-income ratio that is necessary to assume an existing loan or obtain a new loan from an institutional lender. Experience has shown me that roughly 50 percent of all prospective buyers are credit-challenged and cannot qualify for any type of loan, other than from a pawn shop, and maybe not even then. The main reasons for this are insufficient income and a bad credit history that often includes a previous personal bankruptcy or foreclosure. Or, if potential buyers do qualify for a loan, they do not have the down payment necessary to buy the property. Also, many qualified buyers prefer to buy new homes from builders, who are willing to make concessions that an individual selling an existing house cannot afford to make.

Avoid Wasting Your Time with Non-Qualified Prospective Buyers

Years ago, when I was young and dumb, I learned the hard way not to waste my valuable time with non-qualified prospective buyers who cannot qualify for any type of institutional financing. And nowadays, I qualify prospective buyers right upfront by asking them a series of qualifying questions. For example, I recently received a telephone call from a would-be buyer, inquiring about a pre-foreclosure property that I had advertised for sale, and before I went into any sales spiel, I asked her the following four key pre-qualifying questions:

1. Do you currently have $5,000 on hand to pay the down payment?
2. Can you afford a $750 monthly mortgage payment?
3. Do you have a good credit rating?
4. Can you close on the purchase of the property within the next 30 days?

She answered no to all four questions, and I politely ended the conversation. The point in asking pre-qualifying questions during your initial conversation with prospective buyers is to quickly determine if the prospect can qualify to buy the property for sale. And I refuse to do business with prospects who refuse to answer my four basic pre-qualifying questions. I will never forget the woman who called after seeing one of my property for sale signs and demanded that I show her the house that very afternoon. When I told her that I would first have to ask her a few questions before I could show her the house, she went off on a tirade laced with every profane and vulgar word in the English language about how I was going to jail for violating the Fair Housing Act. I held my ground and politely told her to please file a complaint against me with the Tampa HUD office, and I gently hung up the telephone. By the way, I never heard a peep out of her again. But I did wonder where she had learned to swear like a trooper. I am a former U.S. Marine in good standing, and that woman was using the "F" word in ways that I had never heard it used before in any of the barracks that I lived in during my tour of duty. For your information, uniformly asking pre-qualifying questions to all prospective buyers does not in any way violate any of the provisions of the federal Fair Housing Act!

Work with Lenders to Pre-Qualify Your Buyer Prospects

One of the main reasons I obtained a Florida mortgage broker license in 1995 was so that I could learn the ins and outs of exactly how the mortgage loan process worked, from A to Z. I now understand the lending process from application through funding and everything in between. As a result of my getting licensed and taking the required continuing education classes, I know as much about the mortgage lending business as most of the people who do it for a living. And this knowledge has proven to be very useful to me because knowing how to finance a property's purchase is just as important as knowing how to market a property for a fast resale. I recommend that you contact reputable lenders in your area and find three lenders who are interested in working with you to pre-qualify your prospective buyers. By using three lenders, your buyers will have a large selection of loan programs to choose from. This way, when you have prospective buyers who need to obtain their own financing in order to purchase one of your pre-foreclosures, you can send them to one of your lenders to see if they are qualified to borrow under the lender's loan underwriting criteria. And if prospects are not willing to talk with one of your lenders, they automatically disqualify themselves.

Provide Seller-Financed Mortgage Loans to Qualified Buyers at Market Rates

Unlike some investors, I am willing to provide seller-financed second mortgage loans to qualified buyers at market rates with a 10 percent down payment on the property. A *qualified buyer* is an individual or a business entity controlled by an individual with a minimum FICO score of 640. *Market rate* is the advertised interest rate for similar-type mortgage loans being made by institutional lenders. When making seller-financed loans, I recommend that you use the same loan underwriting criteria and loan documentation that institutional lenders use to originate residential loans, which are later sold in the secondary market to Fannie Mae and Freddie Mac. The following are step-by-step guidelines that you must follow when making seller-financed mortgage or deed of trust loans:

Step 1: Buyer completes and signs a Fannie Mae or Freddie Mac residential loan application.

Step 2: Seller obtains the buyer's consumer credit files to include credit scores from Equifax, Experian, and Trans Union credit reporting agencies.

Step 3: Seller obtains a criminal background report on the buyer.

Step 4: Seller evaluates the buyer's creditworthiness and approves or denies the seller-financed loan request.

Step 5: Seller has the proper Fannie Mae or Freddie Mac residential loan documents prepared by a reputable title insurance or escrow company or real estate attorney.

Step 6: Seller transfers title in the property to the buyer at the closing of the transaction.

Residential Loan Application Online

The following web site has a residential loan application that can be filled out online:

www.efanniemae.com/singlefamily/pdf/1003_revised_i.pdf.

Residential Mortgage and Deed of Trust Loan Documents Are Available Online

You can download copies of the conventional residential mortgage or deed of trust loan documents that are used in your state from the following web sites:

Fannie Mae Loan Documents: www.efanniemae.com/singlefamily/ forms_guidelines/mortgage-documents/sec_instr.jhtm1?role=ou

Freddie Mac Loan Documents: www.freddiemac.com/uniform

Provide Buyers with a Limited One-Year Buyer's Protection Plan

To show my buyers that I stand behind the pre-foreclosure properties that I sell, I provide each buyer with a limited, one-year buyer's protection plan, which covers the costs of any repair over $1,000, which has not been caused by the buyer/owner's negligence. Please note that all repair cost estimates must be from reputable repairmen who are properly licensed and insured. The main reason that I provide my buyer's protection plan is to quell any preconceived fears that prospective buyers may have about buying a potentially problem-plagued used property, which could suck up money in repair costs like a Florida sinkhole sucks up fill dirt. And to date, I have not had one buyer/owner who has had to take advantage of my buyer's protection plan. A word of caution: Prior to offering any type of buyer protection plan, make certain that you have the property thoroughly inspected by a professional building inspector to determine the property's condition and to uncover all necessary repairs that need to be made before the property is sold.

Make Money by Selling Your Purchase Agreements to Other Investors

In any real estate market nationwide, there is a group of real estate investors—both active and armchair types—who are looking for properties that they can rent out or resell for a profit. In fact, many busy career professionals, such as doctors, dentists, attorneys, accountants, small business owners, and other individuals with relatively high incomes, are always on the lookout for bargain-priced properties they can add to their portfolios or upgrade and resell. However, heavy professional demand usually prevents such people from having the time, desire, knowledge, skills, and experience necessary to find and negotiate bargain purchases. They want the profits that come with the investments, but they depend upon other investors, oftentimes referred to as wholesalers, to find bargain-priced properties that they can turn around and resell for a fast profit. This is where you, as a pre-foreclosure property wholesaler, can make money: by finding, researching, negotiating, and putting pre-foreclosure properties under contract and then assigning or selling your purchase agreements to other investors. Once your network of buyers is set up, you will be in a position to sell your purchase agreements within a couple of days of signing them. The main advantage of using this strategy is that it does not require a lot of startup capital, and it also greatly reduces your risks and financial liability. This is because your investment in any purchase agreement should never consist of more than a $500 earnest money deposit and $125 to $150 for a title report. And if you use the earnest money deposit clause that is contained in the sample purchase agreement in Chapter 17, your financial liability in any purchase agreement should be limited to the forfeiture of your earnest money deposit as liquidated damages and nothing more. However, I must warn you that you want to deal only with honest, competent, professional investors who have the cash and credit needed to quickly close on a pre-foreclosure property purchase. I am telling you this because you do not want to end up jerking owners in foreclosure around by assigning your purchase agreement to some clueless flake who does not go through with the purchase and ends up leaving the owner stranded. To my way of thinking, pre-foreclosure property investors have an ethical obligation to do everything in their power to ensure that they do not default on any purchase agreement they sign with an owner in foreclosure. And this includes purchase agreements that are assigned to third-party investors! Finally, do not get greedy when you are trying to sell your purchase agreements. Instead, do what I do, and price your agreements for a fast sale. I recommend that you sell your pre-foreclosure property purchase agreements for right around 5 percent of the property's current market value. For example, I would sell a purchase agreement on a property under contract for $130,000 and with a current market value of $165,000 for right around $8,000 ($165,000 multiplied by 5 percent equals $8,250).

Assign or Sell Your Purchase Agreements to Third Parties

First off, understand that what you are really selling when you sell your purchase agreement is your exclusive right to buy a property under contract for a specific purchase price within a certain period of time. And when you sell a purchase agreement to a third party, you transfer the ownership of the purchase agreement through an assignment of real estate purchase agreement, like the sample on page 243. To do this, you as the seller or assignor, and the buyer or assignee buying your purchase agreement would both sign an assignment of real estate purchase agreement in the presence of a notary public, in which you would assign or sell all of your rights and interests in the purchase agreement.

What You Must Know about the Vacancy Exclusion Clause in Insurance Policies

As a pre-foreclosure property investor, you need to know that virtually all property and casualty insurance policies contain what is called a vacancy exclusion clause, which excludes coverage for properties that have been vacant for 30 to 60 days. Each insurance carrier has its own vacancy exclusion period, which is supposed to be in accordance with state insurance statutes. For example, most insurance policies generally have a vacancy exclusion period of 30 days. This means that the insurer could not be held liable for any losses that occur to a property that has been vacant for longer than 30 days. This vacancy exclusion clause is important to pre-foreclosure property investors because it usually takes from 30 to 120 days to sell a property. In the meantime, the property is excluded from insurance coverage, which means that the property owner has violated the terms of the mortgage or deed of trust loan by failing to carry adequate insurance coverage.

FORM 20.3   Sample Assignment of Real Estate Purchase Agreement

---

This agreement is made this tenth day of September 2005 between David D. Jones, known hereinafter as the Assignor, and Donald S. Reed, known hereinafter as the Assignee. Assignor and Assignee hereby agree as follows:

In return for the consideration set forth in this agreement, Assignor hereby assigns, sells, and transfers all of Assignor's title and interest in and rights under the attached agreement entitled, "Purchase Agreement" dated thirteen, August, 2005, hereinafter referred to as the "Agreement," executed by John Q. Burns as Seller and by David D. Jones as Buyer, for the purchase of said property known as 4899 Crenshaw Street, Tampa, Florida 33690, and legally described as Lot 34, Block 17 of the Elliot and Harrison Subdivision, according to map or plat thereof, as recorded in Plat Book 37, Page 79, of the public records of Hillsborough County, Florida.

By accepting this assignment, Assignee agrees to undertake and perform the obligations imposed on Assignor, as buyer, under the aforementioned Agreement. Assignee accepts this assignment subject to all terms and conditions contained in the Agreement, or imposed by law. A copy of the Agreement is attached hereto as Exhibit "A" and incorporated herein as if fully set forth herein.

It is hereby agreed that the obligations of both Assignor and Assignee, hereunder, are not contingent upon the recordation of a deed, or other completion of the purchase of the property, under the Agreement. It is the sole responsibility of Assignee to seek legal or other relief, in the event that the agreement is not performed, as a result of the act or omission of any other party to the Agreement.

In return for the rights assigned by Assignor herein, Assignee hereby agrees to pay Assignor the sum of five thousand five hundred dollars.

All of the provisions of this assignment of purchase agreement shall extend to, bind, and inure to the benefit of heirs, executors, personal representatives, successors, and assigns of Assignor and Assignee.

IN WITNESS WHEREOF, Assignor and Assignee have set their hands the date aforesaid.

David D. Jones   Donald S. Reed
Assignor   Assignee

Robert B. Big   Sally M. Little
Witness   Witness

Plus, the investor risks losing all of his or her equity if the property were to become a total loss while vacant and waiting to be resold.

How Income from the Sale of a Pre-Foreclosure Property Is Taxed

You must understand how income from the sale of a pre-foreclosure property is taxed so that you can structure a tax-efficient sale, which allows you to minimize the amount of income tax that you pay from the resale of your pre-foreclosure property. However, you must know that if you resell a pre-foreclosure property within 12 months of the purchase date, your profit will be taxed as ordinary income. But, you will be able to deduct the cost of purchasing the property, repair costs, mortgage interest paid, real estate taxes paid, cost of insurance, and the cost of reselling the property. You also need to know that you could end up being tagged as a real estate dealer instead of as a real estate investor by the IRS if you buy pre-foreclosures with the intent to immediately resell them. I recommend that you consult with a tax professional who is well versed in real estate tax matters to find the best way for you to conduct business as a real estate investor. You can download the following three IRS publications by logging onto www.irs.gov/forms/pubs.html:

1. Publication 537, "Installment Sales."
2. Publication 946, "How to Depreciate Property."
3. Publication 550, "Investment Income and Expenses."

Tax Information Online

The following web sites provide tax information online:

Internal Revenue Service: www.irs.gov

Internal Revenue Code And Tax Regulations Online: www.tax.cchgroup.com /freecoderegs

Revenue Ruling Bulletins: www.irs.gov/bus_info/bullet.html

Use the *U.S. Master Tax Guide* As Your Tax Reference Guide

Last, I highly recommend that you use the *U.S. Master Tax Guide* as your tax reference guide. It is published annually by the Commerce Clearinghouse and is available online at wwwtax.cchgroup.com.

Pre-Foreclosure Property Investor Resources Online

The following is a listing of over 100 real estate-related web sites, which every serious pre-foreclosure property investor must have bookmarked on his or her personal computer.

Foreclosure Reporting Services Online

Atlanta Foreclosure Report, www.equisystems.com
Record Information Services, www.public-record.com/market/foreclose.htm
Chicago Foreclosure Report, www.chicagoforeclosurereport.com
Foreclosure Access, www.foreclosureaccess.com
The Daily Record, www.mddailyrecord.com
Houston Foreclosure Listing Service, www.foreclosehouston.com
PropertyTrac, www.propertytrac.com
Foreclosure Data NW, www.foreclosuredatanw.com
Foreclosure Reporting Service, www.foreclosure-report.com
Jacksonville Daily Record, www.jaxdailyrecord.com
Daily Business Review, www.dailybusinessreview.com
Information Resource Service, www.irsfl.com
New York Foreclosures, www.newyorkforeclosures.com
REDLOC, www.redloc.com
ForeclosureTrac, www.foreclosuretrac.com
Bates Foreclosure Report, www.brucebates.com
Foreclosure Report, www.foreclosurereport.com
Real Data Corp, www.real-data.com
Midwest Foreclosures, www.midwestforeclosures.com
Foreclosure Listing Service, www.foreclosehouston.com
Foreclosure Disclosure Weekly, www.foreclosuredisclosure.com
RETRAN, www.retran.net
County Records Research, www.countyrecordsresearch.com

Public Property Records Information Online

Public Record Finder, www.publicrecordfinder.com/property.html
Public Records Sources, www.publicrecordsources.com
Access Central, www.access-central.com
Real Estate Public Records, www.real-estate-public-records.com
Search Systems, www.searchsystems.net
Tax Assessor Database, www.pubweb.acns.nwu.edu/~cap440/assess.html
Public Records Online, www.netronline.com/public_records.htm
National Association Of Counties, www.naco.org/counties/counties
Public Records USA, www.factfind.com/public.htm
International Association Of Assessing Officers, www.iaao.org/1234.html
Public Records Research System, www.brbpub.com

Where to Search for People Online

Internet Address Finder, www.iaf.net
Switchboard, www.switchboard.com
Skipease, www.skipease.com
Social Security Administration Death Index, www.ancestry.com/search/rectype
/vital/ssdi/main.htm
Street Address Information, www.melissadate.com/lookups/index.htm
Reverse Telephone Directory, www.reversephonedirectory.com

Crime Information Online

Crime.com, www.crime.com/info/crime_stats/crime_stats.html
Neighborhood crime check, www.apbnews.com/resourcecenter/datacenter/index.html
Nationwide sex registry, www.crimetime.com/bbosex.htm

Environmental Hazardous Waste Information Online

EPA superfund hazardous waste site search, www.epa.gov/superfund/sites
/query/basic.htm
Environmental hazards zip code search, www.scorecard.org
EPA Enviromapper zip code search, www.epa.gov/cgi-bin/enviro/em/empact
/getZipCode.cgi?appl=empact&info=zipcode
HUD environmental maps, www.hud.gov/offices/cio/emaps/index.cfm

Demographic Information Online

FFIEC Geocoding System, www.ffiec.gov/geocode/default.htm
U.S. Census Bureau FactFinder, www.factfinder.census.gov/servlet/BasicFactsServlet

U.S. Census Bureau Gazetteer, www.census.gov/cgi-bin/gazetteer
U.S. Census Bureau QuickFacts, www.quickfacts.census.gov/qfd/index.html
U.S. Census Bureau zip code statistics, www.census.gov/epcd/www/zipstats.html

Maps Online

MapQuest, www.mapquest.com
MapBlast, www.mapblast.com
Maptech, www.mapserver.maptech.com
Expedia, www.expedia.com
Topozone, www.tpozone.com
Yahoo Maps, www.maps.yahoo.com
Maps, www.maps.com

Title Insurance Information Online

American Land Title Association, www.alta.org
TitleWeb, www.titleweb.com
Old Republic National Title Insurance Company, www.orlink.oldrepnatl.com/index.htm
Stewart Title Insurance Company, www.stewart.com
Chicago Title Insurance Company, www.ctic.com
Fidelity National Title Insurance Company, www.fntic.com
First American Title Insurance Company, www.firstam.com/fatic/html/about/site-map.html
Lawyers Title Insurance Corporation, www.landam.com/subsidiaries/LTIC/index.asp

Attorney Locator Services Online

Martindale Hubbell Lawyer Locator, www.martindale.com/locator/home.html
Findlaw, www.findlaw.com/14firms
Lawyers, www.lawyers.com

Comparable Property Sales Data Online

DataQuick, www.dataquick.com
HomeGain, www.homegain.com
REAL-COMP, www.real-comp.com
HomeRadar, www.homeradar.com
Domania Home Price Check, www.domania.com
Yahoo Real Estate, http://realestate.yahoo.com/re/homevalues
OFHEO House Price Index, www.ofheo.gov/HPI.asp
Home Price Forecasts, www.cswcasa.com/products/redex/home

NAR Existing Single-Family Home Sales, www.realtor.org/Research.nsf/Pages /EHSdata

Property Replacement Cost Information Online

Marshall & Swift, www.marshallswift.com
Craftsman Book Company, www.craftsman-book.com
R.S. Means Company, www.rsmeans.com
Construction Cost Calculator, www.get-a-quote.net
Construction Material Calculators, www.constructionworkcenter.com /calculators.html
Building Cost Calculator, www.nt.receptive.com/rsmeans/calculator

Property Appraisal Information Online

Appraisal Foundation, www.appraisalfoundation.org
Appraisal Institute, www.appraisalinstitute.org
Federal Appraisal Subcommittee, www.asc.gov
Real Estate Appraisal Books, www.rwm.net/books.htm
Appraisers Forum, www.appraisersforum.com
Appraisal Today, www.appraisaltoday.com
American Society Of Appraisers, www.appraisers.org
National Association Of Independent Fee Appraisers, www.naifa.com

Property Valuation and Analysis Software Online

Z-Law Real Estate Software Catalog, www.z-law.com
Real Estate Valuation Software, www.atvalue.com
Real Data Real Estate Software, www.realdata.com

Tax Information Online

Internal Revenue Service, www.irs.gov
Internal Revenue Code and Tax Regulations Online, www.tax.cchgroup.com /freecoderegs
Revenue Ruling Bulletins, www.irs.gov/businfo/bullet.html
Technical Advice Memorandums, www.apps.irs.gov/news/efoia/determine.html

Lead-Based Paint Hazard Information Online

EPA National Lead Information Center, www.epa.gov/lead/nlic.htm
Lead-Based Paint Disclosure Fact Sheet, www.epa.gov/opptintr/lead/fs-discl.pdf

Lessor's Lead-Based Paint Disclosure Statement, www.epa.gov/opptintr/lead
/lesr_eng.pdf
HUD Lead-Based Paint Abatement Guidelines, www.lead-info.com
/abatementguidelinesexamp.html
EPA Lead information Pamphlet, www.hud.gov/lea/leapame.pdf

Building and Repair Cost Calculators Online

Construction Cost Calculator, www.get-a-quote.net

Construction Material Calculators, www.constructionworkcenter.com
/calculators.html

Building Cost Calculator, www.nt.receptive.com/rsmeans/calculator

Thomas J. Lucier has been a real estate investor in Tampa, Florida, since 1980. Mr. Lucier is the author of six books on real estate investing and managing Florida residential rental property. He is also a Florida licensed mortgage broker and an active member of the National Association of Real Estate Editors, and the Real Estate Educators Association. Mr. Lucier's real estate investment advice has been published in the *Wall Street Journal, Commercial Investment Real Estate Magazine,* and on CBS MarketWatch and the Bankrate web sites. To read more about Thomas J. Lucier, log onto his web site at www.thomaslucier.com.

And unlike 99 percent of all real estate authors in America, there are no gatekeepers between Thomas J. Lucier and his readers. Tom answers his own e-mail and telephone, and is fully wired to communicate from anywhere within the United States. You can e-mail Thomas J. Lucier directly at tjlucier@thomaslucier.com, or you can call Tom at his office in Tampa, Florida, at (813) 237-6267, to speak with him personally.